THE
PERSIAN LETTERS

MONTESQUIEU

THE
PERSIAN LETTERS

Translated, with Introduction, by
GEORGE R. HEALY

Hackett Publishing Company, Inc.
Indianapolis/Cambridge

Charles-Louis de Secondat, Baron de la Brède et de
Montesquieu: 1689-1755

Copyright © 1964 by the Bobbs-Merrill Company, Inc.
Reprinted 1999 by Hackett Publishing Company, Inc.

Printed in the United States of America

05 04 03 02 01 00 99   1 2 3 4 5 6

For further information, please address
  Hackett Publishing Company, Inc.
  P.O. Box 44937
  Indianapolis, IN 46244-0937

  www.hackettpublishing.com

Library of Congress Cataloging-in-Publication Data

Montesquieu, Charles de Secondat, baron de, 1689-1755.
    [Lettres persanes. English]
    The Persian letters / Montesquieu ; translated, with an
introduction, by George R. Healy.
        p.   cm.
    Includes bibliographical references.
    ISBN 0-87220-490-1 (pbk.) — ISBN 0-87220-491-X (cloth)
    I. Healy, George R., 1923-   . II. Title.
PQ2011.L5E53   1999
843'.5—dc21   99-36814
                                                        CIP

The paper used in this publication meets the minimum require-
ments of American National Standards for Information Sciences—
Permanence of Paper for Printed Materials, ANSI Z39.48-1984.
                            ⊗

CONTENTS

· · · · · · · · · · · · · · · ·

THE PERSIAN LETTERS

Translator's Introduction

In 1720, with *The Persian Letters* finished but in doubt about publishing it, Montesquieu, according to the lively if not unfailingly accurate recollection of the Abbé Guasco,[1] finally took the completed manuscript to Père Desmolets [2] for a reading and an opinion. Desmolets was a priest, a friend, and a literary critic of some distinction; his advice was appropriately mixed. As a priest, he argued that to print the book would be to show small regard for religion and for the obligations of Montesquieu's social position. As a friend, he emphasized that the author's tranquillity might be seriously disturbed by the scandal the book would probably raise. He added as a critic, however, that if Montesquieu chose to disregard his other advice—and Desmolets was sure he would—the book could not fail "to sell like bread."

It happened that he was right on every point. Printed on Dutch presses but judiciously carrying the imprint of a fictitious Cologne publisher and no indication of the author, *The Persian Letters* was duly smuggled into France early in 1721. It created an immediate sensation and, in various religious and political circles, a scandal. It raised vexing difficulties for Montesquieu throughout his life. It also went through multiple printings in the first year, stimulated a number of inferior imitations, and remained a steadily popular title throughout the eighteenth century.

Charles-Louis de Secondat, Baron de la Brède et de Montes-

---

[1] The Abbé Octavien de Guasco, Comte de Clavières (1715?-83), knew Montesquieu well after 1738, but his information on earlier events was based on hearsay; in 1767 he edited and published the *Lettres familières du Président Montesquieu*.

[2] Pierre-Nicolas Desmolets (1678-1760) was a priest, a close acquaintance of Malebranche, and librarian of the Oratory in Paris.

quieu, was thirty-two in 1721. He was the head of a proud provincial family that traced a distinguished record of service and nobility into an adequately remote past. He lived in an ancient, moated château in Guienne, surrounded by extensive, rich, and debt-burdened vineyards. He held the office of *président à mortier* in the *parlement* of Guienne, which sat at Bordeaux.[3] He was an important patron of the learned society of Bordeaux, and a frequent contributor of papers, usually on scientific subjects, to its meetings. In Paris, he was well known in many salons and some boudoirs, having lived there from 1709 to 1713 while studying law, and again for shorter periods whenever his finances permitted the maintenance of a suitable establishment in the capital.

He was, in a word, a man of some consequence. It was the publication of *The Persian Letters,* however, that brought him wide notice throughout France and suddenly raised him far above the crowd of landed and learned dabblers in science and literature. And for twenty-seven years, until as an elderly and almost blind man he published *L'Esprit des lois* in 1748, it was primarily for *The Persian Letters* that he was known, if not unanimously admired.

The Persian Letters is a youthful book, written by a man fascinated, indeed almost overwhelmed, by the empirical possibilities of life, and who hoped some day to be a great naturalist. There are unities in the book: as Montesquieu pointed out in "Some Reflections on *The Persian Letters,*" there is a logical beginning, development, and end to the story involving Usbek and his unhappy harem; there is a remarkable unity to the characterization, and a subtly consistent development of the characters. The essence of the work, however, is in variety rather than unity, or in what Montesquieu called the "disgressions"—the reflective observations provoked in Usbek and Rica

---

3 The thirteen *parlements* were the highest courts in the French judicial system; the more important of them, and especially the *parlement* of Paris, also exercised important political and administrative functions which made them centers of local resistance to the central administration of the crown. The highest magistrates were the *présidents*.

by their wide experience in the West and by their homesick-
ness for Persia. These observations are related and unified
only as experience itself is related and whole; *The Persian
Letters*, Montesquieu emphasized in the "Reflections," does
not have the unity of "ordinary stories." The author's intent
and the form employed to accomplish it are different:

> Finally, in ordinary stories, digressions are permitted only
> when they form in themselves a separate and new story; in
> them philosophic arguments cannot be included, because
> the characters have not been gathered together for the pur-
> pose of speculating, and to make them do so violates the
> nature and design of the work. But in the epistolary form,
> where accident selects the characters and where the subjects
> treated are not dependent upon any preconceived design or
> plan, the author permits himself to join philosophy, poli-
> tics, and ethics to the story, and to bind the whole with a
> secret and, in some respects, hitherto unknown chain. ("Re-
> flections," below, p. 3.)

As has been well remarked, *The Persian Letters* is related to
the later and more fully developed thought of the Enlightenment rather as an overture is related to an opera. Its thought is
diverse, designed more to provoke than to answer. It is prodi-
gal of observations and themes suggested or stated but never
fully explored. It implies more than it tells; it shows the man
working, not the completed work. It is, consequently, a book
as difficult to classify as Montaigne's *Essays* or Bayle's *Dictionary*, and for exactly the same reason: its subjects are as many
and as different as the author, almost uninhibited by literary
forms, chose to select from the rich store of his memory.

For example, while it is not a personal document in any
obvious sense, there is much in *The Persian Letters* that may
reasonably be read as autobiographical. It is not known when
Montesquieu first conceived the book and began its composi-
tion; most scholars discount the date of 1711 given to the first
letter, and argue convincingly that at least the bulk of the
work was written after 1717. In any case, it seems likely that
many of the experiences and observations he attributed to his
Persian travelers were similar to his own, when as a young and

rather innocent aristocrat from the provinces he moved into
the very different world of high Parisian society after 1709.
Without unduly stretching the interpretive point, it is quite
possible to understand the grave Usbek and the vivacious Rica
as representing two quite distinct sides to Montesquieu's own
personality, which evidently was as deeply divided between a
serious, responsible, introspective element, and the more spirited, witty, irreverent, and increasingly sophisticated qualities
that he ascribed to Rica. Biographers of Montesquieu have
argued that he, rather like Usbek, may have fled to Paris to
free himself from the subtle tyrannies imposed by his familial
and social position in Guienne, or to escape the routine of his
legal duties in the *parlement,* which he never liked and which
he was eventually to relinquish—for a high price, as such posts
were coveted, valuable, and venal in the eighteenth century—
in 1726. Like Usbek, too, he seems to have discovered in Paris
that the obligations and spiritual ties to his native lands and
people could not be easily dismissed, even as, with Rica, he
appears to have been more fascinated than shocked by the different mores of "this most bewitching city."

There is something of both Usbek and Rica in most men; to
deny it in Montesquieu would be to deny some of the most
prominent facts of his biography. Few men traveled the Paris-
Bordeaux road more often than he. As he himself fully realized, his personal need was for both cities and for the different
ways of life they represented, and even as he relished the one
he mildly regretted the temporary abandonment of the other.
Throughout his life, Montesquieu was both the deep-rooted
seigneur of La Brède, overseeing his vineyards and gardens in
rough workman's dress, and the elegant, worldly *saloniste.* His
most urbanely Parisian bons mots, contemporaries remarked,
were delivered in southern provincial accents.

If *The Persian Letters* is thus to some degree about Montesquieu, it is also, and in a more serious and significant way than
is sometimes realized, about Persia.

It is of course true that, by any present-day sociological
standard, Montesquieu did not understand Oriental culture.

However carefully he may have used the materials available to him on Persia, they were inadequate for a thorough study. Nor can it be denied that Montesquieu, for all his stubborn empiricism, had in him much of the seventeenth-century rationalist's impatience to generalize on evidence that was more provocative than conclusive. His Persians are thus unquestionably more French than Persian, and the society imaged in their letters is ridden with clichés obviously derived from Galland's translation of *The Thousand and One Nights* and Chardin's *Voyage en Perse*.[4]

It is equally apparent, however, that his purposes were serious, and that his failure to depict an authentic Persia was due more to inadequacies in his sources than to his motives or energies. And failure is a relative term. Usbek and Rica are not very convincing to us as citizens of Ispahan, and probably they convinced few really perceptive readers in 1721. Yet they are not men from Mars, objectively registering the facts of French civilization on minds free of earthly prejudice; nor were they intended by their creator to be simply French *honnêtes hommes* in dress exotic enough to placate the censor. Montesquieu did not invent the device of using presumably innocent Eastern travelers to explore and to criticize European society. His contribution was to raise this rather common literary fiction to a new level of excellence, and his improvement over earlier "Persian Letters" was nowhere more evident than in his ability to give to his characters a cultural identity that had some qualities of verisimilitude. As a result, and as Montesquieu surely intended, there is in *The Persian Letters* a sense of a real confrontation of values, and from the experience the reader gains a somewhat deeper appreciation of the fact that truth is a difficult word, and one that is defined in large measure by cultural and temporal conditions.

There was certainly nothing new about the idea of cultural relativity in the early eighteenth century. Aristotle, the Stoics,

---

4 Antoine Galland (trans.), *Les mille et une nuits* (Paris, 1704-1717); Jean Chardin, *Voyages en Perse et autres lieux de l'Orient* (Amsterdam, 1711).

and Montaigne, to name but three likely contributing sources
of Montesquieu's inspiration, had in one way or another
placed the principle at the center of their thought. To the
men of Montesquieu's generation there was, however, a new
urgency to the idea. Two hundred years of overseas exploration had exposed an overwhelming knowledge of non-Euro-
pean morals and manners, which demanded comparison with
Western values; and by 1700 many men, dissatisfied with the
old ways of thought and desirous of reform even if not yet
noisily insistent upon it, were more than willing to point out
that such comparisons did not always favor the comfortable
old customs and ethics of Europe. In some way, intelligent
men had always known that values changed in time and place;
now, however, the idea began to disturb them seriously. The
platitude had become a real problem, and some adjustment to
this larger context of life had to be made by anyone with a
claim to philosophy.

Some of the *philosophes* made this adjustment with a facility
that prompts one to question the amount of serious thought
they actually turned to the problem; the French Enlightenment was to be densely populated with men who spoke of the
world, yet who remained, essentially, incorrigible little-Euro-
peans. But no such easy resolution would do for Montesquieu,
who was in fact, and notwithstanding the Cartesian side of his
mind, sincerely committed to the empirical and comparative
method that most *philosophes* extolled but comparatively few
really understood and fewer really praticed. Montesquieu had
to know not only that ideas and institutions varied, but how
they varied; before he could in conscience submit his general-
izations, the naturalist in him insisted that he amass as much
of the evidence as it was practically possible to get. Montesquieu must have the details, the abundant and confusing examples; he must somehow make himself feel the differences,
and make his readers feel them. Less extensively than in his
later *L'Esprit des lois,* but no less clearly, *The Persian Letters*
shows this cautiously inductive tendency in his mind. It was
only a tendency, and contemporary critics all agree that he

was a better sociologist in spirit than in accomplishment; but, in the Cartesian context of the early eighteenth century, even to be a sociologist in spirit was something of an accomplishment.

Most obviously and importantly, of course, *The Persian Letters* is not about Persia or Montesquieu, but about France. It is hardly necessary to point out that it is an incomplete France that he dissects and details. There are no peasants in it, few workers, tradesmen, or merchants, and no provinces; with few exceptions Montesquieu's universe is that of "a certain society" in Paris. Yet there is nothing small or unimportant in this conception. If there was a capital of Europe in the early eighteenth century, that city was Paris, and through its streets daily passed the men—and the women—who shaped the tastes and styles and ideas, and often the material destinies, of a continent. Montesquieu's France was limited, yet it teems with the important, the ambitious-to-be-important, and the absurd—who are no less significant for being absurd. Before Usbek's and Rica's bemused scrutiny pass kings, regents, and ministers, tax-farmers and speculators, Jesuits and Jansenists, philosophers and hairdressers, gamblers and lawyers, alchemists and actresses, *nouvellistes* and courtesans. There is even a translator, who must be classed among the absurd.

The France of *The Persian Letters* was a nation at a critical point. In 1715, Louis XIV was dead, Louis XV was a child, and the Regency was evidently confused as to its directions. Once apparently stable values, particularly the political values, were in doubt. The world had somehow and suddenly become larger, more perplexing, and more open to experiment. For a time in the early Regency almost anything seemed politically possible, even—or so it seems in retrospect—a turning aside from the well-marked but not yet inevitable path that led to catastrophe in 1789. For Montesquieu, it must have been an exciting time, partly because he was young in it, and in Paris; partly because the Regent's short-lived "reforms" of the state promised, or, more correctly, hinted at a political arrangement which would reduce some of the centralized power

of the crown and return to the nobility, the *parlements,* and
the provinces some of the freedom and the responsibility removed from them by the work of Richelieu, Mazarin, and
Louis XIV.

This, however, was not to be. The Regency ended not with
the establishment of the vigorous federalism and the checked
and balanced conditions of power which Montesquieu, even as
a young man, deemed imperative to political virtue and security. It ended instead, and portentously, with desperate, unsuccessful, and highly centralized experiments with the national finances. By 1720, France had passed another possible
turning point without turning; the centralized absolutism,
which no longer could be made effectively absolute, was to
survive for two more generations. And with it was to survive,
and then to fall forever, that comfortable belief in the timeless
validity of aristocratic European values which Montesquieu
questioned through his Oriental travelers.

The Persian Letters has a largely deserved reputation for
wit, naughtiness, and negative criticism. To write for a salon
audience without some show of wit would have been to write
without hope of being widely read; to be unconcerned with
love and sex would have been to be something less than
Regency French; and to be other than sharply critical of
many eighteenth-century ideas and institutions would have
been to honor them more than they deserved. Yet the jesting,
the play on sex, and the occasionally embittered denunciations
are, even in sum, but a minor part of the book. Montesquieu
is usually entertaining, but he was not writing an entertainment; he criticized, but almost always with a serious and posi-
tive intent. Many anthologists to the contrary notwithstanding
the burden of *The Persian Letters* is not to be found in Rica's
irreverent observations on popes and kings, or in the tangled
story of Usbek's frustrated wives and eunuchs. It is located
instead in the densely packed and usually humorless essays
and allegories, mostly attributed to Usbek, in which he attempts to straighten out his puzzled mind, and to suggest some

principles by which a confused world might better be organized.

The fundamental problem which Montesquieu considers in *The Persian Letters* is the one that occupied him in one way or another throughout his life: that of discovering, amid all the diversities and relativities of life, the universals or absolutes, or at least the pragmatic constants, in human society. Convinced though he was that most of the traditional "absolutes" of European thought were little more than hearth gods, Montesquieu still could not accept the contrary proposition to which so many other similarly skeptical men have uneasily turned: that there are no values in human relationships except those imposed by force, or agreed upon in selfish and expedient conventions. Montesquieu believed, as did most "enlightened" thinkers of his time, in natural law. It seemed evident to him that such a conviction had been recently and brilliantly vindicated by the discoveries of the natural scientists. Further, it seemed likely to him that among all things, and most importantly in the affairs of men, similarly natural and objective relationships could be uncovered by the diligent use of right reason. Such relationships were law; obedience to that law was morality. "Laws," he was later to state in the famous first sentence of *L'Esprit des lois*, "in their most general signification, are the necessary relations arising from the nature of things." This same idea, though never so briefly put, runs through every discussion of law, justice, and morality in *The Persian Letters*.

This understanding of the problem and its possibilities implies an inductive methodology. If laws arise from "the nature of things," then the attempt to discover law must begin not with any a priori conception, but with the study of the "things," the factual particulars, the actual situation. To Montesquieu, therefore, there was no inherent incompatibility between his belief in immutable natural laws and his tough empirical insistence upon change and diversity. Law, as he understood it, was not an abstract command, for properly it could be said to exist only as a relationship between materially existent subjects; an abstract law, in the sense of a law apart from or antecedent to the "things," was a contradiction in terms. Thus, law is for him "relative," since it is determined by the subjects' presence. Yet it is also absolute in that it objectively exists between subjects regardless of their will, and cannot properly be regarded as a product of convention or force.

It follows, Montesquieu believed, that in human society the natural laws will vary in their explicit content as the material and historical conditions of societies (the "things") vary; but as human beings are fundamentally alike and subject to identical necessities, the natural laws operating between them will —or should—be identical. A just and moral rule in French society may thus not be at all applicable in Persia, with its different material conditions of soil and climate, and its different cultural and historical experience. But as both the French and Persians are men and are therefore alike despite their considerable material differences, there are also natural laws that are equally binding upon both. The institution of marriage, with which Montesquieu was much concerned in *The Persian Letters,* is instructive as an example. Between the sexes, there is a natural need for sexual satisfaction and for the procreation and protection of children; marriage is thus a concrete manifestation of a universal natural law which is determined by the existence of male and female. Marriage, however, is monogamous in Europe and polygamous in Persia; which is the more natural? Montesquieu's answer in *The Persian Letters* is not entirely clear; but, generally, he leads to the conclusion that in its cultural context either form of marriage is—or can be made to be—lawful, moral, and natural.

In this conception of law, there was little that was actually new; Aristotle, for one, had argued in somewhat the same manner, albeit in a terminology that the eighteenth century considered outmoded, and within a larger context that was no longer agreeable. Moreover, as Montesquieu's numerous critics have hastened to point out, the conception presents some serious difficulties. He assumed without epistemological hesitation, for example, that "the nature of things," and the processes which order them and to which they contribute, are objectively and easily knowable. He implied little difference, if any, between a law in physics and a law for society. And there is no question that, in practice, Montesquieu's thought tended always to unify the radically opposed directions implicit in his definition of law. Believing as he did that to a large extent the material and cultural conditions of a society determine its value scheme, he often inclined toward a position of complete moral relativism. Yet at the same time, his commitment to natural law often led him to the profession of "absolute" values which on close examination turn out to be largely gratuitous.

This confusion—if such is the applicable term—was, of course, not unique with Montesquieu in the eighteenth century. Most of the *philosophes* were equally prone to place environmental relativism and natural law in the same close proximity, and with no greater logical success. Yet structural consistency and logic, it is hardly necessary to say, are not equivalent to strength, significance, or truth. On careful reading, many of Montesquieu's seemingly clearest discussions (e.g., the story of the Troglodytes) turn out to be full of unresolved problems. As Joseph Dedieu correctly remarked, Montesquieu's genius was more analytic than synthetic, and many of his "answers" in *The Persian Letters* and elsewhere are thus in fact only a more complex framing of the question.[5] But this is not to doubt the significance of the undertaking, for while it is, of course, true that men cannot live without some answers, it is equally true that, unless their questions are properly framed, any response to them will be incomplete and misleading.

Most of the *philosophes* eventually came to realize the difficulties in such an understanding of natural law, and as the century progressed they increasingly turned from "nature" to "utility" as the basic test of the worth of an idea or institu-

---

[5] In his *Montesquieu: l'homme et l'œuvre* (Paris: Boivin, 1943), p. 175.

tion. It is interesting to note that in 1721 Montesquieu, in this as in so many things at least a generation ahead of his colleagues, was very near the utilitarian position. It will be noted, for example, that in *The Persian Letters* he attacks Louis XIV's revocation of the Edict of Nantes not on the ground that the revocation denies the natural right of every man to worship as his conscience may dictate, but rather because it weakened and divided the state of France, though the king's intent was to strengthen and unify; because, in a word, it did not fulfill the useful purpose for which it was intended. Montesquieu bitterly deplored John Law's financial manipulations, not as abstractly or inherently bad or "unnatural," but largely for the social disruption they caused. Criminal punishment, he argued, must be scaled reasonably to the magnitude of the crime, not for humanitarian reasons rooted in nature, but because if it is not so proportioned, criminal behavior will increase and further harm society. Montesquieu detested political despotism for various and immediate reasons; his many arguments against it in *The Persian Letters,* however, most often come down to the entirely pragmatic and utilitarian objection that despotism simply does not work very well.

To argue the case in terms of utility and workability, however, is only to change the focus of the discussion; utility serves little better than the doctrine of natural law to resolve the problem of values. For just as the natural-law theorist needs an understanding of natural norms that nature itself is not likely to reveal, so too must the utilitarian and pragmatist discover and utilize some standard, some "absolute," by which things may be said to be useful or not, workable or not.

Montesquieu's absolute, in this sense, was society. Metaphysical norms he rejected as unknowable, even if, as he doubted, they existed. The individual he regarded as unworthy; the family and the state as worthy but incomplete. His ideal was the betterment of the human race. "If I knew something useful to me, but prejudicial to my family, I would reject it from my mind," he wrote in his *pensées.* "If I knew something useful to my family, but not to my country, I would try to forget it. If I knew something useful to my country, but prejudicial to Europe, or useful to Europe and prejudicial to the human race, I would regard it as criminal." [6] The best, and by implication the only true way to serve God, Usbek concludes in Letter XLVI, "is to live as a good citizen in the society where Thou hast placed me." "He is," Sorel wrote of Montesquieu, "before all, and above all, a citizen." [7]

It is hard, perhaps impossible, to be a citizen in Montesquieu's terms—to be a member of a family, a state, a culture, and the human race all at once and without contradiction. He never pretended, in *The Persian Letters* or elsewhere, that it was easy or even possible, only that it was a worthwhile goal. In Letter XXX, Rica relates that in Western dress he was not recognized as alien until "someone chanced to inform them that I was a Persian." He then heard murmured all around him, "Ah! Indeed! He is a Persian? How extraordinary! How can anyone be a Persian?" This ingenuous question could be variously phrased. How can anyone be a Frenchman? How can anyone be a European? How can anyone be a man? Montesquieu, when he wrote *The Persian Letters,* did not know; doubtless one of the reasons for his writing was to find out. In no final sense can he be said to have been successful in his search. Yet it was a worthy quest, undertaken sincerely and with spirited intelligence; and as guides in it Rica and Usbek are engaging companions.

GEORGE R. HEALY

---

6 Montesquieu, *Cahiers* (Paris: Grasset, 1941), p. 9.
7 Albert Sorel, *Montesquieu* (2nd edn.; Paris: Hachette, 1889), p. 19.

Selected Bibliography

BIBLIOGRAPHIES

CABEEN, DAVID C. "Montesquieu: A Bibliography," *Bulletin of the New York Public Library,* LI (1947), 359-83, 423-30, 513-25, 545-65, 593-616. Printed separately; New York, 1947.

————. "A Supplementary Montesquieu Bibliography," *Revue internationale de philosophie,* IX (1955), 409-34.

HAVENS, G. R., and D. R. BOND (eds.). "Montesquieu," in *The Eighteenth Century.* Vol. IV (1951) of *A Critical Bibliography of French Literature,* ed. DAVID C. CABEEN. Syracuse, N. Y.: Syracuse University Press, 1947-61.

SELECTED BIOGRAPHIES AND GENERAL STUDIES

BARCKHAUSEN, HENRI. *Montesquieu, ses idées et ses œuvres d'après les papiers de la Brède.* Paris: Hachette, 1907.

DEDIEU, JOSEPH. *Montesquieu.* Paris: Alcan, 1913.

————. *Montesquieu, l'homme et l'œuvre.* Paris: Boivin, *c.* 1943.

FAGUET, ÉMILE. "Montesquieu," in *Dix-huitième siècle; études littéraires.* Paris: Lecène et Oudin, 1890.

SHACKLETON, ROBERT. *Montesquieu: A Critical Biography.* Oxford: Oxford University Press, 1961.

SOREL, ALBERT. *Montesquieu.* Paris: Hachette, 1887.

VIAN, LOUIS. *Histoire de Montesquieu.* Second edn. Paris: Didier, 1879.

CRITICAL AND ANNOTATED EDITIONS

ADAM, ANTOINE (ed.). *Lettres persanes.* Geneva and Lille: Droz, 1954.

BARCKHAUSEN, HENRI (ed.). *Lettres persanes.* 2 vols. Paris: Imprimerie nationale, 1897. Reprinted Paris: Hachette, 1913.

CAILLOIS, ROGER (ed.). *Lettres persanes,* in *Œuvres complètes.* "Pleiade" edn. 2 vols. Paris: Gallimard, 1949.

CARCASSONNE, ÉLIE (ed.). *Lettres persanes.* 2 vols. Paris: Roches, 1929.

VERNIÈRE, PAUL. *Lettres persanes.* Third edition. Paris: Classiques Garnier, 1992.

ENGLISH TRANSLATIONS

DAVIDSON, JOHN (tr.). *The Persian Letters.* London: Routledge, 1891.

LOY, J. ROBERT (tr.). *The Persian Letters.* New York: Meridian, 1961.

The Persian Letters. Anonymous translation. Private edition for subscribers only; London, 1897, 1914.

SELECTED STUDIES OF *The Persian Letters*

BARRIÈRE, P. "Elements bordelais dans les *Lettres persanes,*" *Revue de l'histoire litteraire de la France,* LI (1951), 14-36.

CRISAFULLI, A. S. "Parallels to Ideas in the *Lettres persanes,*" *Publications of the Modern Language Association,* LII (1937), 773-77.

———. "Montesquieu's Story of the Troglodytes: Its Background, Meaning, and Significance," *ibid.,* LVIII (1943), 372-92.

———. "L'Observateur oriental avant les *Lettres persanes,*" *Lettres romanes,* VIII (1954), 91-113.

GOODMAN, DENA. *Criticism in Action: Enlightenment Experiments in Political Writing.* Ithaca: Cornell University Press, 1989. Part I, "Montesquieu: The Epistolary Form of Writing."

GREEN, F. C. "Montesquieu the Novelist, and Some Imitations of the *Lettres persanes,*" *Modern Language Review,* XX (1925), 32-42.

GRIMSLEY, RONALD. "The Idea of Nature in the *Lettres persanes*," *French Studies*, V (1951), 293-306.

KESSLER, SANFORD. "Religion and Liberalism in Montesquieu's *Persian Letters*," *Polity*, 15 (Spring 1983), 380-96.

KRA, PAULINE. "The Invisible Chain of the *Lettres persanes*," *Studies in Voltaire and the 18th Century*, 23 (1963), 3-55.

———. "Religion in Montesquieu's *Lettres persanes*," *ibid.*, 72 (1970), 11-224.

MASSON, ANDRÉ. "Un Chinois inspirateur des *Lettres persanes*," *Revue des Deux Mondes* (May 15, 1951), pp. 348-54.

OAKE, ROGER. "Polygamy in the *Lettres persanes*," *Romanic Review*, XXXII (1941), 56-62.

PUCCI, SUZANNE L. "Orientalism and Representations of Exteriority in Montesquieu's *Lettres persanes*," *The Eighteenth Century*, 26 (1985), 263-79.

SCHAUB, DIANA J. *Erotic Liberalism: Women and Revolution in Montesquieu's* Persian Letters. Lanham: Rowman & Littlefield, 1995.

SHACKLETON, ROBERT. "The Moslem Chronology of the *Lettres persanes*," *French Studies*, VII (1954), 17-27.

SHKLAR, JUDITH. *Montesquieu*. Oxford: Oxford University Press, 1986. Chapter 2, "*The Persian Letters:* How Others See Us."

STAROBINKSI, JEAN. *Blessings in Disguise; or, The Morality of Evil*. Cambridge: Cambridge Univeristy Press, 1993. Chapter 3, "Exile, Satire, Tyranny: Montesquieu's *Persian Letters*."

VALÉRY, PAUL. "Préface aux *Lettres persanes*," in *Variété II*. Paris: Gallimard, 1930.

VAN ITTERBECK, E. "On Dating the *Lettres persanes*," *Lettres Romanes*, XI (1956), 82-83.

VAN ROOSBROECK, G. L. *Persian Letters before Montesquieu*. New York: Institute of French Studies, 1932.

VENTURI, FRANCO. "Oriental Despotism," *Journal of the History of Ideas*, 24 (Jan.-March 1963), 133-42.

Summary of Contents

The Persian Calendar

The Moslem calendar is lunar, the Western calendar, solar; thus, to date an event precisely and easily in both is difficult. Montesquieu resolved the problem by the simple if inaccurate expedient of making the months equivalent, beginning the year in March, as follows:

Moslem Calendar [1]	*Western Calendar*
Maharram (Muharram)	March
Saphar (Safar)	April
Rebiab (Rabia I)	May
Rebiab II (Rabia II)	June
Gemmadi I (Jumada I)	July
Gemmadi II (Jumada II)	August
Rhegeb (Rajab)	September
Chahban (Shaban)	October
Rhamazan (Ramadan)	November
Chalval (Shawwal)	December
Zilcade (Zu'lkadah)	January
Zilhage (Zu'lhijjah)	February

Montesquieu evidently took his information on the calendar from Chardin's *Voyages en Perse et autres lieux de l'Orient,* and he accepted Chardin's spelling with two exceptions: he apparently misread Rebiab for Rebiah, and he also changed Cheval to Chalval.[2] The years, of course, are in the Christian rather than the Mohammedan chronology.

[1] Montesquieu's spellings; the usual English renderings are in parentheses.

[2] For the probable reason that, in French, *cheval* is the word for "horse."

Note on the Translation

Montesquieu revised *The Persian Letters* several times, and like many books anonymously and clandestinely printed in the eighteenth century, it underwent other variations in its publishing history. Establishment of a text true to Montesquieu's considered and final wishes has thus occupied much academic attention, conjecturally for more than a century after Montesquieu's death, and then, after his heirs opened his papers at La Brède to scholars, on the basis of sound research, which is now as complete as it is ever likely to be.

The edition usually accepted as the first appeared in 1721, carried the fictitious imprint "À Cologne, Chez Pierre Marteau," and contained 150 letters. A presumed second and "revised" edition, usually dated 1722 but in some copies 1721, contained 140 letters, thirteen of the original letters and parts of others having been removed, and three new letters (CXI, CXXIV, CXLV) having been added. Why Montesquieu made this revision—if indeed he did—remains a mystery. The material repressed is almost all innocuously concerned with Usbek's problems in Persia, unlikely to offend even the most irritable censor, and there is absolutely no evidence to support the long-held hypothesis that Montesquieu expurgated his work in a counterfeit edition, backdated 1722, so as to remove the opposition of Cardinal de Fleury to his candidacy for the Academy in 1727. Some Montesquieu scholars argue that this edition is actually the first, that is, an earlier draft which somehow got to press. The third edition of 1754 followed with minor variations the text of the "first" 1721 edition; in the 1754 edition, Montesquieu added "Some Reflections on *The Persian Letters*" and in a supplement included the three letters added to the "second" edition, and eight new ones: XV, XXII, LXXVII, XCI, CXLIV, CLVII, CLVIII, CLX. The fourth edition appeared as part of an *Œuvres complètes* in 1758, three years after Montesquieu's death. It was edited by his friend, François Richer, who had access to Montesquieu's papers, and who faithfully carried out his wishes for revision. It contains the 161 letters of the 1754 edition, all worked into the main text, thus abolishing the awkward supplement; except for the relegation of much of Letter CXLIII to footnotes, other changes were minor.

The present translation is based upon a 1761 edition (Amsterdam and Leipzig: Arkstée and Merkus), which is a reprint of that of 1758. Where this text was inexplicably varied from others, and in cases of the inevitable printing errors, I have checked the "definitive" texts of Barckhausen, Carcassonne, Caillois, and Adam, and usually accepted the consensus as a guide; when the variations seemed important or puzzling enough I have indicated the difficulty in a footnote. It has not been my intention to prepare another variorum edition, however, and the reader interested in such detail is referred to the Bibliography (p. xx).

Montesquieu has some hard and probably deserved words to say about translators in Letter CXXVIII, and against them I do not intend to protest much. On the translation, then, I plead only that I have tried to keep as close as I could to the literal sense without completely sacrificing in English the frequently involved but always sturdy symmetry of Montesquieu's French. With occasional misgivings, I have retained Montesquieu's paragraphing; curious as it sometimes appears to be, there is more wisdom in it than I thought at first. With few exceptions, I have also retained his spelling of names; where the modern version of the name is significantly different I have given it in a footnote. I have, however, freely altered his (or his printer's) punctuation, which in customary eighteenth-century style consisted almost entirely of colons and semi-colons. My footnotes in the text are bracketed; Montesquieu's are not.

In a work such as *The Persian Letters,* where almost every page contains an allusion that could be identified, explained, or compared, it is particularily hard to know when to stop footnoting. Generally, I have restricted notation to what appeared most obvious to me: identification of names and places specifically mentioned, Persian and Islamic terms, French institutions and events, without a knowledge of which a passage would make no sense. There is no doubt that the reader's enjoyment is heightened if, for example, he recognizes in Letter XXXV that Usbek's observations on Christian beliefs are exactly those, even to the language, which were made by the Christian missionaries who sought in pagan beliefs some parallels to Christianity; or if, in Letter CXXXI, he recognizes in this 1721 work the ideas Montesquieu was later to develop and make famous in *L'Esprit des lois.* Such discoveries, however, I have presumed to leave to the reader. In making that decision, Montesquieu has been consoling. A good author, he once observed apropos his own elliptical style, should "omit enough of the intermediate ideas so as not to become tedious," and thus make the reader participate actively in the process of discovery. An author and a translator, an epigram and a footnote, are not the same thing, but the dictum seems nonetheless relevant.

G. R. H.

THE PERSIAN LETTERS

Some Reflections on The Persian Letters[1]

Nothing in *The Persian Letters* has given more pleasure than the unexpected discovery of a kind of story in them. It can be seen to have a beginning, a development, and an end, and its various characters are linked in a chain. In proportion as their stay in Europe lengthens, the manners of this part of the world appear to them less astonishing and less bizarre; and they are more or less struck by the bizarre and the astonishing as their personalities differ. On the other hand, the Asiatic seraglio grows more disorderly in proportion to the length of Usbek's absence from it—that is to say, in proportion as frenzy increases and love declines.

Moreover, stories of this sort are usually successful because the characters themselves recount their actual experiences, and this makes us feel their passions better than any mere narration could. This is one of the reasons for the popularity of several charming works which have appeared since the publication of *The Persian Letters*.[2]

Finally, in ordinary stories, digressions are permitted only when they form in themselves a separate and new story; in them philosophic arguments cannot be included, because the characters have not been gathered together for the purpose of speculating, and to make them do so violates the nature and design of the work. But in the epistolary form, where accident selects the characters and where the subjects treated are not dependent upon any preconceived design or plan, the author permits himself to join philosophy, politics, and ethics to the

---

1 [The "Reflections" were first added by Montesquieu to the 1754 edition.]

2 [In a manuscript draft of the "Reflections" found at La Brède, Montesquieu cited Samuel Richardson's *Pamela* (1741) and Mme. de Graffigny's *Lettres peruviennes* (1747) as examples of such "charming works."]

story, and to bind the whole with a secret and, in some respects, hitherto unknown chain.

The Persian Letters had such a prodigious sale when it first appeared that publishers made every effort to obtain sequels. They buttonholed everyone they met. "Sir," they would say, "write me some more *Persian Letters.*"

What I have just said, however, should convince the reader that they can have no sequel, much less any admixture with even the cleverest letters from the hand of another.[3]

Some people have found certain remarks excessively bold; but they are advised to regard the nature of the work itself. The Persians who play such a large part in it found themselves suddenly transplanted in Europe—which is to say, in another world. For a time, therefore, it was necessary to represent them as full of ignorance and prejudice; the author's purpose was to show the formation and development of their ideas. Their first thoughts had to be singular, and it seemed that the author had only to give them that kind of singularity which can harmonize with wit, to depict their sentiments on everything which appeared extraordinary to them. Far from intending to touch upon any principle of our religion, he did not even suspect himself of imprudence. The remarks in question are always found joined to sentiments of surprise and astonishment, never to a sense of inquiry, and much less to one of criticism. In speaking of our religion, these Persians could not be made to appear better instructed than when they spoke of our customs and manners; and if they sometimes find our dogmas strange, their observations are always marked by a complete ignorance of the links between these dogmas and our other truths.

This justification the author submits out of his love for these great truths, to say nothing of his respect for the human race, which he never intended to strike in its most sensitive spot. The reader is thus entreated always to regard these remarks of which I speak as the effects of surprise in men who

---

3 [Probably a reference to Germain Saint-Foix's *Lettres turques,* published with *The Persian Letters* in a 1744 edition.]

were bound to be surprised, or as paradoxes made by men who were in no position to make them. He is asked to notice that the entire charm of the work is in the constant contrast between things as they really are and the singular, naïve, or bizarre way in which they are perceived. Certainly the nature and the design of *The Persian Letters* are so obvious that they can deceive only those who wish to deceive themselves.

Introduction[1]

I am not writing a dedication here, nor do I seek protection for this book. It will be read if it is good; if bad, I am not anxious that it be read.

I have issued these first letters to gauge the public taste; I have many more in my portfolio which I may release later.

This, however, is only on condition that I remain unknown; I shall be silent the moment my name becomes public. I know a woman who walks well enough, but who limps when watched.[2] There are enough faults in this work without also exposing my person to criticism. Were I known, it would be said, "His book is inconsistent with his character; he ought to occupy his time to better purpose; this is not worthy of a serious man." Critics never miss a chance to make such remarks, for they can do so without needlessly exerting their brains.

The Persians who write here were lodged in my home, and we spent our time together. Since they regarded me as a man from another world, they hid nothing from me; indeed, people transplanted from such a distance could have no more secrets. They would show me most of their letters; I copied them. I even fell upon several which they would surely have kept from me, so mortifying were they to Persian vanity and jealousy.

I am, then, only a translator, and all my efforts have been to adapt the work to our taste. I have spared the reader as much as possible of the Asiatic idiom and saved him from a countless number of sublime expressions which would have been supremely boring.

But this is not all I have done for him. I have cut out those

---

1 [The Introduction first appeared in 1721.]

2 [Probably an allusion to Montesquieu's wife, who limped slightly.]

long compliments, which Orientals abuse no less than we, and I have omitted a vast number of those trivialities which barely survive exposure to light, and which always ought to die within the circle of intimate friendship.

If most of those who have published collections of letters had done the same, they would have seen their works disappear completely.

One thing has often astonished me: to see these Persians sometimes as learned as I in the customs and manners of the nation, to the point of knowing the most subtle details and of noticing things which I am sure have escaped many a German who has traveled in France. I attribute this to the long time they have stayed here; I might add that it is easier for an Asiatic to learn about the customs of the French in one year than for a Frenchman to learn Asian customs in four, since the former are as communicative as the latter are reserved.

Usage permits every translator, and even the most barbarous commentator, to adorn the head of his version or his commentary with a panegyric on the original, and to extol its utility, merit, and excellence. I have not done so; it should be easy to guess my reasons. One of the best is that it would be a most tedious thing, put in a place which already is quite tedious itself, namely, a preface.

Usbek to his friend Rustan, at Ispahan

We stayed only one day at Com. After we had made our devotions at the tomb of the virgin who gave birth to twelve prophets, we resumed our journey, and yesterday, twenty-five days after our departure from Ispahan, we arrived at Tauris.[1]

Rica and I are perhaps the first Persians who, urged by a thirst for knowledge, have left their country and renounced the delights of a tranquil life in favor of the laborious search for wisdom.

We were born in a flourishing realm, but we did not believe that its boundaries were those of our knowledge, nor that the light of the Orient should alone illuminate us.

Tell me what they are saying about our journey; do not flatter me: I am not counting on many supporters. Address your letter to Erzeroum,[2] where I will stay for some time. Farewell, my dear Rustan. Rest assured that wherever I am in the world, there you have a faithful friend.

Tauris, the 15th of the moon of Saphar, 1711 [3]

---

1 [Com (Qum) and Tauris (Tabriz) are Persian (Iranian) cities; Ispahan (Isfahan, Esfahan), before it was sacked by the Afghans in 1722, was the capital and chief city of Persia. The virgin venerated in the Com mosque is Fatima, daughter of Mousa al Kassim, the sixth successor of Ali (Hali), Mohammed's son-in-law. Montesquieu evidently confuses her with Mohammed's daughter Fatima, Ali's wife and thus mother of the Alid line if not of "twelve prophets."]

2 [Erzeroum (Erzurum) is the chief city of Turkish Armenia.]

3 [For information on the Persian calendar, see p. xxxv.]

LETTER II

Usbek to the chief black eunuch,
at his seraglio [1] *in Ispahan*

You are the faithful guardian of the most beautiful women in
Persia; to you I have entrusted my dearest worldly possessions;
you hold in your hands the keys to those fated doors that are
opened only for me. While you guard this precious storehouse
of my love, my heart enjoys perfect ease and security. You
stand guard in the silence of the night and the tumult of the
day. Your untiring care sustains virtue when it falters. If the
women you guard should be inclined to stray from their duty,
you would destroy their hopes. You are the scourge of vice and
the pillar of fidelity.

You command them, and you obey them. You execute
blindly their every desire, and you make them execute the laws
of the seraglio in the same way. You take pride in providing
them with the humblest services; you submit with respect and
fear to their legitimate orders; you serve them like the slave
of their slaves. But, resuming your power, you command im-
periously, even as I, whenever you fear relaxation of the laws
of decency and modesty.

Remember always the oblivion from which you, then the
meanest of my slaves, were brought when I put you in this employ and entrusted you with the delights of my heart. Abase
yourself completely in the company of those who share my
love; yet, at the same time, make them feel their entire dependence. Procure every innocent pleasure for them; beguile
their anxieties; amuse them with music, dancing, and de-

---

1 [The words "seraglio" and "harem" have incorrectly come to have
approximately equivalent meanings in English, and throughout *The
Persian Letters* Montesquieu similarly confuses the terms. More correctly,
a seraglio is a princely or royal palace, and harem refers specifically to
the closely guarded women's quarters in a dwelling.]

licious drink; persuade them to meet together frequently. If they wish to go to the country, you may take them, but have any man who enters their presence put to the sword. Exhort them to cleanliness, the image of the soul's purity; speak to them sometimes of me. Would that I could see them again in that charming place they adorn. Farewell.

Tauris, the 18th of the moon of Saphar, 1711

LETTER III

Zachi to Usbek, at Tauris

We ordered the chief enunch to take us to the country; he will tell you that no accident befell us. When we had to leave our litters to cross the river, we got into boxes as is customary; two slaves carried us on their shoulders, and we escaped all onlookers.

How can I have lived on, dear Usbek, in your seraglio at Ispahan, in those places that constantly invoked my past pleasures and every day aroused my desires with new violence? I wandered from apartment to apartment, always seeking you and never finding you, but everywhere coming upon some cruel memory of my departed joy. Sometimes I would find myself in that place where I first received you into my arms; sometimes in that place where you settled the famous quarrel among your women. Each of us claimed to be superior in beauty to the others: we presented ourselves to you after exhausting our imaginations on dress and ornament. With pleasure you saw the miracles of our art; you marveled that we had gone so far in our desire to please you. But you soon made those borrowed charms give way to more natural graces; you destroyed all our work; we had to remove all that ornamentation which had wearied you, and to appear before your gaze in the simplicity of nature. Thinking only of my glorious vic-

tory, I counted modesty as nothing. Happy Usbek, what
charms were displayed before your eyes! Long we saw you
wander from enchantment to enchantment, without settling
your uncertainty. Each new grace sought your tribute; in an
instant we were covered with your kisses. Your curious gaze
penetrated to the most secret places; you made us take a thousand different positions; ever new commands brought ever
new compliance. I confess, Usbek, that a passion stronger than
ambition made me hope to please. I saw myself gradually become the mistress of your heart; you took me, left me, and
then returned, and I found ways to hold you. My triumph
and my rivals' despair were complete. It seemed to us as if
we were alone in the world; nothing around us was any longer
worthy of attention. Would that my rivals had had the courage
to witness the proofs of love that I received from you! If they
had seen my ecstacies, they would have appreciated the difference between my love and theirs; they would have seen that
while they might compete with me in beauty, they could not
match my feeling. . . . But where am I? Where is this vain
recital leading me? It is a misfortune not to be loved at all,
but an affront to be loved no longer. You leave us, Usbek, to
wander in barbarian lands. Do you count it as nothing to be
loved? Alas, you do not even know what you are losing! My
sighs go unheard; my tears flow without your enjoying them.
Love seems to breathe in the seraglio, and heartlessly you flee
farther from it. Ah, dear Usbek, if only you knew how to
be happy!

> *The seraglio at Fatima, the 21st of the moon of*
> *Maharram, 1711*

LETTER IV

Zephis to Usbek, at Erzeroum

The black monster has finally resolved to drive me to despair. He absolutely insists on taking away my slave, Zelida—Zelida, who so affectionately serves me, and so adroitly grooms and graces me. Nor is it enough for him that this separation be painful, he wants to dishonor me as well. That traitor chooses to regard my confidence in her as criminal, and because he finds it tedious to stand behind the door as I always order him to do, he dares suppose he has heard or seen things I cannot even imagine. I am so unhappy! Neither my seclusion nor my virtue puts me beyond his extravagant suspicion. A vile slave attacks me even in your heart, and there I must defend myself. But no; I have too much self-respect to lower myself by justification. I wish no other guarantor of my conduct than you, than your love and mine, and—if I must tell you, dear Usbek—than my tears.

> *The seraglio at Fatima, the 29th of the moon of Maharram, 1711*

LETTER V

Rustan to Usbek, at Erzeroum

You are the subject of every conversation in Ispahan; we speak only of your departure. Some attribute it to a lighthearted whim, others to some sorrow; only your friends defend you, and they persuade no one. No one can understand how you could leave your wives, your friends, and your country to wander in climates unknown to Persians. Rica's mother is inconsolable; she asks you to return her son, whom she says you have taken from her. As for me, my dear Usbek, I feel naturally inclined to favor all you do; but I cannot pardon your absence, and whatever explanations you might give me, my heart will never admit them. Farewell, love me always.

Ispahan, the 28th of the moon of Rebiab I, 1711

LETTER VI

Usbek to his friend Nessir, at Ispahan

One day's journey from Erivan [1] we left Persia and entered the lands held by the Turks. Twelve days later we arrived at Erzeroum, where we will remain for three or four months.

I must admit, Nessir, that I felt a secret sorrow when I lost sight of Persia and found myself among the perfidious Osmanlis; and the farther I went into the lands of these infidels, the more I seemed to become an infidel myself.[2]

My country, my family, and my friends appeared before me; my affections stirred, and a certain troubling uneasiness made me realize that I had undertaken too much for my peace of mind.

But what most afflicts my heart are my wives. I cannot think of them without being devoured by grief.

It is not that I love them, Nessir; in that respect I find myself insensitive to desire. In the crowded seraglio where I have lived, I have destroyed by the acts of loving the very love I

---

1 [Erivan (Yerevan) is a major Armenian city, held by Persia in the eighteenth century, conquered by Russia in 1827, and now capital of Armenia, U. S. S. R.]

2 [Shortly after Mohammed's death Islam was split into two antagonistic sects, the Sunna and Shia. Among other differences is a major dynastic one: the Sunnites trace Mohammed's true succession through his father-in-law Abu Bekr, Omar, Othman, and eventually Osman I (d. 1326), the founder of the Ottoman Turkish empire; the Shiites hold that the true succession derives from Ali (Hali), Mohammed's son-in-law.]

anticipated. But from my very coldness springs a secret jealousy which consumes me. I see a band of women left almost entirely to themselves; I have only sluggards to guard them. Even if my slaves were faithful, I would hardly feel safe; how would it be if they were not? What sorry news might reach me in the distant lands I shall travel! Moreover, this is an evil my friends cannot remedy, a situation forbidden to their investigation. And, in any case, what could they do? Would I not a thousand times prefer hidden impunity to a public punishment? I lay my sorrow in your heart, my dear Nessir; it is the only consolation left me in my present state.

Erzeroum, the 10th of the moon of Rebiab II, 1711

LETTER VII

Fatima to Usbek, at Erzeroum

It is now two months since you left, dear Usbek, but in my dejection I cannot yet persuade myself of it. I wander through the whole seraglio as if you were here; I cannot rid myself of the delusion. What would you have become of a woman who loves you, who used to hold you in her arms, whose only concern was to prove her affection, who is free by birth but enslaved by her violent love?

When I married you I had never seen even the face of a man; and you are still the only man I have been permitted to look upon,[1] since I do not class as men these frightful eunuchs, whose least imperfection is that they are not men. When I compare your beauty and their deformity, I can only esteem myself a happy woman. My imagination cannot conceive of anything more ravishing than the charms of your person. I swear, Usbek, that even though I might be allowed to leave

---

[1] Persian women are much more carefully confined than Turkish or Indian women.

this place where I am confined by the necessity of my condition; even if I could escape my surrounding guard; even if I were allowed to choose from all the men in this capital of nations—Usbek, I swear I would choose only you. In the entire world there can be no other but you worthy of being loved.

Do not suppose that your absence has led me to neglect the beauty you cherish. Though I must be seen by no one, and though the ornaments I affect may be useless for your happiness, still I try to maintain the habit of pleasing, and I never go to bed unless perfumed most deliciously. I recall that happy time when you would come into my arms. A flattering and seductive dream shows me the object of my love; my imagination is lost in its desires, even as it indulges in flattering hopes. Sometimes I think that you are returning to us, disgusted with a difficult journey; then the night passes in dreams that are neither waking nor sleeping. I seek you beside me, but it seems you flee from me; and finally the fire devouring me dissipates these illusions and brings me to myself. By then I am so excited. . . . You may not believe it, Usbek, but it is impossible to live like this, with fire coursing through my veins. Why can't I explain what I feel so keenly, and how can I feel so acutely what I cannot express? In these moments, Usbek, I would give the world for one of your kisses. A woman is indeed unfortunate to have such violent desires when she is deprived of the only one who can satisfy them. Left to herself, without entertainment, she must live with sighs and the fury of aroused passion. Far from being happy, she must even forego the pleasure of serving another's happiness; a useless decoration of the seraglio, she is guarded for the honor, not the enjoyment, of her husband!

How cruel you men are! You are delighted that we have passions we cannot satisfy; you treat us as insensitive, but would be angry if we were; you believe that our long-restrained desires will be kindled at the mere sight of you. It is difficult for a man to make himself loved, and it is easier for you to obtain from the mortification of our senses that which you could not dare to gain by your own merit.

Farewell, dear Usbek, farewell. Be assured I live only to adore you. My soul is filled with you; and your absence, far from encouraging forgetfulness, would further arouse my love if it could be more impassioned than it is.

> *The seraglio at Ispahan, the 12th of the moon of Rebiab I, 1711*

LETTER VIII

Usbek to his friend Rustan, at Ispahan

Your letter reached me at Erzeroum, where I am now. I was certain that my departure would create a stir, but that does not disturb me. Would you have me follow my own counsel or that of my enemies?

From my earliest youth I have been a courtier. Yet I can say that I was not in the slightest corrupted by it; indeed, I formed the great plan of daring to be virtuous even at court. As soon as I recognized vice, I drew away from it, though later I approached it in order to unmask it. I carried truth even to the foot of the throne, and I spoke a language previously unknown there. I disconcerted the flatterers, and I simultaneously astounded the idolaters and the idol.

But when I saw that my sincerity made enemies, that I provoked the jealousy of the ministers but not the favor of the prince, that I maintained myself in a corrupt court only by the weakest of virtues, then I resolved to withdraw. I feigned great attachment to the sciences, and in time the force of this pretense produced real devotion. I no longer took part in intrigues, but retired to a country house. Yet even this behavior had its drawbacks, for while I remained exposed to my enemies' malice, I had shorn myself almost completely of protection from it. Certain secret counsel made me think seriously of myself, and I resolved upon self-exile from my country. My withdrawal from the court supplied a plausible pretext. I went to the king, informed him of my desire to learn the sciences of the West, and insinuated that he might profit from my journey. I found favor in his eyes, and so robbed my enemies of a victim.

And that, Rustan, is the real reason for my journey. Let Ispahan talk; defend me only to my friends. Leave my enemies to their malign interpretations; I am overjoyed that they can harm me no more than this.

I am spoken about now; perhaps I will be soon forgotten, and my friends. . . . No, Rustan, I cannot give in to that sad thought. I will remain always dear to them; I count upon their fidelity, as I do on yours.

Erzeroum, the 20th of the moon of Gemmadi II, 1711

LETTER IX

The chief eunuch to Ibbi, at Erzeroum

You follow your old master in his travels and traverse provinces and kingdoms; you are impervious to grief; each moment shows you something new; everything you see is diverting and time passes without notice.

It is not so with me, constrained as I am in a frightful prison, continually surrounded by the same objects, and consumed by the same regrets. I groan, crushed beneath fifty years of cares and anxieties; in the course of a long life I cannot remember one serene day or one tranquil moment.

When my first master formed the cruel plan of having me guard his wives, and by tantalizing promises, seconded by a thousand threats, obliged me to separate myself from my manhood forever, I, weary of service in miserable employments, calculated that I was sacrificing my passions to repose and wealth. How mistaken I was! My deluded mind saw only the compensation and not the loss; I expected I would be delivered from the attacks of love by an inability to satisfy it. Alas, only the effects of passion were extinguished in me, not the causes; and far from being relieved, I found myself surrounded by constantly exciting things. I entered the seraglio, where everything inspired regret for my loss; I felt continually agitated; a thousand natural charms appeared to my despairing view; and, to crown my sorrows, I always had a happy man to observe. In that troubled time, I never took a woman to my master's bed, never undressed her, but that I turned away with rage in my heart and utter despair in my soul.

So I passed a miserable youth, with no confidant but myself. I alone had to consume the regrets and grief that weighed upon me, and I had to look sternly upon the very women I was tempted to gaze at with tender eyes. For I would have been lost, had they discovered my secret. What advantages would they not have taken then?

I recall one day when, putting a woman into her bath, I felt myself so transported that I lost my head and dared to move my hand into a fearful place. At first thought I supposed that day would be my last. I was fortunate to escape death by torture; but the beautiful creature to whom I thus revealed my weakness sold her silence dearly. I lost all authority over her, and she has since forced me to comply to a thousand things that have endangered my life.

At last the fires of youth went out. I am old, and I find myself peaceful in that respect; I look at women indifferently and give back to them all the scorn and all the torments they made me suffer. I remember constantly that I was born to command them, and when I do command, I seem to become a man again. I hate them, ever since I have been able to regard them dispassionately, and ever since my reason has been freed to see their weaknesses. Although I keep them for another, making them obey gives me secret joy. When I deprive them of anything, the order is entirely mine, and it always produces indirect satisfaction. The seraglio is a little empire that I rule, and ambition, the only passion left me, is somewhat appeased.

I note with gratification that everything depends on me, that I am absolutely necessary; and I willingly accept the hatred of these women, for that confirms me in my post. In this way I am not undeserving of their hate: I block all their pleasures, however innocent; I am an unshakable barrier; they conceive projects and I suddenly frustrate them; I am armed with refusals and bristle with scruples; I mouth only words of duty, virtue, chastity, and modesty; I drive them to despair by continually speaking of the weakness of their sex and the authority of their master. Finally, I lament that I am required to be severe, and I pretend to be concerned that they realize I act only in their best interest and out of true affection for them.

In turn, of course, I suffer an infinity of disagreeable acts, by which these vindictive women seek to retaliate for what I do to them. Their revenge is dreadful. Between us there is a constant ebb and flow of authority and submission. They continually seek to have the most humiliating tasks fall on me; they affect a contempt without parallel; and with no regard for my age, they rouse me ten times nightly for the slightest trifle. I am overwhelmed with orders, commands, whims; they seem to take turns in bothering me with successive fantasies. Often they delight in making me redouble my vigilance, and in bringing me false rumors. Sometimes they tell me of a young man prowling around the walls, or that they heard a noise, or that someone is to receive a letter. All this unnerves me, and they laugh, pleased to see me tormenting myself. At other times they make me suspicious enough to guard their doors day and night. They cleverly feign sickness, swoons, and frights, never lacking pretexts to lead me where they wish. On such occasions my only possible action is blind obedience and limitless compliance; for refusal from someone like me is unheard of, and if I hesitated to obey them they would have the right to punish me. And I would rather die, Ibbi, than descend to that humiliation.

Nor is that all. From one minute to the next I am never certain of my master's favor. In his heart each woman is my enemy, dreaming only of destroying me. They command parts of the day when I am not heard, when they are refused nothing, when I am always wrong. I conduct an angry woman to my master's bed; do you suppose that she labors there for me, that my interests prevail? I have everything to fear from their tears and their sighs, even from their embraces and pleasures. They are in the place of their triumphs; their charms terrify me; their present services to my master efface in a moment all mine past, and responsibility vanishes in a master who is no longer himself.

How often have I gone to bed in favor and awakened in disgrace? The day I was whipped so ignominiously around the seraglio, what had I done? I left a woman in my master's arms; as soon as she saw him enflamed, she burst into a torrent of tears; she complained, and scaled her complaints so well that they augmented exactly in proportion to the love she aroused. How could I defend myself at such a critical moment? I was doomed when I least expected it, the victim of amorous negotiations and a treaty composed of sighs. Such, my dear Ibbi, is the cruel state in which I have always lived.

How fortunate you are! Your duties are only to Usbek personally. It is easy for you to please him, and to hold his favor to the end of your days.

> *The seraglio at Ispahan, the last day of the moon*
> *of Saphar, 1711*

LETTER X

Mirza to his friend Usbek, at Erzeroum

You are the only one who can recompense me for Rica's absence, and only Rica could console me for yours. We miss you, Usbek, for you were the life of our company. How difficult it is to break the bonds formed by both heart and mind.

We are much given to discussion here, usually on moral

questions. The problem was posed yesterday, whether men were made happier by the pleasures and satisfactions of the senses or by the practice of virtue. I have often heard you say that men were born to be virtuous, and that justice is a quality as innate in them as existence. Would you please explain to me what you mean?

I have talked with the mollahs [1] about this, but they drive me to despair with their quotations from the Koran; for I speak to them not as a true believer, but as a man, a citizen, and as the head of a family. Farewell.

Ispahan, the last day of the moon of Saphar, 1711

Usbek to Mirza, at Ispahan

You renounce your judgment, to defer to mine; you even deign to consult me; you believe me capable of instructing you. My dear Mirza, the one thing that flatters me even more than the good opinion you have of me is the friendship that prompts it.

To satisfy your request, I do not believe it necessary to use abstract arguments. There are certain truths of which one must not only be persuaded but must feel; such are the truths of morality. Perhaps this bit of history will touch you more than any philosophical subtleties.

In Arabia there once lived a small tribe called the Troglodytes, descendants of those ancient Troglodytes who, if we can believe the historians, more resembled beasts than men.[1]

---

1 ["Mollah" (mullah, mollak) is an honorific title given to learned religious dignitaries and is roughly equivalent to "theologian."]

1 [In ancient legends (see Herodotus IV), the distant and unknown regions around the southern coasts of the Red Sea were inhabited by savage and fierce cave dwellers, or Troglodytes.]

But the people of whom I speak were not that deformed; they were not shaggy like bears, nor did they hiss, and they had two eyes. However, they were so brutal and ferocious that there was no principle of equity or justice among them.

They had a king of foreign origin who, hoping to correct the brutality of their nature, treated them harshly; but they conspired against him, killed him, and exterminated the entire royal family.

Having struck the blow, they assembled to choose a government, and after much dissent they elected magistrates. No sooner had they been elected, however, than they became intolerable, and they too were massacred.

Freed from this new yoke, the people now consulted only their own savage nature. All of them agreed that they would no longer obey anyone at all; each was to attend only to his personal interests, and to consider none other.

This unanimous resolution was extremely pleasing to all. Each said: "Why should I kill myself working for people who don't matter to me? I will think only of myself. I will be happy; what is it to me if the others are happy or not? I will satisfy all my needs, and after that, I won't care if the other Troglodytes are miserable."

When the month for sowing came, each said, "I will cultivate only as much of my fields as is needed to furnish me with grain for my sustenance; a greater quantity would be useless, and I am not going to trouble myself for nothing."

The land of this little realm was not all alike; some was high and arid, and in the lowlands some was watered by many streams. The first year was very dry, so that land in the high places was completely unproductive, while that which could be irrigated was very fertile. Thus the mountain people almost all perished of hunger, because their merciless neighbors refused to share their harvest.

The next year was very wet, and the high places were extraordinarily productive, while the lowlands were flooded. Again, half of the people cried famine, but they found the others to be as heartless as they themselves had been.

One of the chief men had a very beautiful wife; his neighbor fell in love with her and carried her off. This occasioned a great quarrel, and after many insults and blows they agreed to abide by the decision of a Troglodyte who had had some distinction under the earlier republic. They went to him and asked that he hear their arguments. "What is it to me," the man said, "whether this woman is yours, or yours? I have my field to cultivate; I am not going to waste my time in settling your differences and doing your business while I neglect my own. I ask you to leave me alone and not bother me any longer with your quarrels." Thereupon he left them, and went to work his land. The ravisher, who was the stronger man, swore to die rather than return the woman; and the other, wounded by his neighbor's injustice and the hardness of the judge, was returning home in despair, when he saw in his path a young and pretty woman returning from the well. No longer having a wife, he was attracted to her, and the more so when he discovered that she was the wife of the man he had hoped to employ as a judge, and who had been so insensitive to his misery. He seized her, and carried her off to his house.

Another man possessed a very fertile field, which he cultivated with great care. Two of his neighbors banded together, chased him from his house, and occupied his fields. Between them they made a compact to defend each other from anyone who in turn might seek to overthrow them, and, indeed, they managed to stay there for several months. But one man, tired of sharing what he could have for himself, killed the other and became sole master of the field. His rule did not last long: two other Troglodytes attacked him, and, too weak to defend himself, he was slaughtered.

Yet another Troglodyte, almost naked, saw some wool for sale and asked its price. The merchant said to himself, "At market price I could expect from this wool only enough money to buy two measures of grain; but I will sell it for four times that, so I can get eight measures." The other needed the wool, and paid the price. "I am pleased at this," said the merchant; "now I can buy some grain." "What was that?" the buyer replied. "You need grain? I have some to sell, but the price may astonish you; you know grain is extremely expensive now, for famine reigns everywhere. But give me back my money, and I will give you one measure—but not one bit more, even if you were dying of hunger."

Meanwhile a dreadful disease was ravaging the country. A skillful physician came from a nearby country, and dispensed medicine so effectively that all those in his care were cured. When the disease had died out, he went to those he had treated and requested his fee. But he met with refusals everywhere, and returned to his own country, worn out by the rigors of a long journey. Shortly afterward, he learned that the same disease had sprung up again and was afflicting the ungrateful land even more than before. This time they did not wait for him to come to them but came to him themselves. "Begone," he told them. "Unjust men, your souls contain a poison more fatal than that which you want cured. You do not deserve a place on the earth, because you have no humanity, no sense of the rules of justice. I believe I would offend the gods who are punishing you, if I opposed their just anger."

> *Erzeroum, the 3rd of the moon of Gemmadi II,*
> *1711*

LETTER XII

Usbek to the same, at Ispahan

You have seen, my dear Mirza, how the Troglodytes perished by their wickedness and became victims of their own injustice. Only two families in the entire nation escaped its ruin. For there were in this country two remarkable men, who were humane, just, and lovers of virtue. As much united by their upright hearts as by the corruption all about them, they regarded the general desolation with a pity that became a new bond between them. They labored together for their mutual benefit; their only differences were those that spring from sweet and tender friendship; and in a remote part of the country, apart from compatriots unworthy of their presence, they led a happy and tranquil life. The earth, cultivated by such virtuous hands, seemed to fructify spontaneously.

They loved their wives, and were beloved by them. Their entire attention was directed to educating their children in the ways of virtue; the miseries of their fellow countrymen were constantly represented to them and held up as the sorriest of examples. Above all, they were taught that individual interest is always bound to the common interest, that to try to separate them was to invite ruin, that virtue is not something costly to achieve nor painful to exercise, and that justice for others is a blessing for ourselves.

They soon had the consolation of virtuous fathers, seeing their children develop in their image. The young race grew before their eyes and increased through happy marriages; the community grew, but the bond of union remained, and virtue, far from dispersing in the crowd, was instead strengthened by new examples.

Who could describe the happiness of these Troglodytes? So just a people could not fail to gain the gods' favor. From the moment they first learned of the gods, they learned also to fear them, and religion softened manners that nature had left hard.

They instituted feasts in honor of the gods. Boys and young girls adorned with flowers paid them homage with dancing and the harmonies of rustic music; festival banquets followed at once, joyful yet frugal. In such assemblies untutored nature spoke. There young people learned to exchange their hearts, and blushing virgins were surprised into confessions soon to be ratified by their fathers; there tender mothers delighted to predict sweet and faithful unions to come.

When they prayed in the temple for favor from the gods, it was not their own wealth and abundance they sought—for such wishes were unworthy of these happy Troglodytes, who

knew only how to request good for their fellows. They went
to the altars only to seek health for their parents, unity among
their brethren, love from their wives, and affection and obedience from their children. Girls came to submit the tender
sacrifice of their hearts, asking no other blessing than the
power to make a Troglodyte happy.

In the evening, when the flocks had left the meadows and
the weary oxen returned with the plow, they gathered together at a modest supper, where they sang of the wickedness
and the miseries of the early Troglodytes, of the revival of
virtue in the new people, and of their happiness. They celebrated the grandeur of the gods, their unfailing aid to men
who implore it, and their inevitable vengeance on those who
do not fear them. They next described the delights of a simple
rural life, and the joys of an existence graced with innocence.
Then they gave themselves up to a sleep which care and grief
never disturbed.

Nature supplied their desires as well as their needs. Cupidity
was alien to this happy land, and when they gave presents to
each other, he who presented the gift always believed himself
the favored one. All the Troglodytes considered themselves
members of a single family; their flocks always mingled, and
the only trouble they spared themselves was that of separating
them.

> *Erzeroum, the 6th of the moon of Gemmadi II,*
> *1711*

LETTER XIII

Usbek to the same

I cannot tell you enough of the Troglodytes' virtue. One of
them once said, "Tomorrow my father is to work his field;
but I will get up two hours earlier, and when he goes to his
work, he will find it all done."

Another said to himself: "It seems to me that my sister has taken a liking to a young Troglodyte related to us. I must speak to my father and convince him to arrange a marriage."

Another was told that thieves had carried off his herd. "I am very sorry," he said, "because in it there was a white heifer I intended to sacrifice to the gods."

One man was overheard telling another, "I must go to the temple to give thanks to the gods, for my brother, whom my father and I love so dearly, has recovered his health."

And again, "The field bordering my father's is always exposed to the heat of the sun; I must plant some trees in it, so those who work there may have some place in the shade to rest occasionally."

One day, in a group of Troglodytes, an old man mentioned a youth whom he suspected of committing a crime and reproached him for it. "We don't believe him guilty," the young Troglodytes said, "but if he is, may he be the last member of his family to die!"

Another Troglodyte was informed that strangers had sacked his house and carried off everything in it. "If they had not been wicked men," he answered, "I would wish that the gods grant them a longer use of my things than I had of them myself."

All this prosperity was not unenvied; neighboring tribes banded together and decided, on some pretext, to carry off their herds. As soon as they learned of this decision, the Troglodytes sent ambassadors, who spoke as follows:

"What have the Troglodytes done to you? Have they carried off your women, stolen your animals, or ravished your lands? No, for we are just and fear the gods. What, then, do you ask of us? Do you want wool to make clothing? Do you want milk from our herds, or the fruits of our lands? Lay down your arms, come to us, and we will give you all that. But we swear by all that is most sacred, that if you enter our country as enemies, we will consider you wicked people and treat you like wild beasts."

These words were scornfully rejected, and the barbaric

tribes came armed into the land of the Troglodytes, whom they believed were defended only by their innocence.

They were, however, quite able to defend themselves. They had put their wives and children within their defenses. It was the wickedness of their enemies which horrified them, not their great numbers. In their hearts burned a previously unknown ardor. One wished to die for his father, another for his wife and children; this one for his brothers, that one for his friends; all for the Troglodyte nation. The place of each dying man was at once taken by another, who had not only the common cause to defend but a particular death to avenge.

Such was the struggle between injustice and virtue. The wretched tribes, whose only object was plunder, were not ashamed to flee; thus, though unaffected by the Troglodytes' virtue, they were forced to succumb to it.

> *Erzeroum, the 9th of the moon of Gemmadi II, 1711*

LETTER XIV

Usbek to the same

As the Troglodyte nation grew larger every day, the people felt it appropriate that they choose a king. They agreed that the crown must go to the most just, and their thoughts turned toward a man respected both for his age and his virtue. He, however, had refused to attend the meeting and, stricken with grief, had shut himself into his house.

Deputies were sent to inform him that he had been chosen. "God forbid," he said, "that I should so wrong the Troglodytes as to make them believe that no one among them was more just than I. You offer me the crown, and if you absolutely insist, I must of course accept it; but rest assured that I will die of grief to see the Troglodytes, free since my birth, submit now to a master." With these words he burst into tears. "O miserable day!" he exclaimed. "Why have 1 lived so long?" Then his voice became severe. "I see very well what is happening, Troglodytes. Your virtue is beginning to burden you. In your present leaderless state you must be virtuous in spite of yourselves, for if you were not you could not exist, and you would fall into your ancestors' misery. But this yoke seems too hard; you prefer to submit yourselves to a prince and to obey his laws, which would be less exacting than your own morality. You know that under such laws you will be able to indulge your ambition, acquire riches, and languish in mean pleasures; you know that, so long as you avoid actual crime, you will not need virtue." He stopped for a moment; his tears flowed faster than ever. "And what do you suppose I could do? How could I command anything of a Troglodyte? Would you have an act deemed virtuous because I required it, when it would have been done anyway, by natural instinct? O Troglodytes, I am at the end of my life; the blood grows colder in my veins. I will soon rejoin your revered ancestors; why do you ask me to afflict them, and oblige me to tell them that I have left you under a yoke other than that of virtue?"

Erzeroum, the 10th of the moon of Gemmadi II, 1711

LETTER XV

The chief eunuch to Jaron, the black eunuch, at Erzeroum

I pray that heaven will bring you back to this country, and keep you from all dangers.

Although I have scarcely known that attachment men call friendship and am entirely wrapped up in myself, yet you have made me aware that I still have a heart; and while I was as hard as bronze to all the slaves living under my authority, yet I watched with pleasure your childhood growth.

The time came when my master cast his eyes on you, and even before nature had shown herself in you, the knife separated her from you. I will not say whether I pitied you, or whether I felt pleasure in seeing you raised to my condition. I appeased your tears and cries. I imagined that I saw you born again, and leaving a servitude where you could only obey, to enter a servitude where you would command. I took charge of your education, and while the severity required in instruction kept you for a long time ignorant of my love, yet you were dear to me. I can tell you now that I loved you as a father loves his son, if the names of father and son are consistent with our destiny.

You are about to travel through lands inhabited by Christians, who have never been believers; it is inevitable that you will be somewhat soiled. How can the Prophet watch over you in the midst of so many millions of his enemies? I hope that my master, on his return, will make the pilgrimage to Mecca; in that land of the angels you can purify yourself.

> *The seraglio at Ispahan, the 10th of the moon of*
> *Gemmadi II, 1711*

LETTER XVI

Usbek to the mollah Mohammed Ali, guardian
of the three tombs at Com [1]

Why, divine mollah, do you live in the tombs? You are better qualified to dwell among the stars. No doubt you hide yourself for fear of obscuring the sun, for though you are not

---

[1] [The three tombs at Com are those of Fatima (see above, p. 9, footnote 1) and Sefi I and Abbas II, Shahs of Persia.]

spotted like that star, you do similarly cover yourself with clouds.

Your knowledge is an abyss deeper than the ocean, your mind sharper than Zufagar, Hali's two-pointed sword.[2] You know what happens among the nine choirs of celestial powers.[3] You read the Koran on the breast of our divine Prophet, and when you find a passage obscure, an angel, at his order, unfolds his rapid wings and descends from the throne to reveal the secret to you.

With your aid I could have intimate correspondence with the seraphim; for is it not true, O thirteenth iman,[4] that you are the center where earth and heaven meet, the point of communication between the abyss and the empyrean?

I am among a profane people. Permit me to purify myself through you; suffer me to turn my face toward those sacred places you inhabit. Distinguish me from the wicked, as one distinguishes the black and white thread at dawn.[5] Help me with your counsel. Take care of my soul. Vitalize it with the spirit of the prophets; nourish it with knowledge of paradise; allow me to lay its wounds at your feet. Address your sacred letters to Erzeroum, where I will remain several months.

> *Erzeroum, the 11th of the moon of Gemmadi II,*
> *1711*

---

2 [Zufagar, the sword given by Mohammed to his son-in-law Ali (Hali) was reputed to have a double point, "like a fork."]

3 [In medieval cosmography, there were nine heavenly or celestial spheres, all in motion ultimately through God's power, but in popular and poetic thought these were often inhabited and sometimes locally moved by angelic powers.]

4 [According to the Shiites, there were twelve sacred imans (imams): Ali (Hali) and his eleven descendants. As intercessors between God and man, they were sinless and regarded as the sovereign leaders of Islam. Thus, to address someone sincerely as a "thirteenth iman" would be to pay a high compliment; here, of course, the intent is ironic. In another sense, which Montesquieu often uses, "iman" may refer to the prayer-leader in a mosque; the word, literally translated, simply means "leader."]

5 [In Moslem tradition, day begins when there is light enough to distinguish black and white threads.]

LETTER XVII

Usbek to the same

I cannot calm my impatience, divine mollah; I cannot await your sublime response. I have doubts that must be resolved; I feel my reason wandering; lead it back to the right road. O source of light, come to enlighten me. Destroy with your divine pen the difficulties I am about to propose. Make me blush, in shame and self-pity, at the questions I am about to ask.

Why is it that our Lawgiver forbids us to eat the flesh of swine and all meats that he calls unclean? Why does he forbid us to touch a corpse? And why, to purify our soul, does he require that we incessantly wash our bodies? It seems to me that things are neither pure nor impure in themselves, for I cannot conceive of any inherent quality that can make them that way. Mud appears filthy to us only because it offends our sight, or another of our senses; in itself, however, it is no filthier than gold or diamonds. The notion that we are made unclean by touching a corpse comes to us only because it is naturally repugnant to us. If the bodies of the unwashed did not offend either smell or sight, how could we have imagined that they were impure?

Must the senses, divine mollah, thus be the sole judges of the purity or impurity of things? But objects of sense do not affect all men in the same way. What gives an agreeable sensation to some produces disgust in others; and so it follows that the testimony of the senses cannot here serve as the standard, unless we can say that everyone can decide as his fancy dictates, and distinguish by himself those things that are pure from those that are not.

But would this not, sacred mollah, upset the distinctions established by our divine Prophet, and the fundamental points of the law written by the hand of angels?

Erzeroum, the 20th of the moon of Gemmadi II, 1711

LETTER XVIII

Mohammed Ali, servant of the prophets, to Usbek, at Erzeroum

You are always asking us questions that have already been asked of our holy Prophet a thousand times. Why do you not read the traditional opinions of the learned? Why not go to that pure source of all intelligence? There you would find your doubts resolved.

Unhappy man! Always encumbered by worldly things, and never having an eye fixed on heavenly things, you revere the mollah's condition but dare not embrace and follow it.

O profane ones, who never enter into the secrets of the Eternal! Your light is but abysmal shadow, and the reasonings of your mind are like the dust raised by your feet at noonday in the torrid month of Chahban.

Your mind, at its zenith, is lower than the nadir reached by the least of the imans.[1] Your vain philosophy is the lightning, warning of storm and darkness. You are in the midst of the tempest, wandering at the will of the wind.

It is easy to solve your difficulty, for you need only be told what once occurred when our holy Prophet, tempted by the Christians and harassed by the Jews, confounded both.

The Jew Abdias Ibesalon[2] asked him why God had forbidden the eating of swine's flesh. "There is a reason for this," Mohammed responded. "Swine are unclean animals, as I will convince you." He then made a figure of a man from some mud, threw it to the ground, and cried, "Arise." Immediately,

---

[1] This word is more commonly used by the Turks than the Persians.

[2] Mohammedan tradition. [This anecdote is not to be found in either the Koran or the "Traditions," a collection of the sayings and deeds of Mohammed and his disciples. Montesquieu may have adapted it from the *Voyages d'Adam Olearius, en Muscovie, Tartarie et Perse* (1659), where the story is reported as coming from the Koran, but where it is Jesus, not Mohammed, who is interrogated by the disciples about Noah's experiences on the ark.]

a man stood up and said, "I am Japhet, the son of Noah." "Did you have such white hair when you died?" the holy Prophet asked. "No," he responded, "but when you bade me rise, I believed the day of judgment had arrived, and I was so frightened that my hair instantly turned white."

"Now tell me the entire story of Noah's ark," said God's messenger. Japhet obeyed, and after detailing everything that had happened in the first months, he continued:

"We put the excrement from all the animals on one side of the ark, which made it lean so much that we were in mortal terror, especially our wives, who lamented fearfully. Our father Noah consulted God, and He commanded him to take the elephant and turn his head toward the listing side of the ship. Now this great animal's excrement was so huge that a pig sprang from it." Do you wonder, Usbek, that since that time we have abstained from pork, and that we have regarded swine as unclean animals?

"Moreover, as the pig wallowed constantly in the excrement, he raised such a stench in the ark that he could not avoid sneezing, and from his nose there sprang a rat, which commenced to gnaw everything in sight. This Noah found so intolerable that he once again consulted God, who ordered him to strike the lion on the forehead; and the lion sneezed forth a cat." And do you wonder that these animals are also unclean? How does it seem to you?

When, therefore, you fail to perceive the reason for the impurity of certain things, it is because you are unaware of so much else, and because you do not know what has taken place between God, the angels, and man. You do not know the history of eternity; you have not read the books written in heaven. What has been revealed to you is but a tiny piece of the divine library, and even those like us, who approach heaven a bit more closely even as we exist in this life, are still in darkness and shadows. Farewell. May Mohammed be in your heart.

Com, the last day of the moon of Chahban, 1711

LETTER XIX

Usbek to his friend Rustan, at Ispahan

We remained only eight days at Tocat, and after thirty-five days of travel we have arrived at Smyrna.[1]

From Tocat to Smyrna there is not a single city worthy of the name. I have seen with astonishment the weakness of the Osmanli empire. This sick body does not sustain itself with a mild and temperate regimen, but by violent remedies that continually exhaust and undermine it.

Pashas, who obtain their offices only by bribery, enter the provinces penniless and ravage them like conquered countries. An insolent militia submits only to its own caprices. Forts are dismantled, cities deserted, the countryside desolated, and the cultivation of both the earth and commerce is entirely abandoned.

Impunity rules in this severe government, and the Christian farmers, as well as the Jews who collect taxes, are exposed to a thousand violences.

As ownership of land is insecure, ardor to improve its value has diminished; for no title, no possession prevails against the whims of those in authority.

These barbarians have so completely abandoned the arts that they neglect even the art of war, and while European nations become constantly more refined, these people remain in their outmoded ignorance and consider adopting new instruments of war only after they have been used a thousand times against them.

They have no sea experience and no skill in naval maneuver. It is said that a handful of Christians, issuing from a rock,[2] throw the Ottomans into a sweat, and wear down their authority.

---

1 [Tocat is a city in Turkish Anatolia; Smyrna (Izmir) is a Turkish Mediterranean port.]

2 These are, apparently, the Knights of Malta.

Incapable of commerce themselves, they barely tolerate the industrious and enterprising Europeans who have taken it over; they believe they are granting favors to these foreigners, in permitting them to enrich the country.

In the entire vast land I have traveled, I have found that only Smyrna could be termed a rich and powerful city, and it is the Europeans who have made it so. It is no fault of the Turks that it does not resemble all the others.

There you have, my dear Rustan, a correct idea of this empire, which will be the scene of some conqueror's triumphs in less than two hundred years.

Smyrna, the 2nd of the moon of Rhamazan, 1711

LETTER XX

Usbek to his wife Zachi, at the seraglio at Ispahan

You have offended me, Zachi, and I feel emotions stirring in my heart that you ought to dread, were it not that my distance from you allows you time to amend your conduct and appease the violent jealousy tormenting me.

I hear that you have been found alone with the white eunuch, Nadir, who will pay for his infidelity and perfidy with his head. How could you forget yourself so far as to not feel that you are forbidden to receive a white eunuch in your room, when you have blacks designated to serve you? It is in vain that you tell me that eunuchs are not men, and that your virtue raises you above thoughts that might be aroused by their imperfect resemblance to men. That suffices neither for you nor me. On your part, you have done something forbidden by the rules of the seraglio. As for me, I am dishonored by your exposure to the gaze—what am I saying, to the gaze?— perhaps to the exploitation of a traitor who may have sullied

you with his crimes, and still more with his regrets and his
despairing impotence.

You may perhaps tell me that you have always been faithful. So, how could you not? How could you escape the vigilance of the black eunuchs, who are so astonished at the life
you lead? How could you break the bars and doors imprison-
ing you? You pride yourself on a virtue that is not free, and
perhaps your impure desires have a thousand times already
destroyed the merit and value of your much-vaunted fidelity.

I hope that you have not done what I have cause to suspect;
that the traitor did not put his sacrilegious hands on you; that
you did not prodigally display to his view the delights of his
master; that you remained clothed and kept that feeble barrier
between you; that, struck with holy respect, he lowered his
eyes; that, his audacity failing, he trembled at the punishments
he had brought upon himself. Yet, even if all this were true,
it is as certain that you have acted contrary to your duty. And
since you violated it gratuitously, and without accomplishing
your perverse inclinations, what might you have really done
to satisfy them? What would you do if you could leave that
sacred place, which for you is a harsh prison, even as it is for
your companions an asylum from the assaults of vice, a holy
temple where your sex, despite its natural disadvantages, loses
its weakness and becomes invincible? Left to yourself, what
would you do if you had for your defense only your love for
me, which is so grievously offended, and your duty, which
you have indecently betrayed? Holy are the customs of the
country where you dwell, that withdraw you from the atten-
tions of vile slaves! You must thank me for the manner in
which I make you live, since only in that way do you deserve
to live at all.

You cannot bear the chief eunuch, because he always
watches your conduct and gives you good advice. He is so ugly,
you say, that you cannot look at him without disgust—as if
one should put beautiful things in that sort of post. What
really disturbs you is that you have not in his place the white
eunuch who dishonors you.

But what has your chief slave done to you? He [1] told you that the familiarities you were taking with the young Zelida were contrary to propriety; that is the reason for your hatred.

I ought to be a severe judge, Zachi; but I am only a husband seeking to find you innocent. My love for Roxana, my new wife, does not change the tenderness I must feel for you, who are as beautiful. I divide my love between you both, and Roxana's only advantage is that which virtue can add to beauty.

Smyrna, the 12th of the moon of Zilcade, 1711

LETTER XXI

Usbek to the first white eunuch

You ought to tremble when you open this letter; or, rather, you ought to have done so when you permitted Nadir's treachery. You, who even in cold and enfeebled old age cannot without guilt raise your eyes to the dread objects of my love; you, who have never been allowed even to put a sacrilegious foot on the threshold of that awesome place which screens them from every gaze; you have permitted them, whose conduct is your responsibility, to do what you would not dare to do. Did you not sense the thunderbolt ready to strike them, and you?

And who are you, but vile tools which I can break at my whim? You exist only insofar as you know how to obey; you are in the world only to live under my rule, or to die as I may order; you breathe only because my happiness, my love, and even my jealousy have need of your servility. In short, you can have no other recourse but submission, no soul apart from my will, and no hope except in my happiness.

I know that some of my wives impatiently accept the austere obligations of their duty; that they are weary of those hideous

---

1 [*Elle* ("she") in original texts; the context suggests a misprint.]

things whose duty is to bring them back to their husband; I know all that. But you, who assisted in this disorder, will be punished in a manner that will cause all those who abuse my confidence to tremble.

I swear by every prophet in heaven, and by Hali the greatest of all, that if you swerve from your duty, I will regard your life as I do that of the insects I crush underfoot.

Smyrna, the 12th of the moon of Zilcade, 1711

LETTER XXII

Jaron to the chief eunuch

The farther Usbek travels from the seraglio, the more he thinks of his consecrated women; he sighs and weeps, his grief turns bitter, his suspicions grow stronger. He intends to augment the number of their guards, and he is planning to send me back, with all the blacks who accompany him. His fear is no longer for his own safety, but for those who are more dear to him than his life.

I come, therefore, to live under your rule and to share your worries. Good God, how much must be done just to make one man happy!

Nature seems first to have made women dependent, and then freed them; hence disorder sprang up between the sexes, because their rights were reciprocal. We are now in a new kind of harmony, in which hatred binds women with eunuchs, and love binds men with women.

My face shall become severe, my looks somber, and joy will flee my lips. I will become tranquil in appearance and troubled within. I will be furrowed with grief before the wrinkles of age appear.

I would have enjoyed following my master in his western travels, but my will is his property. He wants me to guard his wives, and I will do so faithfully. I know how to conduct myself with that sex which becomes arrogant unless allowed to be vain, and which is easier to destroy than humiliate. I prostrate myself to your will.

Smyrna, the 12th of the moon of Zilcade, 1711

LETTER XXIII

Usbek to his friend Ibben, at Smyrna

We have arrived at Leghorn after a voyage of forty days. It is a new city and a testament to the genius of the dukes of Tuscany, who have made a swampy village into the most flourishing city in Italy.

The women here enjoy great liberty. They can look at men through a kind of window, called a jalousie; they can go out every day accompanied by some old women; they wear only one veil.[1] Their brothers-in-law, uncles, and nephews can see them, and their husbands hardly ever object.

For a Mohammedan, the first sight of a Christian city is a great spectacle. I do not mean those things which first strike your eyes, such as the differences in the buildings, clothing, and principal customs; rather, I mean something truly singular, which I feel even in the most minute trifles, but which I cannot describe.

We leave tomorrow for Marseilles, where we will stay only briefly. Rica's plan, and mine, is to press on urgently for Paris, which is the capital of the European empire. Travelers always seek out the big cities, as they are a country common to all foreigners. Farewell. Know that I will love you always.

Leghorn, the 12th of the moon of Saphar, 1712

---

[1] The Persians wear four.

LETTER XXIV

Rica to Ibben, at Smyrna

We arrived in Paris a month ago and have since been in constant motion. There is much to do before you can get settled, find the people to whom you are directed, and procure the things which are all needed at the same time.

Paris is as large as Ispahan, and the houses are so tall you would suppose them inhabited only by astrologers. You may well imagine that a city built in the air, with six or seven houses one on top of the other, is thickly populated, and that when everyone is in the streets there is great confusion.

You may not believe that in the month I have been here I have yet to see anyone walk. No people in the world make more use of their vehicles than the French. They run, they fly; the slow carriages of Asia, or the even pace of our camels, would throw them into a fit. However, I am not made for such speed, and as I often go walking without changing my gait, I sometimes get as angry as a Christian; for even if I did not object to being splashed with mud from head to foot, I cannot pardon the elbowing I regularly and periodically receive. One man, passing me from behind, shoves me half around; another, passing on the opposite side, pushes me back to my original position, and I am more weary after a hundred paces than if I had gone ten leagues.

You must know that at present I cannot speak knowingly to you of the manners and customs of the Europeans, for I myself have but the slightest idea of them and so far have had time only to be astonished.

The king of France [1] is the most powerful prince in Europe He does not own gold mines, like his neighbor the king of Spain; but he is wealthier, because his riches are extracted from the vanity of his subjects, which is more inexhaustible than any mine. He has undertaken and sustained great wars

---

1 [Louis XIV.]

with marketable titles as his only source of revenue; and by so prodigious a display of human pride, his troops are paid, his towns fortified, and his fleets equipped.

Moreover, the king is a great magician, for he exercises dominion even over the minds of his subjects and makes them think as he wishes. If he has only a million *écus* in his treasury, and has need of two million, he has only to persuade them that one *écu* is worth two, and they believe it. If he has a hard war to sustain and no money at all, he has only to put in their heads the notion that a piece of paper is money, and they are instantly convinced. So great is his power over their minds that he has even made them believe that he cures all kinds of disease, simply by touching them.[2]

You ought not to be astonished by what I say of this prince, for there is an even stronger magician than he, who is master of the king's mind even as the king is sovereign over his subjects. This magician is called the pope. Sometimes he makes the prince believe that three is only one, or that the bread he eats is not bread, or that the wine drunk is not wine, and a thousand similar things.

And to keep the king always in condition and in the habit of belief, the pope sends him from time to time certain articles of faith to exercise upon. Two years ago he sent him a large document which he called the *Constitution*, and with threat of heavy punishment he insisted that the prince and his subjects believe everything contained in it.[3] He succeeded with

---

[2] [In the Middle Ages the "king's touch" was believed to be efficacious as a cure for scrofula; the practice was widely disbelieved and infrequently followed in the eighteenth century.]

[3] [The papal bull *Unigenitus*, often simply called the *Constitution* in France, was promulgated by Clement XI in September, 1713; Montesquieu thus errs in referring to it in this letter dated 1712. The bull specifically condemned certain propositions in Quesnel's *Réflexions morales sur le Nouveau Testament* (1692); more generally and significantly, it was understood to condemn the Jansenist tradition in the French Catholic Church. Jansenism had its origins in the writings of Cornelius Jansen (1585-1635), Dutch theologian and Bishop of Ypres, and stressed an Augustinian interpretation of grace and free will which appeared to many in the Church as

the prince, who submitted immediately and gave the example
to his subjects; some of them, however, revolted and said that
they would not believe anything in the document. Women
have been the prime movers in this rebellion, which divides
the court, the entire kingdom, and every family, because this
Constitution forbids their reading a book which all the Christians claim has come down from heaven; it is, in fact, their
Koran. Indignant over this outrage to their sex, the women
rose as a body against the *Constitution,* and have brought over
to their side all the men, who are not anxious about their
superiority in this affair. Indeed, one must admit that this
mufti has not reasoned badly; and, by the great Hali, it must
be that he has been instructed in the principles of our sacred
law: for since women are of a creation inferior to ours, and
since our prophets tell us that they cannot enter paradise, why
then should they trouble themselves to read a book intended
only to teach the way to paradise?

I have heard some things ascribed to the king which seem
incredible, and I have no doubt that you will hesitate to believe them.

It is said that while he was making war against all his
neighbors who were leagued against him, he was surrounded
in his own realm by an infinity of invisible enemies.[4] It is
added that while he sought to uncover these enemies for over
thirty years, and with the indefatigable aid of certain dervishes
who hold his confidence,[5] he has not been able to find a single

---

heretically Calvinistic. Austere and puritanical in attitude, the Jansenists
inevitably came into sharp conflict with the Jesuits, and throughout the
reign of Louis XIV the Gallican Church was constantly threatened with
schism. *Unigenitus* brought the issue to an intense climax, and although
theological Jansenism waned in the following years, the dispute soon
assumed important political implications, as the crown supported the bull
and the Jesuits, while the Jansenists, particularly strong in the high courts
of law called the *parlements,* increasingly came to identify religious truth
with opposition to the king. Many prominent Jansenists were women.]

[4] [The Jansenists.]

[5] [The Jesuits. Montesquieu generally uses "dervish" as the equivalent
of "monk."]

one. They live with him; they are at court, in the capital, in the army, in the law courts; nonetheless it is said that he will be unfortunate enough to die without having found them. One might say that they exist in general but not in particular, that they are a body without members. Doubtless, heaven means to punish this prince for not being moderate enough to his vanquished enemies by sending him invisible enemies whose genius and destiny are superior to his.

I will write again to tell you of things far removed from the Persian character and genius. The same earth carries us both, but the men of this country, and those where you are, are certainly different men.

Paris, the 4th of the moon of Rebiab II, 1712

LETTER XXV

Usbek to Ibben, at Smyrna

I have received a letter from your nephew Rhedi, which informs me that he is leaving Smyrna intending to see Italy, and that the sole purpose of his journey is self-instruction, which will make him more worthy of you. I congratulate you on having a nephew who will some day be the consolation of your old age.

Rica is writing you a long letter and tells me that he extensively described this country. His lively mind draws quick conclusions, but I think slowly, and I cannot tell you anything now.

You are the subject of our most tender conversations; we cannot speak enough of the welcome you gave us at Smyrna and of the daily services your friendship rendered to us. May you, generous Ibben, find friends everywhere as grateful and faithful as we.

May I see you again soon, and rediscover those happy days which pass so pleasantly between two friends. Farewell.

Paris, the 4th of the moon of Rebiab II, 1712

LETTER XXVI

Usbek to Roxana, at the seraglio in Ispahan

How fortunate you are, Roxana, to live in the gentle land of Persia and not in these poisoned regions where neither shame nor virtue are known! You are happy indeed! You live in my seraglio as in the bower of innocence, inaccessible to the assaults of mankind; you rejoice in the good fortune that makes it impossible for you to fall. No man has sullied you with lascivious glances; even your father-in-law, during the freedom of the festivals, has never seen your lovely mouth, because you have never failed to cover it with a sacred veil. Happy Roxana, you have never gone to the country without eunuchs going ahead to kill anyone bold enough not to run from your sight. And what difficulties did even I have to undergo—I, to whom heaven sent you for my happiness—before I made myself master of that treasure you defended so staunchly. How disturbed I was, in the first days of our marriage, when you were out of sight! And how impatient I was when I did see you! Yet you would not satisfy my impatience but intensified it by the obstinate refusals of an alarmed modesty; for you confused me with all the other men from whom you must always hide yourself. Do you recall the day when I lost you among your slaves, who betrayed me by hiding you? Or that other time, when, finding your tears impotent to check the passion of my love, you employed your mother's authority? Do you remember how, when all such resources failed, you courageously found others? How you took a dagger and threatened to immolate the husband who loved you, if he persisted in demanding what you cherished even more than you did him? Two months passed in this combat of love and virtue, and you pushed your chaste scruples so far that you would not surrender even after being conquered. Defending your dying virginity to the last, you saw me as an enemy who had outraged you, rather than as a husband who had loved you. For more than three months you could not look at me without blushing; your abashed confusion seemed to reproach me for the advantage I had taken. I did not even enjoy a tranquil possession; for you hid from me every charm and grace as best you could, and so, although I was intoxicated with your greatest favor, I could not obtain the least.

If you had been raised in this country, you would not have been so troubled. Women here have lost all restraint. They present themselves barefaced to men, as if inviting conquest; they seek attention, and they accompany men to the mosques, on walks, even to their rooms; the service of eunuchs is unknown. In place of the noble simplicity and charming modesty which is the rule among you, one finds here a barbaric impudence, to which one cannot grow accustomed.

Yes, Roxana, if you were here you would be incensed at the dreadful ignominy to which your sex has descended. You would run from these abominable places and yearn for that gentle retreat of innocence, where you are secure and afraid of no peril, where, in short, you can love me without fear of ever losing the love you dutifully owe to me.

When you enhance the brilliance of your complexion with lovely coloring, when you perfume all your body with the most precious essences, when you dress in your most beautiful garments, when you seek to distinguish yourself from your companions by the charm of your dancing or the delight of your song, when you graciously compete with them in beauty, sweetness, and vivacity—then I cannot imagine that you have any other object than that of pleasing me. And when I see you blush modestly as your eyes seek mine, when you steal into my heart with soft and flattering words, I cannot, Roxana, doubt your love.

But what am I to think of European women? Their art in making up their complexions, the ornaments they display, the care they give to their bodies, their preoccupation with pleasing are so many stains on their virtue and outrages to their husbands.

It is not, Roxana, that I believe they push impropriety so far as such conduct would have you believe, or that their debauchery goes to the horrid extreme of absolutely violating the marriage bond—a thought to make one tremble. There are few women so abandoned as to go that far; for they all have engraved in their hearts an impression of virtue, which is given at birth, and which education weakens but cannot destroy. They can be lax in the external duties that modesty requires, but nature revolts when it comes to the question of taking the final step. And so, when we imprison you so strictly and guard you with so many slaves, when we curb your over-reaching desires so strongly, it is not because we fear the ultimate infidelity, but because we know that purity can never be too pure, and that the slightest stain can corrupt it.

I pity you, Roxana. Your long-tried chastity deserves a husband who would never leave you, and who himself would restrain those desires which now only your virtue can subdue.

Paris, the 7th of the moon of Rhegeb, 1712

LETTER XXVII

Usbek to Nessir, at Ispahan

We are now in Paris, that proud rival of the City of the Sun.[1]

When I left Smyrna, I charged my friend Ibben to forward you a box containing some presents for you; you will receive

---

1 Ispahan.

this letter in the same way. Although we are five or six hundred leagues apart, we exchange news as easily as if he were at Ispahan and I at Com. I send my letters to Marseilles, where ships leave regularly for Smyrna; from there he forwards my letters bound for Persia by way of the Armenian caravans which depart daily for Ispahan.

Rica enjoys perfect health, for the strength of his constitution, his youth, and his natural gaiety carry him easily over every trial.

I, however, am not so well. Both my body and mind are depressed; I surrender to reflections which become daily more melancholy; my failing health turns my thoughts toward my country and makes this land even more alien.

But I beg you, dear Nessir, not to inform my wives of my condition. If they love me, I would spare them their tears; if they do not, I would prefer not to encourage their boldness.

If my eunuchs believed me in danger, if they could hope that their mean compliance would go unpunished, they would immediately open their ears to the seductive voice of that sex which can make stones hear and make even inanimate things stir.

Farewell, Nessir; I am pleased to be able so to confide in you.

Paris, the 5th of the moon of Chahban, 1712

LETTER XXVIII

Rica to ———

Yesterday I saw a strange thing, though it happens every day in Paris.

All the people gather together after dinner, and play at a kind of dramatic performance which I have heard called comedy. The main action occurs on a platform that is called the stage. On each side of it there are small recesses called boxes, and here men and women play together at a dumb show, rather like those to which we are accustomed in Persia.

In this box, you see a love-afflicted lady portraying her ailment. There, a more animated woman devours her lover with her eyes, and he returns her gaze; every passion shows on their faces and is expressed with an eloquence even more intense because it is mute. These actresses appear only from the waist up, and ordinarily cover their arms modestly with a muff. Down below, there is a swarm of people who ridicule those above them, who in turn laugh at those below.

But those who put themselves to most trouble are certain people selected for the reason that their youth enables them to sustain fatigue. They are required to be everywhere; they come and go by passages known only to them; they climb from story to story with astonishing agility; they are now upstairs and now down; they appear in every box; they dive, so to speak, are lost, and reappear; they often leave the scene of one action, and appear immediately to play in another. And however prodigious the feat may seem, there are even some men carrying crutches but acting just like the others. Finally, they retire to rooms where a private comedy is played, which begins with flattering greetings and continues by embraces; I am told that the slightest acquaintance gives a man the right to squeeze another to death. The place, it seems, inspires tender sentiment. Indeed, they say that even the princesses who rule the place are not really cruel, and excepting the two or three hours of the day when they are barbarously unsocial, they are pleasant enough the rest of the time, and their bad temper leaves them as easily as drunkenness.[1]

---

1 [Rica, innocently making a judgment sometimes shared by more knowledgeable theatergoers, finds the play among the audience more interesting and important than the activities on the stage. Other elements in this passage are not so clear. The "princesses who rule the place" are the actresses, who generally had a reputation for easy virtue, but this does not simply explain the "hours of the day when they are barbarously unsocial." One possible reading, which is at least consistent with Rica's

Everything said here applies in almost the same way to the place called the opera, except that one talks in one and sings in the other. The other day one of my friends took me into a box where one of the principal actresses was undressing. We became so well acquainted that the next day I received this letter from her:

Sir:

Although I have always been the most virtuous actress at the opera, I am now the most miserable woman in the world. Seven or eight months ago, while I was dressing for my part as a priestess of Diana, in the same room you visited yesterday, I was sought out by a young *abbé;* and he, without any respect for my white robe, my veil, or my filet, ravished my innocence. In vain have I fully explained to him the sacrifice I made; he laughs and pretends that I was already very profane when he found me. But all that aside, I have become so noticeably pregnant that I no longer dare to appear on the stage, since I am extremely delicate in matters of honor, and I continue to maintain that it is easier for a wellborn woman to lose her virtue than her modesty. You must know that this young *abbé* would never have succeeded against this sense of delicacy, had he not promised marriage; such a legitimate motive encouraged me to neglect certain minor and ordinary formalities, and to begin where I should have ended. But since his infidelity has dishonored me, I no longer wish to remain at the opera, where, between you and me, they scarcely pay me enough to live; for as I grow older and lose my charms, my salary, though it is always the same, seems steadily to diminish. I have learned from a man in your retinue that there are unlimited possibilities for a good dancer in your country, and that if I were at Ispahan my fortune would soon be made. If you would be willing to grant me your protection and to take me with you to your country, you would deserve credit for aiding a woman whose virtue and conduct would not be unworthy of your benevolence. I am. . . .

Paris, the 2nd of the moon of Chalval, 1712

mistaken ideas of the theater, would be that the actresses were "unsocial" and frenzied while on stage, but otherwise quite decently human.]

Rica to Ibben, at Smyrna

The pope is the head of the Christians; he is an old idol, revered by custom. At one time he was formidable even to princes, for he deposed them as readily as our magnificent sultans depose kings of Irimetta or Georgia.[1] But they no longer fear him. He proclaims himself as the successor of one of the first Christians, called St. Peter; and it is a rich succession indeed, for he has immense treasures and a large country under his rule.

The bishops are administrators subordinate to him, and they have, under his authority, two very different functions. When assembled together they make, as he does, articles of faith. As individuals, their only function is to dispense with obedience to the law. For you should know that the Christian religion is burdened with a multitude of practices very difficult to follow, and as it is judged harder to fulfill these duties than to have bishops to dispense with them, the latter course has been followed in the interest of public utility. So, if someone does not wish to observe the Rhamazan,[2] or prefers not to subject himself to the formalities of marriage, or wishes to break his vows, or to marry within prohibited bans, or sometimes even to get release from an oath, he has only to go to the bishop or the pope, who immediately grants dispensation.

The bishops do not make articles of faith of their own accord. There are multitudes of doctors, dervishes for the most part, who raise among themselves thousands of new religious

---

1 [Irimetta (Imeretia) and Georgia, in the seventeenth and eighteenth centuries, were petty Caucasian kingdoms dominated alternately by the Persians and the Turks; the area is now part of the Soviet Union.]

2 [Rhamazan (Ramadan) is the ninth month of the Persian calendar, during which strict fasting is to be observed during daylight hours; here, of course, read "Lent."]

questions; they are allowed to dispute for a long time, and the quarrel lasts until a decision comes to terminate it.

I can also assure you that there has never been a realm so prone to civil wars as that of Christ.

Those who publicize some novel proposition are at first called heretics. Each heresy is given a name, which is a rally-ing cry for those supporting it. But no one is a heretic unless he wishes to be, for he needs only to split the difference and to offer some subtle distinction to his accusers, and no matter what the distinction is, or whether it is intelligible or not, it renders a man pure as snow and worthy of being called ortho-dox.

What I have said is good only for France and Germany, for I have heard that in Spain and Portugal there are dervishes who do not understand a joke, and who have a man burned as if he were straw. Whoever falls into the hands of these men is fortunate only if he has always prayed to God with little bits of wood in hand, has worn two bits of cloth attached to two ribbons, and has sometimes been in a province called Galicia! [3] Otherwise, the poor devil is really in trouble. Even though he swears like a pagan that he is orthodox, they may not agree, and burn him for a heretic. It is useless for him to submit distinctions, for he will be in ashes before they even consider giving him a hearing.

Other judges presume the innocence of the accused; these always presume him guilty. In doubt they hold to the rule of inclining to severity, evidently because they consider mankind as evil. On the other hand, however, they hold such a high opinion of men that they judge them incapable of lying, for they accept testimony from deadly enemies, notorious women, and people living by some infamous profession. In passing sentence, the judges pay those condemned a little compliment, telling them that they are sorry to see them so poorly dressed

---

[3] [The references are to a rosary, a scapular, and the pilgrimage shrine of St. James of Campostello in the Spanish province of Galicia.]

in their brimstone shirts,[4] that the judges themselves are gentle men who abhor bloodletting, and are in despair at having to condemn them. Then, to console themselves, they confiscate to their own profit all the possessions of these poor wretches.

Happy the land inhabited by the children of the prophets! There these sad spectacles are unknown.[5] The holy religion brought by the angels trusts truth alone for its defense, and does not need these violent means for its preservation.

Paris, the 4th of the moon of Chalval, 1712

LETTER XXX

Rica to the same, at Smyrna

The people of Paris are extravagantly curious. When I arrived I was studied as if I had dropped from the sky; old men, women, children, all wanted to see me. If I went out everyone went to the windows; if I was at the Tuileries,[1] a circle immediately formed around me, the women even forming a rainbow of a thousand subtle colors; if I went to the theater, I found a hundred lorgnettes focused on me. In short, no man has been more often scrutinized than I. Sometimes I had to smile on hearing people, who had scarcely ventured beyond their own rooms, say to each other, "He certainly does look Persian." Even more remarkable, I found my portrait every-

---

[4] [Those condemned by the Inquisition appeared for sentencing dressed in shirts colored to suggest the flames of their presumed post-mortem destination.]

[5] The Persians are the most tolerant of all the Mohammedans.

[1] [The Tuileries was a royal palace, begun by Catherine de' Medici in 1564 and later enlarged and connected by wings to the Louvre; it was destroyed by the Paris Commune in 1871. It is the Tuileries gardens to which Rica refers.]

where; I saw myself multiplied in every shop and on every mantelpiece, so much did they fear they would not see enough of me.

Such excessive honor could not fail to be burdensome. I did not believe I was such a rare and curious person, and although I have a good opinion of myself I did not think that I, a mere foreigner, should be disturbing the equilibrium of a great city. Consequently, I resolved to exchange my Persian clothes for European, to see if there was truly something astonishing in my appearance. The experiment gave me a measure of my real value, for shorn of my foreign ornaments I was judged more objectively. Quite properly might I complain of my tailor, who had caused me instantly to lose the attention and esteem of the public. I immediately became the most frightful nonentity, and sometimes I remained in a group for an hour without anyone looking at me or offering me an occasion to speak. However, if someone chanced to inform them that I was a Persian, I soon heard a murmur all around me: "Ah! Indeed! He is a Persian? How extraordinary! How can anyone be a Persian?"

Paris, the 6th of the moon of Chalval, 1712

LETTER XXXI

Rhedi to Usbek, at Paris

My dear Usbek, I am now in Venice. One may have seen every city in the world and yet be surprised, on arriving in Venice, to see a city whose towers and mosques astonishingly spring out of the water, and whose innumerable people live in a place more appropriate for fish.

But this heathen city lacks the world's most precious treasure: fresh water. Here it is impossible to accomplish a single legal ablution, and the place is held in abomination by our holy Prophet, who never looks down on it from heaven except in anger.

That aside, my dear Usbek, I would be delighted to live in a city that so constantly fascinates me. I am instructing myself in the secrets of commerce, in the affairs of princes, and in the form of their government. Nor am I neglecting to study European superstitions. I am also applying myself to medicine, physics, and astronomy, and I study the arts. And so I am clearing from my eyes the clouds that covered them in my native country.

Venice, the 16th of the moon of Chalval, 1712

LETTER XXXII

Rica to ———

The other day I visited a place where about three hundred people are meagerly housed.[1] It did not take long, for the church and buildings are undeserving of attention. The people living there are quite gay, and several were playing cards or other games I do not know. One of these men left at the same time as I, and hearing me ask directions to the Marais—the most remote section of Paris [2]—he told me he was going there and asked me to follow him. He was a wonderful guide, who led me through all the crowds and adroitly protected me from carriages and coaches. We had almost arrived, when curiosity overcame me. "My good friend," I said, "may I not know who

---

1 [*L'Hospice des Quinze-vingts*, an asylum founded in 1254 by Louis IX (St. Louis) for three hundred men blinded by the Saracens.]

2 [The Marais, claimed from swampland during the reign of Henri IV and developed into an impressive residential district in the seventeenth century, lies on the right bank of the Seine in the third and fourth *arrondissements*. Even in the early eighteenth century, it was not so remote a district as Rica indicates.]

you are?" "I am blind, sir," he responded. "What!" I said. "Blind? Then why did you not ask that good man playing cards with you to conduct us?" "He is also blind," he replied. "For four hundred years that house has lodged three hundred blind people. But I must leave you. There is the street you wanted; I am going with the crowd into that church, and I assure you that I will be less in their way than they in mine."

Paris, the 17th of the moon of Chalval, 1712

Usbek to Rhedi, at Venice

The duties put on wine make it so expensive in Paris that one might think the intention was to fulfill the precepts of the divine Koran, which prohibits the drinking of it.

When I consider the disastrous effects of that liquor, I can only conclude that it is nature's most fearful gift to man. If anything has blighted the lives and reputations of our monarchs, it has been their intemperance, for that is the chief and poisoned source of their injustices and cruelties.

To the shame of these men it must be said that, though the law forbids our princes to use wine, they drink to an excess that degrades them beneath humanity itself. Christian princes, however, are permitted this usage, and it apparently does not cause them to do any wrong. The human mind is contradiction itself. In licentious debauchery men revolt furiously against all precept, and the law made to encourage us to righteousness instead often serves only to increase our guilt.

But when I disapprove of the use of that liquor that deprives us of reason, I do not condemn those drinks which brighten the mind.[1] It is the wisdom of Orientals to seek as

---

[1][Probably a reference to coffee.]

carefully for remedies for sadness as for the most dangerous diseases. When something bad happens to a European, his only resource is to read a philosopher called Seneca; [2] but Asiatics, more sensible and in this matter better physicians, drink those brews that can make men gay and charm them into forgetting their sorrows.

There is nothing so distressing as the consolations to be drawn from the necessity of evil, the uselessness of remedies, the inevitability of fate, and the wretchedness of the human condition. It is a mockery to try to lessen an evil by recalling that man is born miserable; how much better it is to raise the mind away from such reflections, and to treat man as a feeling, rather than a reasoning being.

The soul, while united to the body, is continually tyrannized by it. We fall into dejection and sadness whenever our blood moves too slowly, when our humors are impure or not sufficient in quantity. If we drink things which can change the disposition of our body, however, our soul then becomes capable again of receiving delightful impressions, and it knows an inward pleasure in sensing its machine regain, so to speak, its motion and life.

Paris, the 25th of the moon of Zilcade, 1713

LETTER XXXIV

Usbek to Ibben, at Smyrna

Persian women are more beautiful than French women, but the French are prettier. It is as difficult not to love the former, as it is not to be pleased with the latter; the first are more tender and modest, the others more gay and spirited.

2 [Seneca, Lucius Annaeus, (4 B.C.?–A.D. 65) was a Roman philosopher and sometime advisor to the Emperor Nero; among his works are moral essays essentially Stoic in character.]

What makes Persian women so fine is the regular life they lead. They do not gamble or stay up late; they do not drink wine and almost never expose themselves to the air. The seraglio, it must be admitted, is better made for health than pleasure; life in it is uniform and unstimulating, turning on duty and subordination; its very pleasures and delights are grave and severe, and almost never tasted except as indications of authority and dependence.

Even the men in Persia lack the gaiety of the French, and in them cannot be seen that freedom of spirit, that contented air I find here in all ranks and conditions.

It is still worse in Turkey, where entire families can be found in which no one from father to son has laughed since the founding of the monarchy.

This Asiatic gravity comes from a lack of social intercourse; they see each other only when forced by ceremonial obligations. Friendship, that gentle engagement of the heart which smooths and sweetens life here, is almost unknown to them. They retire into their houses, where they always find the same company awaiting them; each family's mode of life is, as it were, isolated.

One day, when I was discussing this matter with a man of this country, he said to me: "What most offends me among your customs is that you are required to live with slaves whose minds and hearts always reflect the baseness of their condition; these servile creatures, who beset you from infancy, weaken and eventually destroy in you those sentiments of virtue implanted by nature.

"Forget your prejudices and tell me: What can you expect of an education received from a wretch whose honor consists in guarding someone else's wives, and who prides himself on man's most loathsome employment; whose only virtue—fidelity —is despicable because it springs from envy, jealousy, and despair; who, burning with vengeance against both sexes and spurned by each, consents to be tyrannized by the stronger so that he can afflict the weaker; whose imperfection, ugliness, and deformity define the worth of his position, but who is

esteemed only because he is unworthy; who is forever riveted
to the door to which he is assigned, harder than the bolts and
bars securing it, and yet boasts of fifty years of life in this mean
post, where, as the instrument of his master's jealousy, he has
exercised all his vileness?"

Paris, the 14th of the moon of Zilhage, 1713

LETTER XXXV

*Usbek to his cousin Gemchid, dervish of the
glorious monastery of Tauris*

Sublime dervish, what is your opinion of the Christians? Do
you believe that on the Day of Judgment they will be galloped
off to hell, along with the infidel Turks who will serve as asses
for the Jews? I well know that they cannot enter the sanctuary
of the prophets, and that the great Hali's mission was not to
them. But do you think they will be condemned to eternal
punishment because they have been so unfortunate as not to
have mosques in their country? Will God punish them for not
practicing a religion which he has not made known to them?
I may tell you that I have often questioned these Christians to
see if they had any idea of the great Hali, the most perfect of
men, and I have found that they have never heard of him.

They do not at all resemble those infidels our holy prophets
put to the sword because they refused to believe in divine miracles; rather, they are like those unfortunates who lived in the
shadows of idolatry before the holy light illuminated the face
of our great Prophet.

Besides, if their religion is examined closely, there will be
found in it some seminal evidence of our dogmas. I have often
admired the secret workings of Providence, which seems in
this way to have prepared them for general conversion. I
have heard of a book written by one of their learned men,

entitled *Polygamy Triumphant,* which proves that polygamy is
ordained for Christians.[1] Their baptism is similar to our required ablutions, the Christians erring only in assigning too
much efficacy to the first ablution, which they believe suffices
for all others. Their priests and monks pray, as do ours, seven
times daily. They hope to enjoy a paradise where their resur-
rected bodies will enable them to taste a thousand delights.
Like us, they have days of fasting and mortification, which
they hope will influence the divine mercy. They worship good
angels and despise the bad. They stand in holy credulity before the miracles which God dispenses through his servants.
They recognize their unworthiness, as we do, and the need for
an intercessor with God. Everywhere I see Mohammedanism,
though I cannot find Mohammed. Truth cannot be contained;
it always breaks the clouds surrounding it. A day will come
when the Eternal will behold only true believers on the earth,
for time, which consumes everything, eventually destroys even
error. All men will be astonished to find themselves under the
same standard; everything, even the law, will be consummated;
and the holy will be raised from the earth and carried away
to the celestial archives.

Paris, the 20th of the moon of Zilhage, 1713

LETTER XXXVI

Usbek to Rhedi, at Venice

Coffee is very much consumed in Paris, and there are a great
number of public houses where it is served. In some of these
houses people gather to gossip; in others they play chess.
There is one where the coffee is prepared in such a way that it

---

1 [Theophilus Alatheus (pseudonym for Johann Leyser), *Polygamia
triumphatrix* (Amsterdam, *c.* 1682); a large, rare, and reputedly dull and
well-forgotten work by a German Lutheran pastor.]

turns those drinking it into wits; at least everyone leaving the place believes himself four times wittier than when he entered.

What shocks me about these clever minds, however, is that they render no useful service to their country and amuse their talents with puerilities. For example, when I arrived in Paris I found them in heated dispute on the most insignificant matter conceivable. It concerned the reputation of an old Greek poet whose birthplace and time of death have been unknown for two thousand years.[1] Both sides agreed that he was a fine poet; the only question was on the degree of merit that should be ascribed to him. Each wished to determine his value, but among these distributors of reputation, some carried greater weight than others, and there you have the whole quarrel. It was indeed lively, and such gross insults and bitter jests were exchanged that I marveled as much at the manner of the dispute as at its subject. "If someone," I said to myself, "were foolish enough to attack the reputation of some honest citizen in the presence of these defenders of this Greek poet, he would surely be hotly rebuked; for I suppose that this zeal, so touchy about the reputation of the dead, would indeed blaze up in defense of the living! But however that may be," I added, "God preserve me from ever attracting the enmity of the censors of this poet, who is not safe from implacable hatred even after two thousand years in the tomb! They are now beating the air; what would happen if their fury was stirred by the actual presence of an enemy?"

Those of whom I speak carry on their quarrels in the vulgar tongue and must be distinguished from another kind of disputants, who employ a barbarous language [2] that seems somehow to increase the passion and obstinancy of the combatants.

---

1 [Homer. The dispute, a considerable incident in the so-called "Quarrel of the Ancients and Moderns," was occasioned by Houdar de La Motte's translation of the *Iliad* (1714) and Mme. Dacier's spirited comment on it in her *Causes de la corruption du goût* (1714); La Motte responded in 1715 with *Réflexions sur la critique*. Montesquieu, dating this letter in 1713, is in chronological error.]

2 [Scholastic Latin.]

There are places where these people may be seen, mixed in dark and confused struggle; they feed on subtle distinctions and live for obscure reasoning and false inferences. Such a trade, in which one ought to die of hunger, actually does produce some returns, for a whole nation, driven from its own country, has crossed the seas to establish itself in France, bringing nothing with it to provide for the necessities of life except a formidable talent for argumentation.[3] Farewell.

Paris, the last day of the moon of Zilhage, 1713

LETTER XXXVII

Usbek to Ibben, at Smyrna

The king of France is old. We have no examples in our histories of a monarch who has reigned for such a long time. It is said that to a very high degree he possesses the talent for making himself obeyed, and that he governs his family, his court, and his state with equal ability. He has often been heard to say that of all the world's governments, that of the Turks, or that of our august sultan,[1] pleased him most. So highly does he esteem Oriental statecraft!

I have studied his character and found contradictions I cannot resolve. For example: he has a minister of eighteen and a mistress of eighty;[2] he loves his religion but does not suffer

---

[3] [Escaping from English persecution after 1689, a number of Irish priests found asylum in France, where a seminary was established for them.]

[1] [Montesquieu uses the word "sultan" to indicate no specific ruler of Persia, whereas elsewhere he uses the more correct "shah" for a particular one.]

[2] [Louis XIV had no such youthful minister in 1713. The reference may be to the Marquis de Barbézieux, the fifth son of Louvois, who was Secretary of State in 1691 at twenty-three, or to the Marquis de Cany, who

those who tell him he must rigorously observe it; he flees from the tumult of the cities and he is personally reticent, yet he is occupied from morning to night with making the world talk about him; he loves trophies and victories, but he fears a good general at the head of his own troops as much as if he were commanding the enemy; he is unique in that he is glutted with riches beyond any princely dreams, and yet at the same time he is afflicted by a poverty that no ordinary person would tolerate.

He enjoys giving favors to those who serve him, but he pays as liberally for the obsequious diligence or, rather, the busy laziness of his courtiers, as for the arduous campaigns of his captains. The man who undresses him, or who hands him his napkin at the table, often receives precedence over someone who captures forts or wins battles for him. He does not believe that his sovereign grandeur ought to be restrictive in the distribution of favors, and he heaps benefits on some men without investigating their real merit, believing that a man is made excellent simply by his decision to honor him. Thus, he has given a small pension to a man who ran two leagues from the enemy, and a handsome governorship to another who ran four.

He is magnificent, especially in his building. There are more statues in his palace gardens than there are citizens in a great city. His personal guard is as powerful as that of the prince before whom all thrones tremble,[3] his armies are as large, his resources as great, and his finances as inexhaustible.

Paris, the 7th of the moon of Maharram, 1713

---

was eighteen in 1708 and who exercised many of the functions of the ministry without, however, the title of Secretary. The "mistress of eighty" is Mme. de Maintenon, who was seventy-eight in 1713, and who had been secretly married to Louis for many years.]

3 [The Persian shah.]

LETTER XXXVIII

Rica to Ibben, at Smyrna

It is an important question among men, whether it is better to allow women their liberty or to take it from them. It seems to me that there are good arguments on both sides. If the Europeans say that there is little generosity in making those we love unhappy, we Asiatics can respond that there is something debasing to men in renouncing the authority which nature has given them over women. If they tell us that a number of imprisoned women is troublesome, we answer that ten obedient women are less bother than one who does not obey. But let us in turn observe that Europeans cannot be happy with unfaithful women; and they can answer that the fidelity we value so much does not prevent the disgust which always follows satisfaction of the passions, that our wives are too much with us, that such a tranquil possession leaves nothing to desire or to fear, and that a bit of coquetry is like salt, which piques the taste and prevents spoilage. Probably a wiser man than I would be embarrassed to decide this question; for if we Asiatics do well to seek means of calming our uneasiness, the Europeans also do well in not being uneasy.

"After all," they say, "though we may be unfortunate as husbands, we can always find compensation as lovers. For a man to complain justly of his wife's infidelity there need be only three people in the world; but things even out as soon as there are four."

Another question asks if the natural law requires the submission of women to men. "No," a gallant philosopher told me the other day, "nature never dictated such a law, and the authority we hold over them is nothing but tyranny. They permit it only because they are gentler than we, and consequently more humane and reasonable; these advantages, which would give superiority to them if we were reasonable, make them instead lose it, because we are not.

"Now if it is true that we hold only tyrannical power over women, it is not less true that they have a natural authority over us—that of beauty, which nothing can resist. Our power is not universal; beauty's power is. Why, then, should we be privileged? Is it because we are stronger? But this is a truly unjust standard, for we seek all sorts of ways to weaken their courage. Power would be equal if education were equal. Test them in the talents that education cannot enfeeble, and then we shall see if we are so strong."

It must be admitted, however it shocks our customs, that among the most civilized nations women have always dominated their husbands. This was legally established in Egypt in honor of Isis, and in Babylon in honor of Semiramis. It is said of the Romans that they commanded all nations but obeyed their wives. I will not speak of the Sarmatians, who were truly slaves to their women, since they were too barbarous to be used as an example.[1]

You see, my dear Ibben, how I adopt the taste of this country, where extraordinary opinions are fondly upheld, and everything is reduced to paradox. The Prophet has decided this question, and ordained the rights of the sexes. "Wives," he said, "ought to honor their husbands, and husbands ought to honor their wives; but men have the advantage of being created one degree superior to women."[2]

Paris, the 26th of the moon of Gemmadi II, 1713

---

[1] [Sarmatia is the ancient name for the land north of the Black Sea; according to Herodotus (IV. 110-117), the Sarmatians were the children of the union of the Scythians and the Amazons.]

[2] [This may refer to a passage in the Koran (sura 2, 228) discussing the rights and duties of divorced women: "and it is not lawful to them [women] that they hide what God has created in their wombs, if they believe in God and in the Last Day. Their husbands will do better to take them back [in that case] if they wish for reconciliation; for, the same is due to them as from them; but the men should have precedence over them." See also, in a discussion of punishment for refractory wives (sura 4, 38): "Men stand superior to women in that God hath preferred some of them over others."]

LETTER XXXIX

Hagi [1] *Ibbi to the Jew Ben Joshua, Mohammedan proselyte, at Smyrna*

It seems to me, Ben Joshua, that the birth of extraordinary men is always accompanied by startling prodigies, as if nature were going through a kind of crisis, and the celestial power could not deliver itself without effort.

There is no birth so marvelous as that of Mohammed. God, by providential decrees, had resolved from the beginning to send this great Prophet to mankind so that Satan might be chained, and two thousand years before Adam He created a light that passed from elect to elect, from one ancestor of Mohammed to another, until at last it reached him, as an authentic sign of his descent from the patriarchs.

It was also because of this very Prophet that God decreed that no child could be conceived immaculately, and that man should be circumcised.

He came into the world already circumcised, and joy shone upon his face from the moment of his birth. The earth quaked three times, as if it were itself giving birth. Every idol fell prostrate, and the thrones of kings were overturned. Lucifer was hurled into the depths of the sea; he escaped the abyss only after swimming for forty days, and fleeing to Mount Cabes,[2] he cried to the angels with a frightful voice.

That night God put an impassable barrier between men and women. The art of magicians and necromancers lost its power. And from heaven was heard a voice saying, "I have sent forth to the earth my faithful friend."

According to the testimony of the Arab historian, Isben Aben,[3] all the birds, the clouds, the winds, and the hosts of

---

[1] A "hagi" is a man who has made the pilgrimage to Mecca.

[2] [The location of this mountain is undetermined.]

[3] [Such an Arab historian is not easily identifiable.]

angels gathered to raise the child and disputed the privilege. The birds warbled that they were most capable of caring for him because they could most easily gather fruits from so many different places. The winds murmured and said, "Rather let us do it, as we can send to him from everywhere the most agreeable odors." "No, no," said the clouds, "no, to our care he should be given, for we can refresh him at any moment with water." From on high the indignant angels then complained, "And what will be left for us to do?" But the dispute was ended by a voice from heaven: "He will not be taken out of mortal hands, for the breasts that suckle him, the hands that touch him, the house wherein he lives, and the bed on which he lies shall all be blessed."

After so much conclusive testimony, my dear Joshua, one must have an iron heart not to believe the sacred law. What more could heaven have done to authorize his divine mission without overturning nature and destroying the very men it sought to convince?

Paris, the 20th of the moon of Rhegeb, 1713

LETTER XL

Usbek to Ibben, at Smyrna

When a great man dies, people gather in a mosque to hear a funeral oration, a discourse in his praise from which it would be very difficult to make a correct estimate of the deceased's merits.

I would abolish all funeral pomp. One should cry for men at their birth rather than at their death. What is the use of these ceremonies and all the lugubrious displays made to the dying man in his last moments? Do not the tears of his family and friends only serve to exaggerate the loss he is about to suffer?

We are so blinded we do not know when to grieve and when to rejoice; our sorrow and our gaiety are almost always false.

When I see the Great Mogul foolishly put himself each year in the balance to be weighed like an ox, and when I see the people rejoice that he has become more corpulent—which is to say, less able to govern them—then I weep, Ibben, for the extravagance of mankind.

Paris, the 20th of the moon of Rhegeb, 1713

LETTER XLI

The chief black eunuch to Usbek

Ismael, one of your black eunuchs, has just died, magnificent lord, and I must replace him. Since eunuchs are extremely scarce at present, I thought of utilizing one of your black slaves now in the country, but so far I have been unable to persuade him to undergo what would consecrate him to this service. Realizing that it would be to his advantage in the long run to make the change, I decided the other day to employ slightly more rigorous arguments. With the aid of the superintendent of your gardens, I ordered that, whatever his wishes, he was to be put into the proper condition to render you the service nearest to your heart, and to live as I do in those fearful places he dares not now even glimpse. But he began to shriek as if we were going to skin him alive, and he struggled so much that he escaped our hands and the fateful knife. I have just learned that he intends to write to you for mercy, and he will maintain that I have conceived this project only to be revenged for certain sarcastic remarks he has reportedly made about me. However, I swear to you by the hundred thousand proph-

ets that I have acted only for the good of your service, which
is the only thing dear to me and the sole object of my
thoughts. I prostrate myself at your feet.

> *The seraglio of Fatima, the 7th of the moon of
> Maharram, 1713*

LETTER XLII

Pharan to Usbek, his sovereign lord

If you were here, magnificent lord, I would appear before you
entirely covered with white paper, though even that would
not be enough to write a full account of the insults heaped
upon me since your departure by your chief black eunuch, the
most malignant of men.

Using as a pretext certain jests he claims I have made about
his unfortunate condition, he has victimized me with an inexhaustible vengeance. He has stirred against me the cruel
superintendent of your gardens who, since your departure, has
laid impossible tasks upon me. Yet, even though I thought
a thousand times that I would die in doing them, I never once
lost the ardor to serve you. How many times have I said to myself, "My master is the gentlest of men, yet I am the most unhappy slave on earth!"

I confess, magnificent lord, that I did not believe I was fated
to even worse miseries, but this evil eunuch had yet to crown
his wickedness. Some days ago, and on his own authority, he
destined me to guard your consecrated wives, which is to say
he condemned me to a punishment which to me would be a
thousand times more cruel than death. Those infants who
have been unfortunate enough to receive such treatment from
their cruel parents can perhaps console themselves with the
thought that they have never known any other condition; but

if I were so degraded by losing what makes me human, I would die of grief even if I survived the barbarous operation.

I kiss your feet, sublime lord, in profoundest humility. Act, so that I may feel the effects of your renowned virtue, and so that it may not be said that your orders added another to the miserable of the world.

> *The gardens of Fatima, the 7th of the moon of Maharram, 1713*

LETTER XLIII

Usbek to Pharan, at the gardens of Fatima

Be joyful in your heart, acknowledge these sacred words, and bid the chief eunuch and the superintendent of gardens to kiss them. I forbid them to undertake anything against you; tell them to buy the missing eunuch. Acquit yourself of your duties as if I were continually watching, and know that while my bounty is great, even greater will be your punishment if you abuse it.

> *Paris, the 25th of the moon of Rhegeb, 1713*

LETTER XLIV

Usbek to Rhedi, at Venice

There are three privileged orders in France: the Church, the sword, and the robe.[1] Each has a sovereign contempt for the

---

1 [French society was traditionally "ordered" into three classes, or estates: the clergy, the nobility, and the third estate which included everyone else.

other two; and so, for example, when a man deserves to be despised because he is a fool, he is often scorned only for being a lawyer.

Everyone, including the meanest artisan, disputes the excellence of his chosen craft, and everyone holds himself superior to the others in different professions, according to the exalted notions he has of his own calling.

Men all more or less resemble that woman from the province of Erivan who received some favor from one of our monarchs, and, in lavishing blessings upon him, expressed a thousand times the wish that heaven might make him governor of Erivan.

I have read in a travel account how some of the crew of a French vessel anchored off the Guinea coast went ashore to purchase some sheep. They were led to the king, who was seated under a tree administering justice to his subjects. On his throne—that is, a block of wood—he sat as proudly as if it had been the seat of the Great Mogul. He had three or four guards armed with wooden spears; a parasol served as a canopy to keep off the sun; all his ornaments, and those of his wife, the queen, consisted of their black skin and a few rings. Yet this prince, whose vanity was greater even than his wretchedness, asked the strangers if he was much spoken about in France. He believed that his name must have carried from pole to pole, and unlike the conqueror who is said to have reduced the earth to silence,[2] this one supposed that the universe must be talking about him.

After the khan of Tatary has dined, a herald proclaims that all the princes of the earth may now begin to eat if they choose. That barbarian who eats only milk, who has no roof

---

The nobility was divided into the nobility of the sword, usually the older families whose patents dated from the time when a noble's chief function was warfare; and the nobility of the robe, whose patents usually derived from legal, political, or personal service to the crown, though many families originally purchased the positions which conferred their titles. The nobility of the sword was considered the superior rank.]

2 [Alexander the Great.]

over his head, and who lives by brigandage, regards all the kings of the world as his slaves and insults them regularly twice each day.

Paris, the 28th of the moon of Rhegeb, 1713

LETTER XLV

Rica to Usbek, at ———

Yesterday morning when I was still in bed, I heard a violent knocking on my door, which was suddenly opened, or banged in by a man whom I know only casually, and who seemed to be quite beside himself.

His clothing was modest to say the least; his wig was set crookedly and had not even been combed; he had not taken time to have his black waistcoat mended; generally he had renounced for that day the prudent precautions he customarily took to disguise the sad state of his dress.

"Get up," he said, "I need you all day today, for I have a thousand purchases to make and it will be good to have you along. First we must go to the rue Saint-Honoré to speak with a notary who is commissioned to sell an estate worth five hundred thousand livres; I want him to give me preference in the matter. And on my way here I stopped for a moment in the faubourg Saint-Germain, where I rented a house for two thousand *écus;* I hope to sign the contract today."

As soon as I was dressed, or almost dressed, my man rushed me down to the street. "Let us begin," he said, "by buying and equipping a coach." And in fact we bought in less than an hour not only a coach but merchandise worth a hundred thousand francs.

This was all done with such dispatch because he never haggled, kept no account, and paid no money. I reflected on all this, but as the man appeared to be such a strange combination of weath and poverty I did not know what to think. Finally I broke my silence, and taking him aside, I said, "Sir, who is to pay for all this?" "I am," he said. "Come to my room and I will show you immense treasures, riches that the greatest monarchs envy—but not you, for you will always share them with me." I followed him. We climbed to the fifth floor and then scaled a ladder to the sixth, which was a garret open to the four winds and furnished with nothing but two or three dozen earthenware basins filled with various liquids. "I got up very early," he told me, "and as I have been doing for twenty-five years, I first went to look in on my project. I saw that the great day had arrived, the day that would make me richer than any man in the world. Do you see that reddish liquid? It now contains every quality that philosophers require to transmute metals. I have extracted from it those grains you see there, which are pure gold in their color, even though lacking a bit in weight. The secret discovered by Nicolas Flamel, but hunted in vain by Raymond Lulle [1] and a million others, is now mine; today I happily find myself an initiate. God grant that I use these vast treasures he has given me only for his glory!"

Transported with anger, I left and descended, or rather threw myself down the stairs, leaving this man of great wealth in his garret. Farewell, my dear Usbek. I will come to see you tomorrow, and if you like we can return together to Paris.

Paris, the last of the moon of Rhegeb, 1713

---

1 [Nicolas Flamel (1330-1418) mysteriously acquired great wealth and was widely believed to have found the philosopher's stone. Raymond Lulle (Ramón Lull, 1235?-1315), a Catalan Franciscan from Palma, wrote extensively on all the sciences and, rightly or wrongly, was considered a great alchemist.]

LETTER XLVI

Usbek to Rhedi, at Venice

I see here people who dispute endlessly about religion, but who at the same time apparently compete to see who can least observe it.

These people are not better Christians than others; they are not even better citizens. This strikes me as important, for whatever religion one professes, its principal parts consist always in obedience to the law, love of fellow man, and reverence for one's parents.

In fact, ought not the first object of a religious man be to please the deity who has established the religion he professes? But doubtless the surest way to do this is to observe society's rules and to do our duty to men. For whatever our religion, as soon as we suppose its existence, we must also suppose that God loves men, since he establishes a religion for their happiness. And since he loves men, one is assured of pleasing him by loving them—that is to say, by practicing in their behalf all the obligations of charity and humanity, and by never violating the laws under which men live.

One is much more certain of pleasing God in that way than in observing this or that ceremony, for ceremonies have no intrinsic excellence; they are good only relatively, and on the supposition that God has ordained them. But this is a matter of great discussion, and since one must choose the ceremonies of one religion from two thousand, it is easy to be mistaken.

A man made this prayer to God every day: "Lord, I understand nothing of the continual disputes about Thy nature, and though I wish to serve Thee according to Thy will, every man I consult would have me serve Thee according to his. When I wish to pray to Thee, I know not what language in which to speak, nor do I know what posture I should assume. One tells me I must pray standing, another wants me to sit down, and still another requires that I kneel. And this is not all, for some pretend that I must wash myself every morning in cold water, and others insist that Thou wilt regard me with horror if I do not cut off a small bit of flesh. I happened the other day to eat a rabbit in an inn. Three men present made me tremble, for each maintained that I had grievously offended Thee; one [1] because that animal is unclean, the second [2] because it had been strangled, and the third [3] because it was not fish. A Brahman, who was passing by and whom I asked to judge, told me: 'They are all wrong, since you evidently did not kill the animal yourself.' [4] 'Oh, but I did,' I told him. 'Ah!' he said in a severe voice. 'Then you have committed an abominable act which God will never pardon, for how do you know that the soul of your father has not passed into that beast?' All these things, Lord, trouble me deeply. I cannot move my head without threatening to offend Thee, even though I want to please Thee and to employ for that purpose the life which I owe to Thee. I may be mistaken; yet I believe that the best way to achieve this end is to live as a good citizen in the society where Thou hast placed me, and to be a good father to the family Thou hast given to me."

Paris, the 8th of the moon of Chahban, 1713

Zachi to Usbek, at Paris

I have great news for you. I am reconciled with Zephis, and the seraglio, which had taken sides in our quarrel, is reunited.

---

[1] A Jew.

[2] A Turk.

[3] An Armenian. [This seems to be an error, as Armenians are not forbidden to eat the flesh of animals.]

[4] [A Brahman is forbidden animal flesh; his indulgence here is inexplicable.]

Now only you are needed in this peaceful abode; return, my dear Usbek, return and make love triumphant here.

I gave a magnificent banquet for Zephis, to which your mother, your wives, and your principal concubines were invited; your aunts and several of your cousins also came, arriving on horseback and covered with clouds of clothing and veils.

The next day we left for the country, where we hoped to enjoy more freedom. We mounted our camels, four of us to each carriage. As we had decided rather spontaneously to leave, there was no time to have the *courouc* proclaimed,[1] but the ever vigilant chief eunuch took the extra precaution of adding a curtain to the cloth covering us, which was so heavy that we could see absolutely no one.

When we came to the river that must be crossed, we got into a box, as is proper, and were carried over in the boat. We were told that the river was swarming with people, and that one curious fellow, approaching too close to our place of confinement, received a blow that forever deprived him of the light of day; another, found bathing naked at the bank of the stream, met the same fate. So did your faithful eunuchs sacrifice these two unfortunates to your honor and ours.

But hear the rest of our adventures. When we were in the middle of the river a violent wind arose, and such a fearful cloud covered the sky that the boatmen began to despair. Frightened by this peril, almost all of us fainted away. I recall hearing the voices of the eunuchs raised in argument. Some maintained that we must be told of our danger and released from our prison, but their leader insisted that he would die rather than allow his master to be so dishonored, and that he would drive his dagger into the chest of anyone daring to make such proposals. One of my slaves, quite beside herself and all undressed, ran to help me, but a black eunuch

---

1 [*Courouc* ("forbidden" or "back, back") was the shout of the eunuchs and horsemen who accompanied the women's litters of a king or very important man.]

seized her brutally and rushed her back to her original place. Then I fainted, to recover only after the danger was past.

How difficult journeys are for women! Men are exposed only to threats against their lives, but we women are constantly fearful of losing either life or virtue. Farewell, dear Usbek, I will love you always.

> *The seraglio at Fatima, the 2nd of the moon of*
> *Rhamazan, 1713*

LETTER XLVIII

Usbek to Rhedi, at Venice

Those who find pleasure in self-instruction are never idle, and although I am not charged with any affairs of importance, still I am continually occupied. I spend my time observing, and each evening I write down what I have noticed, what I have seen and heard during the day. Everything interests and surprises me; I am like a child whose tender senses are vividly impressed by the slightest things.

Perhaps you will not believe it, but we are graciously accepted into all circles of society. I believe I owe much of this to Rica's lively mind and natural gaiety, which make him seek out everyone, and at the same time make him sought after. Our foreign appearance no longer offends anyone; indeed, we are delighted at the surprise people show on finding us somewhat refined, for the French do not suppose that our climates can produce real men. However, it must be admitted that they are well worth undeceiving.

I spent a few days at a country house near Paris, the home of a man of some distinction who delights in entertaining. He has a most pleasant wife, who combines great modesty with a gaiety that the secluded life has destroyed in Persian women.

Stranger that I was, I had nothing better to do than to study the crowd of people constantly coming and going and always presenting something new. I was much pleased with the simple manner of a man I had noticed from the outset, and we found ourselves mutually attracted and continually together.

One day while we were talking privately, leaving the general conversation to the others, I said to him: "You may find me more curious than polite, but I beg you to allow me to question you a bit, for I am bored with doing nothing, and with living among people with whom I have little in common. For two days my mind has been constantly tortured by every one of these people, for I could not understand them in a thousand years; to me they are as invisible as the wives of our monarch." "You have only to ask," he replied, "and I will tell you everything you want to know, particularly since I believe you are a discreet man and will not abuse my confidence."

"Who is that man," I said, "who told us so much about the dinners he has given for the great? The one who is so familiar with your dukes and who speaks so often of your ministers, who, I understand, are very difficult to see? He must be a man of quality, but his appearance is so mean that he scarcely honors the class; furthermore, I discovered in him no signs of education. I am a foreigner, but it seems to me that generally there are certain marks of good breeding common to all nations, which I do not find in him. Is it that your aristocracy is worse trained than others?" He laughed. "That man," he said, "is a tax-farmer, and as superior in wealth as he is deficient in birth.[1] He might entertain the best society in Paris at his table if he would only resolve never to eat there himself. For, as you see, he is exceedingly impertinent; but he has an excellent cook, to whom he is not ungrateful: all day you have heard his praises of the man."

"And that big man dressed in black," I asked, "whom that

---

[1] [Tax collection in eighteenth-century France was "farmed," i.e., contracted by bid to men, usually of the middle class, who made the collections, submitted to the government the amount stipulated by the contract, and kept for themselves whatever additional sums were collected, which frequently were considerable.]

lady has arranged to have placed next to her? How is it that his dress is so solemn, while his manner is gay and his complexion florid? He smiles graciously to everyone speaking to him, and his costume, though more modest, is more carefully arranged than that of your women." "That," the man answered, "is a priest and, what is worse, a confessor. Such as he is, he knows more about women than their husbands; he understands their weaknesses, and they know his." "Ah!" I said; "and does he always talk of something called grace?" "No, not always," he replied. "In the ear of a pretty woman he speaks more freely of the fall from grace; he thunders in public but is gentle as a lamb in private." "He seems to receive much attention and to be held in great respect," I observed. "Ha! What respect! He is a necessary man. He brightens a lonely life with his small counsel, his officious concern, and his regular visits. He cures a headache better than any man alive; he is an excellent fellow."

"Now, if I am not becoming troublesome, tell me about that badly dressed man opposite us, who grimaces and speaks a different language than the others. He doesn't have wit enough to talk well, but he talks nonetheless." "That," he answered, "is a poet, the caricature of humanity. His sort maintains they are born to be what they are, and, I might add, what they remain throughout their lives—which is to say, almost always the most ridiculous of mankind, spared by no one, and plentifully scorned by all. Hunger has brought him here, and he has been well received by the master and mistress of the house, whose bounty and good nature alike are offered to all. He wrote their epithalamium when they were married, and since the marriage has turned out as well as he predicted, that is the best thing he has ever written.

"With your Oriental prejudices," he added, "you may find it hard to believe that we have happy marriages here, and that there are some wives whose virtue alone is a sufficient guard. The couple here enjoy an absolutely untroubled peace and are liked and esteemed by everyone. Of course, it is true that their good nature requires that they be hospitable to all sorts of people, and thus one sometimes finds here an unfortunately motley group. But I don't really disapprove of this, for one must take men as they come, and the people who are considered good company are often only those whose vices are most refined; perhaps with people as with poisons, the subtlest are the most dangerous."

"And that old man," I whispered, "with such a sullen appearance? I first took him to be a foreigner; for, quite apart from his clothes, he censures everything done in France and disapproves of your government." "He is an old soldier," he said, "memorable to all listeners by the tedious accounts of his exploits. He finds it insufferable that France could win battles without him, or to hear a seige praised at which he did not mount the breach. He believes himself so necessary to our history that he supposed it ended when he did; he regards the wounds he received as marking the dissolution of the monarchy; and unlike those philosophers who maintain that we can enjoy only the present and that the past is nothing, he enjoys only the past and exists only in the campaigns he has made. He breathes only the air of history, while true heroes ought to live in the future." "But why has he left the service?" I asked. "He has not left the service; the service has left him," he answered. "He is retained in a small post, where he will relate his adventures to the end of his days, but further than this along the road to honor he will never go." "But why?" I said. "We have a policy in France never to advance officers whose patience has been worn out as subalterns. We regard them as men whose genius has been dwarfed by details, and who, in accustoming themselves to petty concerns, are made incapable of anything great. We believe that unless a man has the qualities of a general by thirty he will never have them. If he cannot encompass in a glance the changing situations in terrain covering several leagues, if he hasn't the sort of mind that can exploit any victorious advantage, or employ every resource in defeat, we believe he can never be trained to such talents. It is for this reason that we have brilliant posts for the great, those sublime men to whom heaven has granted not only courage but heroic genius, and subaltern employments for those with inferior gifts. Of this number there are those who have grown old in obscure wars. They can succeed in doing no more than what they have done all their lives, and it would not do to give them new assignments in their declining years."

A moment later my curiosity was again aroused, and I said: "I promise to ask no more questions if you will only answer this one. Who is that tall young man who wears his own hair, and has more impertinence than wit? Why does he speak louder than the others and consider himself so important to the world?" "He is a great lady's-man," he answered. But at this point some people entered, others left, we got up, someone came over to speak to my friend, and so I was left in ignorance about him. However, a moment later it chanced that this young man found himself next to me, and he said, "It is a fine day, sir; would you care to join me for a walk in the garden?" I answered as civilly as possible, and we went out. "I came to the country," he told me, "to please the mistress of the house, with whom I am not on bad terms. Of course, there is another woman who will not be pleased by this, but what can you do? I visit the prettiest women in Paris, but I never attach myself to any one and give them all good cause to worry; for, just between you and me, I am not much good." "Evidently, sir," I said, "you have some commitment or office which prevents you from attending them more assiduously?" "No, sir, I have no vocation other than that of enraging husbands and making fathers despair. I like to alarm women who think they have me caught, by putting them an inch away from losing me. I belong to a crowd of young men who divide up Paris in this way, and keep it wondering about our every move." "If I understand, then," I said, "you make a greater stir than the bravest soldier and are more highly regarded than a great magistrate. If you were in Persia, however, you would not relish such advantages; you would be considered more fit to guard our women than to please them." The blood mounted to my face, and I believe that had I gone on speaking, I could not have prevented myself from being rude to him.

What can be said of a country where such people are tolerated; where they allow such tradesmen to survive; where infidelity, treachery, rape, perfidy, and injustice lead to distinction; where a man is esteemed for tearing a daughter away from her father or a wife from her husband, and so disturbing the sweetest and holiest of societal bonds? Happy are the children of Hali, who defend their families from shame and seduction! Daylight itself is no more pure than the fires burning in the hearts of our wives, and our daughters tremble to contemplate the day when they must lose the virtue which makes them like the angels and the celestial powers. Dear land of my birth, on which the sun first shines, you have not been sullied by the horrid crimes that make that star hide itself when it approaches the gloomy West!

Paris, the 4th [2] of the moon of Rhamazan, 1713

LETTER XLIX

Rica to Usbek, at ———

The other day an extraordinarily dressed dervish visited me in my room. His beard fell almost to the rope girdling his waist; he was barefoot, and his gown was coarse, gray, and peaked at various places. The total impression was so bizarre that my first idea was to send for a painter to make a sketch.

He began by paying me a big compliment, in which he informed me that he was not only a man of merit, but a Capuchin.[1] "I am told, sir," he added, "that you will soon be re-

---

[2] [Some texts read "the 5th."]

[1] [A Capuchin is a mendicant friar of a religious order recognized in 1528 as independent of the parent Franciscan order.]

turning to the Persian court, where you hold a distinguished
rank. I have come to ask your protection, and to beg you to
obtain from your king a small establishment near Casbin [2] for
two or three members of our order." "Do you, father, wish to
go to Persia?" I asked him. "Me, sir!" he said. "I'll take good
care not to. I am the provincial here, and I wouldn't trade my
position for any Capuchin office in the world." "Then why
the devil did you ask?" "Because," he replied, "if we had this
monastery, our Italian fathers would send out two or three
monks." "So you know these monks?" I said. "No, sir, I do
not." "Bah! Then what concern of yours is it that they go to
Persia? A fine project indeed, to send two Capuchins to
breathe the air of Casbin! For this it is imperative to petition
monarchs! So this is what is meant by your fine colonies! Get
out! You and your type are not made to be transplanted, and
you would better creep along in the places where you have
been engendered."

Paris, the 15th of the moon of Rhamazan, 1713

Usbek [1] *to* ————

I have known people in whom virtue was so natural that they
were not even aware of it. Carried along as if by instinct, they
fulfilled their duty without hesitation; and far from pointing
out their excellent qualities in conversation, they themselves
seemed to be quite unconscious of them. These are the people
I admire, and not those men who seem surprised by their

---

2 [Casbin (Qazvin) is a city which was formerly the ancient capital of
Persia.]

1 [Editions earlier than 1758 ascribe this letter to Rica.]

virtue, and who regard a good act as a kind of prodigy which ought to stimulate wonder in the telling of it.

If modesty is a virtue necessary to those who are graced by heaven with great talents, what can be said of those insects who dare to display a pride which would dishonor the greatest of men?

On all sides I see people ceaselessly talking about themselves. Their conversations are a mirror always reflecting their impertinent features. They will tell you of the slightest things that happened to them, expecting that their interest will make the thing important in your eyes. They have done everything, seen everything, said everything, thought everything; they are a model for mankind, a subject of limitless comparisons, an inexhaustible source of examples. Ah, how insipid self-praise is!

A few days ago a man of this sort burdened us for two hours with himself, his merits, and his talents. However, as perpetual motion is impossible in nature, he finally stopped, and as the conversation was returned to us, we seized it.

A man, apparently in rather ill temper, began by complaining of the tedium of most conversations, dominated by fools either describing themselves or relating everything to themselves. "You are right," our talkative friend interrupted, "no one acts as I do. I never praise myself. I am wealthy, well-born, generous, and my friends say I have some wit, but I never speak of that, and if I have certain good qualities, the one I value most highly is my modesty."

I was stupified by this braggart, and while he continued to talk on loudly, I said to myself, "Happy is he with enough vanity never to speak boastfully of himself, who fears the ridicule of others, and who never hurts another's pride by exhibiting his own!"

Paris, the 20th of the moon of Rhamazan, 1713

LETTER LI

Nargum, Persian envoy in Muscovy, to Usbek, in Paris

In letters from Ispahan I am informed that you have left Persia and are now actually in Paris. Why must I learn such news from others and not from you?

The orders of the king of kings [1] have kept me in this country for five years now, where I have concluded several important negotiations.

You are aware that the czar is the only Christian prince whose interests are allied to those of Persia, since he is as much an enemy of the Turks as we are.

His empire is larger than ours, for there are reckoned to be a thousand leagues between Moscow and the limit of his dominions on the frontier of China.

He is absolute master over the lives and the property of his subjects, who, excepting four families,[2] are all slaves. Even that lieutenant of the prophets, the king of kings whose footstool is the sky, exercises no more redoubtable power.

Considering the frightful climate of Muscovy, one would never suppose that it would be much of a punishment to be exiled from it; however, whenever a noble is disgraced, he is banished to Siberia.

Just as the law of our Prophet forbids us to drink wine, so the prince's law forbids the Muscovites.

Their manner of receiving guests is not at all Persian. As soon as the stranger enters a house, the husband presents his

---

[1] [The shah of Persia.]

[2] [Montesquieu's source for this mistaken observation on slavery and privilege in Russia has not been identified. Some of the names likely to be known to a Westerner with little real knowledge of Russian institutions are the Dolgorukii, Golitsyn, Naryshkin, Miloslavskii, and, of course, the Romanov; but which of these are referred to here, if any, is unknown.]

wife to be kissed, and this is considered an act of courtesy to the husband.

Although fathers ordinarily stipulate in the marriage contract that their daughters are not to be whipped by their husbands, you have no idea how much Muscovite women like to be beaten.[3] They cannot believe that they possess the heart of their husbands if they are not properly beaten; any other conduct on his part is a mark of unpardonable indifference. Here is a letter written recently from a Muscovite wife to her mother:

My dear Mother,

I am the unhappiest woman in the world, for while I have done everything to make my husband love me, yet I have not succeeded. Yesterday, having a thousand things to do about the house, I went out and stayed away all day; when I returned I was sure he would really beat me, but he never said a word. My sister is treated much better: her husband thrashes her every day, and if she but looks at another man he instantly knocks her down. They love each other very much and live in perfect understanding.

That is what makes her so proud, but I will not give her the chance to scorn me much longer. I have determined at all costs to make my husband love me, and I will make him so angry that he will be forced to give me some marks of affection. No one shall say that I have not been beaten, and that I live in a house where no one thinks of me. I will cry as loudly as I can at the slightest touch, so that people will assume that all is going well, and if any neighbors come to my aid, I believe I would strangle them. Dear Mother, I beg you to point out to my husband how unworthily he is treating me. My father, who is an excellent man, did not act this way. In fact, I recall thinking as a little girl that sometimes he loved you too much. I embrace you, dear Mother.

The Muscovites cannot leave their country even to travel; so, separated from other nations by their own laws, they have become even more attached to their old customs and cannot believe it possible for there to be others.

---

[3] These customs have changed.

But the presently reigning prince [4] wants to change every-thing. He has quarreled mightily with his subjects about their beards, and the clergy and monks have struggled as greatly to retain their ignorance.

He makes every effort to nurture the arts and neglects noth-ing that might spread through Europe and Asia the glory of his nation, forgotten until now, and scarcely known even to itself.

Restless and always agitated, he wanders over his vast estates leaving everywhere the marks of his natural severity.

Then he leaves them, as if they were too small to hold him, to seek other lands and new kingdoms in Europe.

I embrace you, my dear Usbek, and beg you to send me your news.

Moscow, the 2nd of the moon of Chalval, 1713

LETTER LII

Rica to Usbek, at ———

I was much amused at a social gathering the other day. There were women of all ages present: one of eighty, another of sixty, and one of forty, who had a niece of about twenty or twenty-one. Instinct led me to choose the youngest, and she whispered to me, "What do you think of my aunt, who at her age tries to play the beauty and wants to have lovers?" "She is wrong," I said. "Such plans become only you." A moment later, I found myself talking to the aunt. "What do you think," she asked me, "of that woman over there, who is at least sixty, but who spent more than an hour today in prettying herself?" "It is a waste of time," I told her. "One must have your charms to justify caring for them." I then went over to the unfortunate woman of sixty, pitying her deeply until she whispered, "Have

---

4 [Peter I, "the Great" (1672-1725).]

you ever seen anything so absurd? Look at that woman of eighty, wearing flame-colored ribbons! She wants to look young and has succeeded only in being childish." "Ah! Good Lord!" I said to myself. "Do we feel only the ridiculousness of others? And yet perhaps it is a good thing," I thought further, "that we can find some consolation in the follies of others." However, I was in a mood to be amused, and I told myself that, having mounted sufficiently high, we might now try the descent. I began with the oldest. "Madame, you so closely resemble that woman to whom I was just talking that you seem to be sisters, I suppose of about the same age." "Quite right, sir," she said. "When one of us dies the other should have real cause for alarm, for I doubt that we are two days apart in age." Leaving this decrepit creature I went over to the one of sixty. "Madame, you must settle a bet I have made. I have wagered that you and that lady over there," indicating the woman of forty, "were the same age." "Upon my word," she said, "I don't believe there is a difference of six months." So far, so good; let us continue. I descended further, this time to the woman of forty. "Madame, would you please tell me if you are joking when you call that girl, over at the other table, your niece? You are surely as young as she; there is even something faded about her face that is quite missing in yours, and the lively colors of your complexion. . . ." "Listen," she said, "I am really her aunt, but her mother was at least twenty-five years older than I. We were not even of the same marriage, and I have heard my departed sister say that her daughter and I were born the same year." "Just as I had said, madame; my astonishment was justified."

My dear Usbek, women who feel that the loss of their charms is prematurely aging them long to be young again. And how can they help deceiving others when they make such an effort to deceive themselves and to rid their minds of this most painful of all thoughts?

Paris, the 3rd of the moon of Chalval, 1713

LETTER LIII

Zelis to Usbek, at Paris

No passion was ever stronger or more violent than that of the white eunuch Cosrou for my slave Zelida; he has asked her in marriage with such ardor that I can no longer refuse him. And why should I resist when her mother does not, and when Zelida herself appears content with this idea of a mock marriage and the empty shadow it offers to her?

What can she want with this unfortunate creature, who will be a husband only in his jealousy; whose coldness can be changed only to impotent despair; who will constantly recall the memory of what he once was, but only to remind her of what he is no longer; who will always be ready but never able to possess her; and who, continually deceiving both himself and her, will remind her at every instant of the misfortune of her condition?

And again! To be always in dreams and fantasies; to live only in imagination; to be always close to pleasure but never in it; to languish in a wretch's arms, responding not to his sighs but to his regrets!

What contempt we must feel for such a man, who is made solely to guard and not to possess. I search for love but cannot see it.

I am speaking frankly to you, because you like my artlessness and prefer my free and responsive attitude toward pleasure to that affected modesty of my companions.

I have heard you say many times that eunuchs do voluptuously enjoy women in some way that we cannot understand; that nature compensates them for their loss, having means with which to repair their damaged condition; that one may cease to be a man and yet feel desire; and that in such a state one acquires another sense and exchanges, as it were, one pleasure for another.

If this is the case I would pity Zelida less. At least it is something to live with people not totally miserable.

Send me your orders on this affair, and let me know if you want this marriage to take place in the seraglio. Farewell.

> *The seraglio at Ispahan, the 5th of the moon of Chalval, 1713*

LETTER LIV

Rica to Usbek, at ———

This morning I was in my room, which as you know is separated from the others by such a thin, grilled partition that one can hear everything said in the adjoining room. A man, pacing the floor in great strides, said to another: "I don't know why it is, but everything seems to turn against me. For at least three days I have not said one noteworthy thing. I find myself thrown pell-mell into conversation, with no one paying the least attention or speaking to me twice. I had prepared various sallies to enliven my conversation, but no one lets me get them off. I had a fine story to tell, but whenever an opportunity approached people evaded it as if on purpose. For four days several witticisms have been growing stale in my head without my ever using them. If this continues, I fear I will end up as a fool; it seems I am under an unlucky star and cannot escape it. Yesterday I hoped to shine with three or four old women who certainly did not impose themselves, and I should have said the most charming things imaginable; but though I directed the conversation for more than a quarter-hour they never once followed my point, and like the fatal sisters, they cut the thread of my every discourse.[1] Let me tell

---

[1] [In Greek and Roman mythology, fate was represented by three sisters, one who spun the thread of life, another who decided its length, and the third who cut it off.]

you, a reputation for wit is hard to achieve, and I don't know how you managed it." "I have an idea," the other replied; "let's work together on this and form an association for the production of wit. Every day we will agree on our subject of conversation, and we will help each other so well that if someone tries to interrupt one of us, the other will draw him aside, with good taste if possible, otherwise with force. We will agree upon the places where approval should be voiced, where to smile, and where to burst into full laughter. You will see that we will give tone to every conversation, and that people will admire our lively wit and apt repartees. We can arrange everything by a system of headshaking. You will shine one day, the next you will be my foil. We will go together to a house; I will point to you and exclaim, 'I must tell you of an amusing reply this gentleman just made to a man we met in the street.' Then, turning to you, I will say, 'He certainly didn't expect it and was very surprised.' I will recite some of my poems and you will say, 'I was there when he composed them; it was at supper and took only a moment.' Sometimes we will mock each other, and people will say, 'Look how they attack each other, and how they defend themselves! There's nothing spared here—let's see how he gets away from that one! Wonderful! What brilliance! A regular battle!' No need to tell them we rehearsed it all the night before. We must buy some books, some collections of bright sayings composed for people without wit but hopeful of counterfeiting it; everything depends on having good models. In six months we should be ready to sustain an hour's talk entirely filled with bons mots. But we must also be attentive to the fate of our witticisms; for it is not enough to make a bon mot, it must be spread and scattered in all directions. Otherwise all is lost, and I assure you that nothing is so disconcerting as to watch one of your witty remarks die in the ear of some fool—though there is, of course, the compensation in such cases that some of the stupid things we say similarly disappear also. Now there, my friend, is the course before us. Do what I say and I promise you a place in the Academy in less than six months. And once there you can abandon all your art, for you will then be judged a man of wit regardless of what you do; thus your efforts need not be protracted. They say that in France a man immediately catches what is called the *esprit de corps* of the social circle he enters; so will you, and I only fear that you will be overwhelmed with applause."

Paris, the 6th of the moon of Zilcade, 1714

LETTER LV

Rica to Ibben, at Smyrna

Among Europeans the first quarter-hour of marriage settles all difficulties, for the last favors are always awarded on the day of the marriage ceremony. Women here are not like those in Persia, who sometimes dispute the terrain for several months. Nothing is more obvious; if they lose nothing, it is because they have nothing to lose. Thus—shameful thing!—they always know exactly the moment of their defeat, and without consulting the stars one can predict almost to the hour the time of their children's birth.

The French seldom speak of their wives; they are afraid to do so in the presence of people who know them better than they do.

Among the French there are certain unhappy men whom no one consoles—jealous husbands. There are men hated by everyone—jealous husbands. And there are men universally scorned —also jealous husbands.

Consequently there is no country with fewer jealous husbands than France. Their tranquillity, however, is not based upon confidence in their wives but on the poor opinion they have of them. All the wise precautions of the Asiatics—the

covering veils, the confining prisons, the vigilant eunuchs—
seem to the French better calculated to exercise rather than to
discourage the ingenuity of women. Here husbands accept
their lot with good grace and regard infidelities as fated by the
stars. Any husband desiring to possess his wife to the exclusion
of everyone else would be considered disruptive of the public
happiness, a madman wanting to enjoy the sunlight and to
forbid it to all others.

Here a husband who loves his wife is a man without sufficient merit to win the love of another woman. He is a person
who abuses the authority given him by law to supply pleasures
he could not otherwise gain, who uses his advantages to the
prejudice of society at large, who appropriates for his own use
what has been given to him only in pawn, and who acts, in
so far as he can, to overturn the tacit agreements made for the
happiness of both sexes. An Asiatic, married to a beautiful
woman, tries hard to conceal the fact; here it is no cause for
anxiety, for diversion elsewhere is always possible. A prince
consoles himself for the loss of one place by taking another;
when the Turks took Baghdad from us, did we not in turn
take the fortress of Candahar from the Mogul? [1]

A man who generally tolerates the infidelities of his wife is
not disapproved but praised for his prudence; only in particular cases is he felt to be dishonored.

It is not that there are no virtuous women; there are, and
one may say that they are distinguished. My guide always
pointed them out to me, but they were all so ugly that one
would have to be a saint not to hate virtue.

After what I have said of the manners of this country, you
will readily see that the French do not admire constancy much.
They believe it is as ridiculous to swear abiding love to one
woman as it is to maintain that they will forever be in good
health, or invariably happy. When they promise always to
love a woman, they suppose that she, in turn, promises that

---

[1] [The Turks captured Baghdad in 1638; Candahar (Kandahar), now in
Afghanistan, was taken by the Persians in 1649.]

she will always be lovable; if she breaks her word, they no longer feel bound to theirs.

Paris, the 7th of the moon of Zilcade, 1714

LETTER LVI

Usbek to Ibben, at Smyrna

Gambling is much practiced in Europe. In fact, one of the ranks of society is that of gambler, and this title by itself supplies the place of birth, wealth, and integrity. Everyone of course knows that it is often a mistake to admit indiscriminately all gamblers to the ranks of honorable men, but they have all agreed not to correct the error.

Women are especially addicted. It is true that in youth they are not likely to give themselves up to it except as it aids a dearer passion, but as they grow older their love for gaming grows younger, and when all other passions have left them, this one fills the void.

Wishing to ruin their husbands, they employ means suitable to every age, from the tenderest youth to the most decrepit old age. Clothes and luxurious display begin the disorder, coquetry increases it, and gambling completes it.

I have often seen nine or ten women, or rather nine or ten centuries, seated about a table. I have watched them in their hopes, their fears, their joys, and especially in their anger. You would have said that they would never again be calm, and that life would leave them sooner than their despair; you would have been in doubt whether they were paying their creditors or their legatees.

It seems that our holy Prophet especially intended to remove from us everything that could unsettle our reason. He has prohibited the use of wine, which shrouds man's mind,

and by express decree he has forbidden games of chance. Moreover, when it was not possible for him to remove the cause of
passion from us, he has subdued it. Among us love produces
neither trouble nor frenzy; it is a languid passion that leaves
our souls calm. A plurality of wives saves us from their domination and tempers the violence of our desires.

Paris, the 18th of the moon of Zilcade, 1714

LETTER LVII

Usbek to Rhedi, at Venice

The libertines here maintain an immense number of prostitutes; and the devout, an innumerable crowd of dervishes.
These dervishes make three vows, of obedience, poverty, and
chastity. It is said that the first is the best observed; as for the
second, I assure you it certainly is not; I leave it to you to
judge the third.

But however rich these dervishes are, they never give up the
appearance of poverty; our glorious sultan would as soon
renounce his magnificent and sublime titles. And they are
right, for their reputation for poverty prevents them from ever
being poor.

Physicians and some of these dervishes called confessors are
here either excessively esteemed or excessively scorned; however, it is said that expectant heirs generally prefer physicians
to confessors.

The other day I went to a convent of these dervishes. One
of them, whose white hair made him venerable, welcomed me
graciously and conducted me through the entire house. In the
garden we fell into discussion. "Father," I said to him, "what
is your function in this community?" "Sir," he replied, apparently very pleased with my question, "I am a casuist." "Casuist?" I asked. "Since I have been in France I have never heard

of that office." "What! You don't know what a casuist is? Then listen and I will give you an explanation which will leave nothing to be desired. There are two kinds of sin: mortal, which absolutely excludes one from paradise, and venial, which truly offends God, but does not irritate him to the point of denying beatitude. Now all our art consists in distinguishing carefully between these two kinds of sin; for excepting a few libertines, all Christians wish to gain paradise, but hardly anyone wants to enter except by the cheapest possible means. When one understands what constitutes mortal sin, he will try not to commit it, and the business is done. There are some men who do not aspire to great perfection, and not being ambitious they do not care for the best places; they would enter heaven as easily as they can, satisfied only to be there, and they undertake neither more nor less than what is necessary for the purpose. There are people who would attack heaven rather than not obtain it, and who would say to God: 'Lord, I have entirely fulfilled your conditions, and you cannot hold back on your promises. Since I have not done more than you required, I release you from granting me more than you promised.'

"Thus we are indispensable, sir. And this is not all; you must see something else. The act itself does not constitute a crime, but rather the knowledge of him who commits it. Anyone doing wrong is safe in his conscience if he believes it not to be bad, and as there are an infinite number of equivocal actions, a casuist can give to them a quality of goodness they do not have simply by declaring them good. Provided he can persuade the person that his intent is not evil, he can absolve him entirely.

"I tell you here the secret of a craft in which I have grown old, and I indicate to you its refinements; there is a twist that can be given to everything, even to those things apparently least susceptible." "Father," I said to him, "that is fine, but how do you reconcile yourself with heaven? If the Sophy [1]

---

1 ["Sophy" was the title once used by the kings of Persia.]

had at his court a man who acted toward him as you act against your God, a man who differentiated his orders and told his subjects which laws they ought to obey and which they might violate, he would have him impaled on the spot." I bowed to my dervish and left without waiting for his response.

Paris, the 23rd of the moon of Maharram, 1714

LETTER LVIII

Rica to Rhedi, at Venice

My dear Rhedi, there are many trades in Paris. Here, for a small sum, a man obligingly offers the secret of making gold.

Another promises that you will sleep with ethereal spirits, provided that for only thirty years you do not see a woman.

You will also find soothsayers so clever that they can tell you your entire life, if only they may have a quarter-hour conversation with your servants.

Clever women turn virginity into a flower which perishes and is reborn daily, and which is plucked the hundredth time more painfully than the first.

There are others whose art repairs all the injuries of time, who know how to re-establish a dazzling facial beauty, and how to bring a woman down even from the summit of age to the most tender youth.

All these people live or try to live in a city that is the mother of invention.

The revenues of these citizens cannot be taxed, for they consist only in cleverness and industry. Each has his own and exploits it as best he can.

He who would number the lawyers [1] who proceed against

---

1 [Montesquieu's term is *gens de loi,* which generally means "lawyers." Some scholars have suggested that "law" (*loi*) in this context be read as "Holy Writ" or "Koran."]

the income of any mosque could as easily count the sands of the sea or the slaves of our monarch.

A multitude of masters of languages, arts, and sciences teach what they do not know; and this is a considerable talent, for it takes much less wit to teach what you know than what you do not.

One cannot die here except suddenly. This is the only way death can work, for in every corner there are people who have infallible remedies against every conceivable malady.

All the shops are hung with invisible nets that catch every customer. Sometimes, however, one can escape cheaply, for a young shopgirl will coax a man for an hour to make him buy a pack of toothpicks.

Everyone leaves this city more cautious than when he arrived, for as one is forced by others to part with so much of his wealth, in time he learns to conserve it. This is the only benefit available to foreigners in this bewitching city.

Paris, the 10th of the moon of Saphar, 1714

LETTER LIX

Rica to Usbek, at ———

The other day I visited a house where a very mixed group of people had gathered. The conversation, I discovered, was dominated by two old women who had vainly labored all morning to make themselves youthful. "It must be admitted," one of them said, "that the men today are much different from those we knew in our youth. Then they were polished, gracious, and obliging, but now I find them only insupportably coarse." "Everything has changed," said a man evidently afflicted with gout. "Times are not what they were. Forty years ago everyone was healthy, gay, and sprightly, asking only to laugh and dance; now everyone is intolerably sad." A moment later the conversation turned to politics. "Bah!" said an old noble. "The state is no longer really governed. Find me today a minister like M. Colbert.[1] I knew him well, M. Colbert; he was one of my friends, and he always paid my pension before anyone else's; he maintained real order in the economy! Everyone was comfortably off; now I am ruined." An ecclesiastic then spoke. "Sir, you are speaking of the most miraculous days of our invincible monarch; and was there anything ever done that was as magnificent as his efforts to extirpate heresy?"[2] "And don't neglect the abolition of dueling," said yet another man, most contentedly. "A judicious remark," someone whispered to me; "that man is delighted with the edict, and he observes it so well that six months ago he accepted a hundred blows with a stick, rather than violate it."

It seems to me, Usbek, that we judge things only by applying them secretly to ourselves. I am not surprised that Negroes paint the devil in dazzling white and their gods in carbon black; or that the Venus of certain peoples has breasts that hang to her thighs; or, finally, that all idolaters have represented their gods in human shape and assign to them all their own attributes. It is well said that if triangles were to create a god, they would describe him with three sides.

My dear Usbek, when I see men crawling on this atom—that is, the earth, and only a dot in the universe—and proposing themselves as the exact model for providence, I find such extravagance and such pettiness impossible to reconcile.

Paris, the 14th of the moon of Saphar, 1714

---

1 [Jean-Baptiste Colbert (1619-83) was Controller-General of Finance, an indefatigable exponent of mercantilistic economic policies, and, at least until 1671, the most influential minister in Louis XIV's government.]

2 [In 1685 Louis XIV, distressed by the official recognition and tolerance granted to Protestants by Henry IV's Edict of Nantes (1598) and convinced by his advisors that the remaining Protestant minority was negligible, revoked the Edict. The persecution following the revocation resulted in an extensive, though illegal, emigration of Protestants from France, with lamentable consequences for much French industry and commerce.]

LETTER LX

Usbek to Ibben, at Smyrna

You ask me if there are Jews in France. Know that wherever there is money there are Jews. You ask me what they do. Precisely what they do in Persia, for nothing so resembles an Asiatic Jew as a European Jew.

Among Christians, as among us, they display an invincible devotion to their religion, which amounts almost to folly.

The Jewish religion is like an old tree trunk which has produced two branches—Mohammedanism and Christianity—that now cover the earth. Or, perhaps, it is like a mother whose two daughters have burdened her with a thousand wounds, for in religious matters the nearest of kin are the worst enemies. But however badly she has been treated by them, she never ceases to glory in their birth, for she uses both of them to embrace the entire world, just as her great age embraces all time.

The Jews thus regard themselves as the source of all holiness and the origin of all religions; and they see us, on the other hand, as heretics who have changed the law, or rather, as rebellious Jews.

If the change had come about gradually, they suppose they might have been easily seduced; but, as it happened suddenly and violently, and as they can mark the day and hour of the birth of either daughter, they are scandalized to discover that we had a beginning, and they hold themselves firm to a religion as old as the world itself.

They have never been less troubled in Europe than they are now. The Christians are beginning to lose that spirit of intolerance which animated them. It is now seen that it was a mistake to chase the Jews from Spain, and to persecute French Christians whose belief differed a bit from that of the king. They now perceive that zeal for the expansion of religion is different from dutiful devotion to it, and that love and observance of a religion need not require hatred and persecution of those who do not so believe.

Would that our Mussulmans thought as sensibly on this subject as do the Christians; that peace were established once and for all between Hali and Abu Bekr,[1] and that the merits of those holy prophets were left to God's decision. I would have them honored by acts of veneration and respect, not by vain preferences. Let us seek to merit their favor, whether God has placed them at his right hand or even beneath the footstool of his throne.

Paris, the 18th of the moon of Saphar, 1714

LETTER LXI

Usbek to Rhedi, at Venice

The other day, I went into a famous church called Notre Dame, and while I was admiring that superb edifice I had occasion to talk with an ecclesiastic who was also there out of curiosity. The conversation turned on the tranquillity of his profession. "Most people," he said to me, "envy the happiness of our condition, and they are right. However, there are some disadvantages, for although we are largely separated from the world, yet we are drawn into it on a thousand occasions. Thus we have a very difficult role to sustain.

"Worldly people are astonishing: they can suffer neither our censure nor our praise. If we try to reform them, they find us ridiculous; but if we approve, they regard us as men out of character. Nothing is as humiliating as the thought that you are scandalizing even the impious. And so we are obliged to be equivocal and to influence the libertines not by consistent action but by making them uncertain about how we will re-

---

1 [See above, p. 14, footnote 2.]

ceive their observations. This requires great ability; the state of neutrality is a hard one. Worldly people who risk everything, who give in to all fancies, who follow or abandon them as they are successful or not, fare much better.

"And this is not all. We cannot maintain in the world that happy and peaceful way of life which everyone considers so desirable. As soon as we appear, we are forced into dispute. We are asked, for instance, to prove the value of prayer to a man who does not believe in God, or the necessity of fasting to someone who has always denied the immortality of the soul; the task is laborious, and there is no laughter on our side. Furthermore, we are constantly tormented by a desire to convert others to our opinions, for this is, as it were, the essence of our profession; yet it is as ridiculous as if Europeans worked to improve human nature by bleaching the skin of the Africans. We disturb the state and torment ourselves by trying to establish religious doctrines which are not at all fundamental; we resemble that conqueror of China who drove his subjects to revolt by insisting that they cut their hair and fingernails.[1]

"There is danger even in our zeal to enforce the duties of our holy religion among those for whom we are responsible, and it cannot be accompanied by too much prudence. An emperor named Theodosius once put to the sword every inhabitant of a city, even the women and children. Appearing shortly afterward before a church, he found that a bishop named Ambrose had closed the doors to him as a sacrilegious murderer. That was a heroic action. But when the emperor, having finally made the penance that his crime required, was later admitted to the church and went to sit among the priests, that same bishop made him sit elsewhere.[2] And that was the action of a fanatic, for in truth, excessive zeal should be avoided.

[1] [The Manchu Emperor Shun-Chih issued such an edict in 1645. There was much individual resistance to it but no general revolt.]

[2] [After the massacre of civilians at Salonica in 390, as punishment for the city's rebellion against his garrisons, the Roman Emperor Theodosius was refused entrance to the cathedral by St. Ambrose, Bishop of Milan, until satisfactory penance was done.]

What difference did it make either to religion or to the state
whether this prince had or had not a place among the priests?"

Paris, the 1st of the moon of Rebiab I, 1714

LETTER LXII

Zelis to Usbek, at Paris

As your daughter is now seven years old, I have decided it
is time to bring her into the inner apartments of the seraglio,
and not to wait until she is ten to entrust her to the black
eunuchs. A young girl cannot be deprived too early of the
liberties of infancy and given a holy education within the
walls sacred to modesty.

I am not of the opinion of those mothers who confine their
daughters only when they are almost ready to be married, who
condemn them to the seraglio rather than consecrating them
to it, and who force them to accept a way of life which they
ought to have taught them to love. Must we expect everything
from the force of reason and nothing from the gentle power
of habit?

It is vain to talk to us of the subordinate position in which
we are put by nature. It is not enough to make us feel this;
rather, we must be made to practice submission, so that it
sustains us in those critical moments when the passions begin
to arouse and encourage us to independence.

If we were attached to you only by duty, we might sometimes forget it; if we were held only by inclination, a stronger
inclination might weaken it. But when the laws give us to one
man, they remove us so far from all others that we might as
well be a hundred thousand leagues away.

Nature, ever active in the service of men, has not been content to give them desires; she has also ordained that we too
should desire and thus become the animated instruments of
men's happiness. She has set us afire with passion, that men

might be peaceful. She has destined us to restore to men the insensibility they sometimes lose, though it is never possible for us to enjoy that happy state into which we put them.

Yet do not suppose, Usbek, that your situation is happier than mine. I have tasted here a thousand pleasures you could not understand. My imagination has worked ceaselessly to make me realize their value, and I have lived while you have only languished.

Even in this prison holding me I am freer than you. You can only redouble your efforts to guard me, that I may enjoy your uneasiness; your every suspicion, jealousy, and annoyance are so many marks of your dependence.

Proceed, dear Usbek. Have me watched night and day, do not trust in merely ordinary precautions. Increase my happiness by assuring your own, and know that I dread nothing but your indifference.

> *The seraglio at Ispahan, the 2nd of the moon of Rebiab I, 1714*

LETTER LXIII

Rica to Usbek, at ———

I do believe that you intend to spend your entire life in the country. At first I lost you for only two or three days, but here it is fifteen since I last saw you. Of course, you live in a charming house and in agreeable society where you can think at your ease, and one needs nothing more to make him forget the whole universe.

As for me, I lead about the same kind of life I did when you were with me. I go into society and try to understand it; my mind is gradually losing its Asiatic cast, and I am adjusting easily to European manners. I am no longer surprised to find five or six women together in a house with five or six men; in fact, I have decided it is not a bad idea.

For I must say that I have become acquainted with women only since I have been here, and I have learned more about them in a month here than I would in thirty years in the seraglio.

Among us character is uniform because it is forced; one never sees people as they are but as they have been obliged to be. In that servitude of heart and mind, only the monotonous language of fear is heard, and nature's various and changing expressions are silent.

Dissimulation, that art so necessary to us and so much practiced, is unknown here; everything is said, and seen, and heard. Hearts are as open as faces, and in manners, in virtue, even in vice one always perceives something naïve.

To please women, one must have a certain talent rather different from what pleases them even more. It consists of a kind of badinage, which amuses them because it seems to promise them at every instant what can be performed only very occasionally.

This banter, naturally appropriate to the boudoir, gradually seems to be forming the character of the nation; they joke in the council room, they joke at the head of an army, they joke with an ambassador. Professions appear ridiculous in proportion to the seriousness of their pretensions, and a doctor would not seem as absurd if his garments were less lugubrious, and if he jested a bit while killing his patients.

Paris, the 10th of the moon of Rebiab I, 1714

LETTER LXIV

The chief of the black eunuchs to Usbek, at Paris

I cannot tell you, magnificent lord, how perplexed I am. The seraglio is in dreadful confusion and disorder, your wives fight among themselves, your eunuchs are divided, nothing but complaints, mutterings, and reproaches are heard. My remonstrances are despised; everything seems to be permitted in this time of license, and in the seraglio I am nothing but an empty title.

There is not one of your wives who does not consider herself superior to all the others in birth, beauty, wealth, wit, or in your love; not one who does not advance some of these in claim for preference. Every moment I lose that long-suffering patience which, unfortunately for me, has succeeded only in displeasing them all. My prudence, even my kindness—a rare and alien virtue in the post I occupy—have been useless.

May I reveal to you, great lord, the cause of all these disorders? It is entirely in your heart and in the tender feelings you have for these women. If you would not restrain my hand, if you would allow me to punish instead of remonstrating, if instead of listening to their complaints and tears you would send them to weep before me, who am never affected, then I could soon fit on them the yoke they ought to bear and exhaust their proud and independent tempers.

Carried away at the age of fifteen from the depths of my native Africa, I was first sold to a master who had more than twenty wives or concubines. Judging from my grave and taciturn manner that I was appropriate for the seraglio, he ordered that I be prepared for it, and I was forced to an operation which was at first painful but had good consequences, as it gave to me the ear and the confidence of my masters. I entered the new world of the seraglio. The chief eunuch, the most severe man I had ever seen, governed there by an absolute rule. Divisions and quarrels were unheard of there; a profound silence reigned everywhere; all the women were put to bed and were awakened at exactly the same hour throughout the year; they entered the bath in turn, and left it at the slightest sign from us; the rest of the time they were almost always shut up in their rooms. He had one rule—that they maintain themselves in strictest cleanliness—and on this matter he was inexpressibly careful, and the slightest refusal to obey was mercilessly punished. "I am a slave," he said, "but a slave of your master and mine, and I wield over you the power he has granted me. It is he who chastises you, not I, who am only his hand." Those women never entered my master's room unless they were called; they received that favor joyfully and did not complain if they were deprived of it. Even I, the least of the black slaves in that peaceful seraglio, was a thousand times more respected than I am in yours, where I command all.

As soon as the chief eunuch had recognized my genius, he regarded me with favor and spoke of me to my master, as a man capable of carrying out his intentions and of succeeding to the post he occupied; my extreme youth did not disturb him, as he believed my diligence would make up for inexperience. Shall I tell you? I made such progress in gaining his confidence that he no longer hesitated to put into my hands the keys to those fearful places he had so long guarded. It was under this great master that I learned the difficult art of commanding, and I was formed according to the maxims of inflexible government. Under him I studied the hearts of women; it was he who taught me to profit from their weaknesses and not to be astonished by their arrogance. It was often his pleasure to watch me drive them to the ultimate limits of obedience; then he made them return gradually and directed me for a time to appear compliant. But he was best seen in those moments when, close to despair, they beseeched even as they reproached him; unmoved by their tears, he exulted in his triumph. "Now you see," he would say contentedly, "how women must be governed. Their number does not disconcert me; I could rule all those of our great monarch as well. How can a man hope to capture their hearts, if his faithful eunuchs had not first broken their spirits?"

He was as shrewd as he was firm. He read their thoughts and their dissimulations; neither their studied gestures nor their composed faces hid anything from him. He knew their every hidden act and their most secret words. He used some of them to learn about the others, and he was pleased to reward the slightest confidence. As they approached their husband only when summoned, the eunuch called whom he

willed and directed his master's eyes toward those he wished
to favor; this distinction was their reward for some revealed
secret. He had persuaded his master that good order required
that the choice be his, so that his authority would be greater.
That was his manner of governing, great lord, in a seraglio
which I believe was the best ordered in all of Persia.

Free my hands, permit me to force obedience, and in a week
order will take the place of confusion. This your glory demands and your safety requires.

> *Your seraglio at Ispahan, the 9th of the moon of
> Rebiab I, 1714*

LETTER LXV

Usbek to his wives, at the seraglio at Ispahan

I understand that the seraglio is in disorder, that it is full of
quarrels and intestine divisions. When I left, did I not request
peace and good understanding from you? Did you promise this
only to deceive me?

It is you who will be deceived if I choose to follow the
advice given me by the chief eunuch, if I choose to use my
authority to make you live as I have exhorted you to do.

I will not employ violent means, however, until I have tried
all others. For your own good, then, do what you have not
been willing to do for mine.

The chief eunuch has a heavy complaint: he says you pay
no heed to him. How can you reconcile such conduct with the
modesty of your condition? During my absence, is not your
virtue entrusted to him? It is a sacred treasure, of which he is
the depository. But the contempt you show for him makes it
apparent that those charged with making you live according
to the laws of honor are irksome to you.

So change your conduct, I beg you. Act in such a way that

I can again reject the propositions made to me, which are contrary to your liberty and repose.

For I wish you to forget that I am your master and to remember me only as your husband.

Paris, the 5th of the moon of Chahban, 1714

LETTER LXVI

Rica to ———

People here are much infatuated with the sciences, but I question whether they are very learned. He who doubts everything as a philosopher dares to deny nothing as a theologian, yet such a contradictory person is perfectly self-satisfied provided that you agree with his distinctions.

The passion of most of the French is to be thought witty, and the passion of those who wish to be considered wits is to write books.

A worse misconception cannot be imagined, for while nature seems wisely to have provided that the stupidities of men should be transient, books immortalize them. A fool should be content with boring everyone who has lived with him, but he further undertakes to torment future generations. He wants his folly to triumph over the oblivion which he should welcome like the sleep of the tomb; he wants to inform posterity that he has lived, and to have it forever remembered that he was a fool.

Of all authors, I most despise the compilers, who search everywhere in the works of others for fragments which they then fit into their own, much as you would piece turf into a lawn. They are no better authors than the printers who select and combine letters and thus, contributing only their manual labor, make a book. I would have original books respected, and it seems to me that there is something profane in tearing constituent pieces from their sanctuary and exposing them to a scorn they do not deserve.

When a man has nothing to say, why is he not silent? Who cares for these repetitions? Let me suggest a new plan. You are a clever man! Come to my library; put the books from the top shelf on the bottom, and move the others from bottom to top; you have created a masterpiece!

I write to you on this subject, ———, because I am outraged by a book I have just finished, one so large that it might be expected to contain the universal science, but which has broken my head without putting anything into it. Farewell.

Paris, the 8th of the moon of Chahban, 1714

LETTER LXVII

Ibben to Usbek, at Paris

Three vessels have arrived here without bringing any news from you. Are you ill? Or does it please you to alarm me?

If you do not care for me in a country where you have no connections, what will it be like when you return to Persia and to your family? But perhaps I am mistaken. You are amiable enough to find friends anywhere; the heart is a citizen of all countries, and how can a generous nature prevent itself from forming attachments? I confess, I respect old friends, but I am not opposed to making new ones everywhere.

In whatever lands I have visited, I have lived as if I had to spend my life there. I have felt the same attraction to virtuous people, the same compassion, or rather love, for the unfortunate, the same esteem for those whose prosperity has not blinded them. Such is my character, Usbek; wherever I find men I choose friends.

There is a Guebre [1] here who, I believe, holds after you the
first place in my heart; he is the very soul of honor. Special
reasons have required him to retire in this city, where he lives
peacefully upon the income from an honest trade, and with a
wife he loves. His life is marked by many generous acts, and
although he seeks obscurity he has more heroism in his heart
than the greatest of monarchs.

I have frequently spoken to him of you, and I show him all
your letters. I notice that this gives him pleasure, and I perceive already that you have a friend, though unknown to you.

Here you will find his principal adventures; though most
reluctant to write them, he could not refuse them to my friendship, and I confide them to yours.

THE STORY OF APHERIDON AND ASTARTE

I was born among the Guebres, whose religion is perhaps the
oldest in the world. Unhappily, love came to me before reason, and
although I was only six I could not live apart from my sister. My
eyes followed her everywhere; and if she left for only a moment,
she returned to find me in tears; each day increased my love as much
as my age. My father, surprised at such strong feelings, would have
been willing to let us marry, in accordance with the ancient custom
of the Guebres introduced by Cambyses; [2] but fear of the Mohammedans, under whose yoke we lived, prevented our people from
thinking of such sacred unions, which are ordered rather than permitted by our religion, and which are the artless images of a union
already formed by nature.

So, seeing that it would have been dangerous to follow my in-

---

1 [Guebre (also Gueber, Gheber, Gabar) was the derogatory term, meaning "unbeliever," given by the Mohammedans to the followers of the
religion of Zoroaster or Zarathustra. Once dominant in Persia, Zoroastrianism declined rapidly after the Mohammedan conquest in the seventh century, and by the eighteenth century it was represented only by a few
thousand Guebres in Persia, and by the Parsees who emigrated to the
vicinity of Bombay in India.]

2 [Cambyses, son of Cyrus and king of the Persians from 529 to 521 B.C.,
according to Herodotus (III. 31), set aside the laws against incest in his
own case by marrying his sister.]

clination and his, my father resolved to extinguish the flame, which he believed was just starting but in fact was already at its height. He made up a pretext for a journey, taking me with him and leaving my sister with one of his relatives, as my mother had died two years before. I need not describe the despair at our separation; I embraced my sister, who was bathed in tears, but I shed none myself, as grief had made me insensible. We arrived at Tiflis,[3] where my father, having entrusted my education to a relative, left me and returned home.

Some time later I learned that through a friend's influence he had my sister placed in the king's harem, as a servant to a sultana. I could not have been more overcome had I learned of her death; for apart from the fact that I could now no longer hope to see her, her entry into the harem made her a Mohammedan, and according to the prejudices of that religion she could now regard me only with horror. Nonetheless, unable to live any longer at Tiflis and tired both of myself and of life, I returned to Ispahan. My first words to my father were bitter ones; I accused him of having put his daughter into a place one could enter only by changing his religion. "You have brought down upon your family," I told him, "the anger of God and of the Sun that shines upon you; you have done more than if you had polluted the elements, by soiling the soul of your daughter, which is no less pure. I will die of sorrow and love, and may my death be the only torment that God makes you suffer!" With these words I left, and for two years I passed my life watching the walls of the harem, wondering just where my sister could be, and exposing myself daily to the danger of having my throat cut by the eunuchs who patrolled that dread place.

Eventually my father died, and the sultana whom my sister served, jealously watching her grow more beautiful every day, married her to a eunuch who desired her passionately. In this way my sister left the seraglio and with her eunuch took a house in Ispahan.

For more than three months I was unable to speak to her, for the eunuch, the most jealous of men, always put me off by various pretexts. Finally, when I was allowed into the harem, he made me speak to her through a lattice, and even the eyes of a lynx would have been unable to discover her under the covering of clothes and veils; I recognized only the sound of her voice. Oh my emotion, to find

---

3 [Tiflis (Tbilis) is the capital of Georgia, in the eighteenth century an independent kingdom, and since 1799 part of Russia.]

myself so close and yet so far from her! I contained it, however, for
I was carefully watched; she, it seemed to me, wept a bit. Her husband tried to make some poor excuse, but I treated him as the
meanest slave. He was much annoyed when he heard me speak to my
sister in the ancient tongue of Persia, our sacred language and unknown to him. "What, my sister," I said, "is it true that you have
renounced your ancestral religion? I know that in entering the
harem you had to profess Mohammedanism; but tell me, has your
heart been able to consent to your mouth's agreement to leave a
religion which permits me to love you? And for whom have you
renounced that religion we ought to cherish? For a wretch still
marked by the chains he has worn, who would be the least of men,
even if he were one." "My brother," she said, "that man you're
speaking of is my husband. I must honor him however unworthy he
appears to you, and I would also be the least of women if. . . ."
"Ah, my sister," I said, "you are a Guebre; he is not your husband
and cannot be. Had you been faithful to your ancestors you could
regard him only as a monster." "Alas!" she said, "how distant that
religion now seems to me! I had scarcely learned its precepts before
I had to forget them. You can see that the tongue in which I speak
to you is no longer familiar to me, and that I express myself only
with great difficulty. But be assured that the memory of our childhood will always delight me, that since then I have known only false
joys, that a day never passes but that I think of you, that you have
had a greater part in my marriage than you know, for I resolved to
go through with it only because I thus hoped to see you again. But
this day, which has already cost me so much, will yet cost more! For
I see you quite beside yourself and my husband quivering with
jealous rage. I will never see you again; I am doubtless speaking to
you for the last time in my life; and if that be so, my brother, it will
not be a long one." With these words she was overcome, and knowing herself to be unable to continue the conversation, she left me,
the most desolated of men.

Three or four days later I asked to see my sister; the barbarous
eunuch would have liked to prevent me, but apart from the fact
that his sort of husband has not the same authority over their wives
as do others, he was so hopelessly in love with my sister that he
could refuse her nothing. I saw her in the same place and covered
with the same veils; as she was accompanied by two slaves, I again

had recourse to our special language. "My sister," I said to her, "why can I see you only under these frightful conditions? These walls that imprison you, these bolts and bars, these wretched guardians watching you make me furious. How can you have lost that sweet liberty enjoyed by your ancestors? Your mother, who was so chaste, gave to her husband as a pledge of her virtue only virtue itself. They both lived happily in mutual trust, and the simplicity of their morality was for them a thousand times more precious than the false glitter you seem to enjoy in this sumptuous house. In losing your religion you have also lost your liberty, your happiness, and that precious equality which honors your sex. What is even worse, you are and can only be not the wife but the slave of a slave who has been degraded from humanity." "Ah, my brother," she said, "respect my husband and the religion I have embraced, for according to that religion I can neither listen nor talk to you without committing a crime." "What, sister!" I said, quite carried away. "Do you really believe that religion to be true?" "Ah," she said, "how well it would be for me if it were not! I made so great a sacrifice for it that I must believe in it, and if my doubts. . . . " With these words she stopped. "Yes, your doubts, my sister, are well founded whatever they are. What can you expect from a religion which makes you unhappy in this world and leaves no hope for the other? Recall that ours is the oldest in the world, that it has always flourished in Persia, and that it has no origins beyond this empire, whose beginnings are lost in time; Mohammedanism was introduced here only by chance and has been established not by persuasion but by conquest. If our native princes had not been so weak, you would still see reigning the cult of those ancient Magi. Go back into those remote centuries, where everything speaks to you of Magianism and nothing of the Mohammedan sect, which was still in its infancy thousands of years later." "But," she said, "if my religion is more recent than yours, it is at least more pure, since it worships only God, while you still revere the sun and stars, fire, and even the elements." "I see, my sister, that among the Mussulmans you have learned to slander our sacred religion. We worship neither stars nor elements, nor have our fathers ever so worshipped; they never built temples to them or made sacrifices but offered to them only the lesser reverence due to the works and manifestations of the deity. But, my sister, in the name of the God who enlightens us, do take this holy book I have brought. It is the book of our lawgiver Zoroaster.[4] Read it without prejudice; receive into your heart the rays of light which will shine upon you as you read; remember your ancestors who have so long honored the Sun in the holy city of Balk; [5] and finally, remember me, whose only hope of peace, of fortune, of life lies in your conversion." Entirely transported, I left her alone to decide the most momentous event of my life.

I returned two days later. I said nothing, awaiting in silence the sentence of life or death. "You are loved, my brother," she said, "and by a Guebre. I struggled long, but, by the gods, how love removes difficulties! How relieved I am! I am no longer afraid of loving you too much; I cannot put bounds upon my love, and now even that excess is legitimate. Ah, how that agrees with my heart! But you, who knew so well how to break the chains which my mind had forged, when will you break those holding my hands? From this moment I give myself to you; show by the speed of your acceptance how dear this gift is to you. My brother, the first time I am able to embrace you I believe I will die in your arms." I can never express the joy I felt at these words; I believed myself to be, and I saw myself in a moment becoming in fact, the happiest of men. I saw almost achieved every desire I had formed in twenty-five years of life, and I saw vanish all the sadness which had made that life so painful. But when I accustomed myself to these sweet thoughts, I discovered that I was not so near my happiness as I first supposed, even though I had surmounted the greatest obstacle. It remained to deceive the vigilance of her guards. I dared not confide my life's secret to anyone; my sister and I had only each other for aid. If I failed the attempt, I ran the risk of being impaled; but I did not see

---

4 [The *Avesta*, the sacred book containing the teachings of Zoroaster, religious reformer of ancient Persia. Zoroastrianism, the dominant religion of Persia before the Mohammedan conquest, is dualistic in doctrine, emphasizing the universal sway of the opposed forces of good, led by Ormuzd, and evil, led by Ahriman; however, it teaches the millennial victory of Ormuzd, following man's free acceptance of regenerative good. There was also a strong element of polytheism in the Zoroastrians' veneration of the elements, which led them to refuse to bury or burn dead bodies, on the ground that to do so would be to pollute either earth or fire.]

5 [Balk (ancient Bactra) is a small city in Afghanistan; it was traditionally the birthplace of Zoroaster.]

that pain as any more cruel than the failure itself. We agreed that she would have me send a clock which her father had left her; that in it I would put a file to cut the lattice of a window opening onto the street, as well as a knotted rope for the descent; that thereafter I would no longer visit her but wait under the window each night until she could execute her plan. As she had not found a favorable time, for fifteen entire nights I waited without seeing anyone. Finally, on the sixteenth, I heard a file working; from time to time the work was interrupted, and in those intervals my dread was inexpressible. After an hour's work, I saw her attach the rope and let herself down to fall into my arms. I no longer sensed any danger and stood motionless there for a long time; then I took her out of town, where I had a horse all readied. With her mounted behind me, we fled with all imaginable speed from the place that could be so dangerous to us. Before daybreak we arrived at a Guebre's house in a deserted spot where he had retired to live frugally by the work of his hands. We did not consider it prudent to remain there, and at his suggestion we entered a dense forest and lodged in the hollow of an old oak tree until the noise of our flight had quieted. Here in this remote place we stayed, seen by no one, ceaselessly repeating our undying love and waiting for the time when a Guebre priest could perform the marriage ceremony prescribed by our sacred books. "Sister," I said to her, "how holy is this union, made by nature and soon to be reaffirmed by our sacred law!" At last a priest arrived to calm our amorous impatience. In the peasant's house he performed the ceremonies of marriage, gave us his blessing, and a thousand times wished us the vigor of Gustaspes and the holiness of Horoaspes.[6] Shortly thereafter we left Persia, where we were not safe, and went to Georgia. Here we lived a year, every day more charmed with each other. However, as my money began to run out, and as I feared poverty for my sister's sake if not my own, I left her to seek aid from our relatives. Never was there a more tender parting. But my journey was not only useless but disastrous: for I found not only that all our property had been confiscated, but that my relatives were almost powerless to help me; and I obtained only as much money as was needed for my return trip. But then, to my

---

6 [Gustaspes (Gushtasp, Vistasp), king of Persia (*c.* 600 B.C.), according to legend was converted by Zoroaster and then officially imposed the religion upon his realm. Horoaspes (Aurvataspa) was the legendary father of Gustaspes.]

great despair, my sister was not to be found! Some days before my return the Tartars had invaded the city where she lived, and finding her beautiful, they carried her off and sold her to some Jews on their way to Turkey, leaving behind only the little girl born to her a few months before. I followed the Jews and met them three leagues away; but my prayers and tears were in vain, for they insisted upon thirty tomans and would not relent a single one. After appealing to everyone, and imploring protection from both Turkish and Christian priests, I went to an Armenian merchant and sold myself and my daughter to him for thirty-five tomans. Then I went to the Jews, gave them thirty tomans, and took the other five to my sister, whom I had not yet seen. "You are free, my sister," I said to her, "and I can embrace you. Here are five tomans; I am sorry that I could not sell myself for more." "What!" she said, "you have sold yourself?" "Yes," I said. "Ah, unhappy man, what have you done? Was I not miserable enough without your working to intensify it? Your freedom consoled me; your slavery will drive me to the tomb. Oh, my brother! Your love is cruel! And my daughter—I do not see her?" "I have sold her too," I said. We both burst into tears, having no strength to say more. Finally I went to find my master, and my sister arrived there almost as soon as I did. She threw herself at his feet. "I ask slavery of you," she said, "as others ask for liberty. Take me; you can sell me for a higher price than my husband's." A struggle then took place, which brought tears to my master's eyes. "Unhappy man," she said, "did you think I could accept freedom at the price of yours? Master, you behold two unfortunates who will die if you separate us. I give myself to you. Pay me; perhaps this money and my services may someday obtain from you what I do not now dare to ask. It is to your interest not to separate us; consider that his life depends on mine." The Armenian was a gentle man and was touched by our calamity. "If you both will serve me faithfully and with zeal, I promise that in a year I will grant you freedom. I see that neither of you deserves the pain of your lot. If, when you are free, you are as happy as you deserve to be, and if fortune favors you, I am certain that you will compensate me for the loss I shall suffer." We both embraced his knees and followed him on his journey. We comforted each other in our servile tasks, and I was delighted when I was able to do my sister's work.

The end of the year came, and our master kept his word and freed us. We returned to Tiflis, where I found an old friend of my father who was successfully practicing medicine. He lent me some money, with which I made several negotiations. Various affairs later called me to Smyrna, where I established myself. I have lived here for six years, enjoying the most amiable and pleasant society in the world. Unity reigns in my family, and I would not change places with all the kings in the world. I have been fortunate enough to meet again the Armenian merchant to whom I owe everything, and I have been able to do some important services for him.

Smyrna, the 27th of the moon of Gemmadi II, 1714

LETTER LXVIII

Rica to Usbek, at ⸺

The other day I dined at the home of a magistrate, who had invited me several times. After speaking of various things, I said to him, "Sir, it seems to me that your profession is very laborious." "Not to the degree you imagine," he replied. "As we treat it, it is only an amusement." "But how is that? Isn't your head always full of other people's business? Aren't you continually involved in uninteresting things?" "You are right. These affairs do not interest us, for the reason that we take no interest in them. That explains why our profession is not as fatiguing as you supposed." When I saw him take the matter so casually, I continued and said, "Sir, I have not seen your study." "I believe it, for I have none. When I took this position, I needed money to pay for it, so I sold my library; the bookseller who bought it left me, of its vast number of volumes, only my account book. Not that I regret them; we judges are not inflated with vain knowledge. What use have we of all those volumes of law? Almost all their cases are hypothetical, and exceptions to the general rule." "But might not this be, sir," I said, "because you have made them exceptions? For why, after all, should every nation on earth have laws if they are not applicable? And how can they be applied if they are not known?" "If you knew the courts," the magistrate answered, "you would not speak as you do. We have living books, called advocates; they do the work for us and undertake to instruct us." "And do they not sometimes undertake to deceive you?" I rejoined. "Would you not do well to guard yourself against their strategems? They have weapons to attack your justice; it would be well if you were also equipped to defend it and did not rush into combat lightly clad against men armed to the teeth."

Paris, the 13th of the moon of Chahban, 1714

LETTER LXIX

Usbek to Rhedi, at Venice

You would never have dreamed that I could become more of a metaphysician than I already was; yet such is the case, as you will be convinced after wading through this philosophic flood.

The most intelligent philosophers, reflecting on the nature of God, have declared him to be a supremely perfect being; but they have much abused this idea. They have enumerated every perfection of which man is capable or can conceive, and each of these they have ascribed to the idea of the deity, not thinking that these attributes are often contradictory and cannot subsist in the same subject without destroying each other.

Western poets tell how a painter, wanting to make a portrait of the goddess of beauty, took from each of the assembled beauties of Greece her most lovely feature and combined them into a single likeness of the most beautiful of all goddesses.[1]

---

1 [Zeuxis (fifth century B.C.), a Greek painter, was reputed to have used five different models when he painted Helen for the Agrigentides.]

If a man had concluded, on that account, that she was both blond and brunette, had both blue and dark eyes, or that she was gentle and haughty at the same time, he would have passed for a fool.

God often lacks a perfection which would imply a larger imperfection; but he is limited only by himself and is his own necessity. Thus, although God is all-powerful, he can neither break his promises nor deceive men. Frequently, indeed, impotence is not in him but in relative things; and that is why he cannot alter the essences of things.

So there is no reason to be surprised that some of our learned men have dared to deny the infinite prescience of God, on the ground that it is incompatible with his justice.

However bold this idea may be, metaphysics sustains it wonderfully. According to its principles, it is not possible that God should foresee things dependent upon the determination of free causes, since what has not happened does not exist and consequently cannot be known. For nothing, having no properties, cannot be perceived; and God cannot read a volition that does not exist, nor see in the mind something which is not there. Until the mind is determined, the action by which it is determined is not in it.

The mind is the agent of its own determination, but there are occasions when it is so undetermined that it does not know which way to decide. Often, in fact, it acts only to use its liberty, so that God cannot see the decision in advance, either in the mind's action or in the action of things upon it.

How could God foresee things dependent upon the determination of free causes? He could see them only in two ways: by conjecture, which contradicts infinite foreknowledge; or as necessary effects infallibly following from a cause equally infallible, which is even more contradictory, for then the mind is presumed free but in fact is no more free than a billiard ball is free to move when struck by another.

But do not think that I wish to limit God's knowledge. Just as he can make creatures act as his fancy wills, so he knows all that he wishes to know. However, though he can see everything, he does not always use this power. Ordinarily he leaves to the creature the power of acting or not acting, so that it may choose either a right or wrong course; this is why he renounces his right to act upon an agent and to determine it. But when he wishes to know something he always does, because he has only to will that it happen as he foresees it, and to determine creatures as he wills. Thus he draws what will happen out of the number of things purely possible, fixing by his decrees the future determination of minds, and taking from them the power he granted to them to act or not to act.

If I may employ a comparison on a subject which transcends all comparisons: a monarch does not know what his ambassador will do on an important matter; but if he wants to know, he has only to order him to act in such a way, and he can be assured that the event will happen as he planned.

The Koran and the books of the Jews everywhere testify against the dogma of absolute prescience. In them God seems always unaware of the mind's future decisions, and it appears that this was the first truth Moses taught to men.

God placed Adam in the earthly paradise on condition that he not eat of a certain fruit—an absurd command for a being aware of the future determinations of men's minds. Could such a being put conditions on his favors without making them a mockery? It is as if a man, knowing of the capture of Baghdad, should say to another, "I will give you one hundred tomans if Baghdad is not taken." Would this not be a miserable joke?

My dear Rhedi, why all this philosophy? God is so high above us that we do not see even his clouds. We know him only in his commandments. He is an immense, infinite spirit. In his grandeur we may see our weakness. To be constantly humble is to be constantly adoring.

Paris, the last day of the moon of Chahban, 1714

LETTER LXX

Zelis to Usbek, at Paris

Soliman, whom you love, is in despair over an affront he has just received. Three months ago a flighty young man named Suphis asked his daughter in marriage. He seemed content with the girl's appearance, as it was described by the women who had seen her since childhood; the dowry was agreed upon, and all seemed to be passing without incident. Yesterday, following the preliminary ceremonies, the girl set out on horseback, accompanied by her eunuch and covered head to foot, as is customary. However, as soon as she arrived at the house of her intended husband, he locked the door against her and swore he would not receive her unless the dowry were increased. Her relatives dashed about trying to arrange the matter, and after considerable resistance Soliman agreed to make a small gift to his son-in-law. The marriage ceremonies accomplished, the girl was conducted to bed with sufficient violence, but an hour later this unbalanced fellow sprang up furiously, cut her face in several places, announced that she was not a virgin, and sent her back to her father. No one could be more afflicted by this injury than he. Some people maintain that the girl is innocent. Fathers are truly unfortunate to be exposed to such insults! If my daughter were so treated, I believe I would die of grief.

> *The seraglio at Fatima, the 9th of the moon of*
> *Gemmadi I, 1714*

Usbek to Zelis

I pity Soliman, the more so because his misfortune is without remedy; his son-in-law has only claimed his liberty under the law. I find that law hard, as it exposes a family's honor to the whim of a fool. It has been vainly said that we have certain sure tests of the truth, but this is an old error which we have lately corrected, and our physicians supply invincible reasons why these tests are uncertain. Even Christians regard them as imaginary, though they are clearly established in their holy books, and though their ancient lawgiver [1] has made the innocence or guilt of all girls depend upon them.

I learn with pleasure of the care you are giving to your daughter's education. God grant that her husband may find her as lovely and as pure as Fatima, that she have ten eunuchs to guard her, that she become the honor and ornament of the seraglio to which she is destined, that she have above her head only gilded ceilings and walk on only the richest carpets! And to crown these wishes, may my eyes see her in all her glory!

Paris, the 5th of the moon of Chalval, 1714

Rica to Usbek, at ———

I found myself the other day in a group where I met a man very pleased with himself. In a quarter of an hour he decided three questions of morality, four historical problems, and

---

1 [Moses. See Deuteronomy 22:13-21.]

five points in physics. I have never seen such a universal decider;[1] his mind was never disturbed by the slightest doubt. We left the sciences to talk of the news of the day; he decided the news of the day. I wanted to trap him and said to myself, "I must put myself on strong ground and take refuge in my own country." So I spoke to him about Persia, but scarcely had I said four words when he contradicted me twice, on the authority of Tavernier and Chardin.[2] "Good heavens," I said to myself, "what kind of man is this? He will next know the streets of Ispahan better than I!" My part, I soon discovered, was to be silent and let him talk; and he is still dogmatizing.

Paris, the 8th of the moon of Zilcade, 1715

Rica to ————

I have heard much talk about a kind of tribunal called the French Academy. There is no less respected court in the world; for it is said that as soon as it decides something, the people break its commands and substitute other laws, which it is bound to follow.

To establish its authority it issued a code of its decisions some time ago. This child of so many fathers was close to old age at birth, and although it was legitimate, an earlier-born bastard almost smothered it in infancy.[1]

[1] [Montesquieu's word, coined for the purpose, is *décisionnaire.*]

[2] [Jean-Baptiste Tavernier, *Les six voyages en Turquie, en Perse et aux Indes* (Amsterdam, 1676), and Jean Chardin, *Voyages en Perse et autres lieux de l'Orient* (Amsterdam, 1711), were Montesquieu's most important sources for his knowledge of Persia and its customs.]

[1] [The French Academy, charged with purifying and standardizing the French language, published its "definitive" dictionary in 1694 after much scholarly hesitation. The "earlier-born bastard" is Antoine Furetière's

Those who compose this tribunal have no other function than to chatter incessantly, and eulogy is about the only subject of their eternal babble. As soon as they are initiated into its mysteries, a mania to eulogize seizes them, and it never leaves.

This body has forty heads, entirely filled with figures of speech, metaphors, and antitheses. So many mouths can speak only in exclamations, and its ears are attuned only to cadence and harmony. There is no question of eyes, as the body seems made for talk rather than sight. It is not firm on its feet, for its scourge—time—shakes it constantly and destroys all its accomplishments. They say that formerly its hands were grasping, but I will say nothing of that, and leave the decision to those who know better than I.[2]

Such oddities, ——, do not exist in our Persia. Our minds do not incline toward singular and bizarre institutions, for in our simple customs and artless manners we seek always what is natural.

Paris, the 27th of the moon of Zilhage, 1715

---

dictionary which was published in 1690. Furetière was expelled from the Academy in 1685 on the ground that he was using his colleagues' work for his own purposes. While Furetière died in 1688, two years before the appearance of his dictionary, the sale of that dictionary was nevertheless prohibited.]

2 [Perhaps a reference to the story told of the prominent academician Jean Chapelain (1598-1674). In the seventeenth century it was customary for the Academy to hold a religious service when one of its members died, with the expenses borne by the director of the moment. In office as director despite efforts to be released when Chancellor Séguier died, Chapelain so represented his poverty and inability to perform his duty that a collection was taken up for him which was, according to rumor, considerably greater than the expenses. This story, widely circulated by Chapelain's detractors, appears to have little foundation.

There is another incident to which this passage might also refer. Auger de Mauléon de Granier entered the Academy in 1635 but was excluded by Richelieu the next spring for supposedly misappropriating funds entrusted to him by a religious sisterhood.]

LETTER LXXIV

Usbek to Rica,[1] *at* ———

Some days past a man I know said to me, "I promised to introduce you into the best houses in Paris, and I will now take
you to the home of a great noble, one of the men who best
represents the realm."

"And what does that mean, sir? Is it that he is more polished
or more affable than the others?" "No," he said. "Ah, I understand; he makes his superiority constantly felt by those who
approach him. In that case I would as soon be excused; I
grant him everything and accept my condemnation as an inferior."

Yet I had to go, and I saw a little man who was so proud,
who took snuff with such haughtiness, who blew his nose so
violently and spat with such indifference, and who caressed
his dogs in such an offensive manner, that I could only be
amazed. "Good heavens," I said to myself, "if I acted like that
at the court in Persia, I acted a great fool!" Surely, Rica, we
would have been the natural inferiors, had we insulted in a
hundred petty ways those people who visited us every day to
show their good will. They knew well that we were above
them, and if they did not, our favors made them aware of it
every day. Having no need to make ourselves respected, we
did all we could to make ourselves liked. We were accessible
to the humblest, and although we lived in a grandeur that
tends to harden feelings, they found us sensitive; we descended
to their needs, keeping only our hearts above them. But when
it was a matter of sustaining the prince's majesty in public
ceremonies, or of building respect for the nation in the eyes
of foreigners; when, finally, it was necessary to bestir soldiery

---

1 [Early editions have this letter *Rica to Usbek*. Its content and style,
however, clearly indicate Usbek as the author, and it has been so ascribed
since the 1758 edition.]

in dangerous situations, then we drew ourselves up a hundred times higher than we had ever descended, we resumed our haughty aspect, and not infrequently were we deemed to have represented ourselves rather well.

Paris, the 10th of the moon of Saphar, 1715

LETTER LXXV

Usbek to Rhedi, at Venice

I must admit that I have not noticed among the Christians that lively faith in their religion which one finds in Mussulmans. With them there are great distances from profession to belief, from belief to conviction, and from conviction to practice. Their religion is less a subject of sanctification than a subject for dispute, which is open to everyone. Courtiers, soldiers, even women rise up against ecclesiastics, demanding that they prove to them what they have resolved not to believe. It is not that they have rationally so decided, or that they have taken the trouble to examine the truth or falsehood of the religion they reject; rather they are rebels, who have felt the yoke and thrown it off before learning what it is. Moreover, they are no more firm in their incredulity than in their faith; they live in an ebb and flow which carries them constantly between belief and disbelief. One of them once told me: "I believe in the immortality of the soul in periods of six months. My opinions depend entirely upon my body's constitution. According to the level of my animal spirits, the adequacy of my digestion, the rarity or heaviness of the air I breathe, or the solidity of the food I eat, I am alternately a Spinozist, a Socinian, a Catholic, an unbeliever, or a zealot. When the physician is close to my bed, the confessor has an advantage on me. I easily prevent religion from afflicting me when I am well, but I permit it to console me when I am ill. When I possess nothing more of earthly hope, religion comes and seizes me with its promises; I am pleased to surrender to it and to die on the side of hope."

Long ago the Christian princes freed all the slaves in their realms, because they said Christianity makes all men equal. It is true that this religious act was very useful to them, for by it they lessened the power of the nobles over the common people. Since then they have conquered lands where they have seen it was to their advantage to hold slaves, whom they have permitted to be bought and sold, forgetting that religious principle which once so deeply affected them. What can I say about this? The truth of one time is the error of another. Why should we not act like Christians? We were foolish to refuse settlements and easy conquests in pleasant climates,[1] only because the water there was not sufficiently pure for bathing according to the dictates of the sacred Koran.

I give thanks to the all-powerful God, who sent his great prophet Hali, that I profess a religion which transcends all human interests and is as pure as the heavens from which it descended.

Paris, the 13th of the moon of Saphar, 1715

LETTER LXXVI

Usbek to his friend Ibben, at Smyrna

European laws are ferocious against those who kill themselves. They are, so to speak, made to die twice, for they are hauled ignominiously through the streets, proclaimed infamous, and their property is confiscated.

It seems to me, Ibben, that these laws are most unjust. If I

---

[1] The Mohammedans had no desire to take Venice, because they could not find water there for their purifications.

am laden with sorrow, misery, and contempt, why should anyone want to prevent me from putting an end to my cares and cruelly deprive me of a remedy which lies in my hands?

Why should anyone demand that I labor for a society which I am willing to leave, or require me against my wish to hold to an agreement to which I did not consent? Society is based on mutual advantage; but when that society becomes onerous to me, who is to prevent my renouncing it? Life has been given to me as a favor, which I can return when it is that no longer. When the cause ceases, so should the effect.

Will the prince demand that I remain his subject if I receive no advantages from subjugation? Can my fellow citizens insist upon an unjust distribution which brings utility to them but despair to me? Does God, unlike other benefactors, want to condemn me to receive favors that crush me?

"But," some will say, "you disturb the providential order of things. God has united your soul and body, and in separating them you oppose his designs and resist his will."

What can this mean? Do I disturb the providential order when I change the mode of matter, when I make a ball square, a ball that the first laws of movement—that is, the laws of creation and conservation—have made round? Certainly not; I simply use a right given to me, and in that sense I can disrupt all of nature as I will, and no one can say that I am opposing providence.

When my soul shall be separated from my body, will there be any less order and arrangement in the universe? Do you believe that any new combination will be less perfect or less dependent upon the general laws, or that the universe will have lost something, or that the works of God will be less great or, rather, less immense?

Do you think that my body, having become a blade of wheat, a worm, or a piece of lawn, would be changed into a work less worthy of nature, and would my soul, freed of everything terrestrial, become less sublime?

All such ideas, my dear Ibben, have no other source but our pride. We do not appreciate our insignificance, and in spite of what we are, we want to be counted in the universe and to figure prominently in it. We suppose that the annihilation of a being as perfect as we are would degrade all of nature, and we cannot conceive that one man more or less in the world—what am I saying?—all men, a hundred million heads [1] such as ours are but an insubstantial and fragile atom, which God perceives only because his knowledge is so vast.

Paris, the 15th of the moon of Saphar, 1715

Ibben to Usbek, at Paris

My dear Usbek, it seems to me that for a true Mussulman misfortunes are not so much punishments as they are warnings. Very precious are those days when we are led to expiate our offenses. It is prosperous times which should be curtailed. Of what avail is all our impatience but to show us that we want to be happy independent of Him who grants all felicity, because He is felicity itself?

If a being is composed of two beings, and if the acknowledgment of the necessity of preserving that union is the chief mark of submission to the commands of the Creator, then that necessity should be a religious law. And if that necessity of preserving unity is the best guarantee of men's actions, then it should be made a civil law.

Smyrna, the last day of the moon of Saphar, 1715

---

1 [The 1721-1722 editions have *terres* ("earths") instead of *têtes* ("heads").]

LETTER LXXVIII

Rica to Usbek, at ———

I am sending you a copy of a letter written by a Frenchman in Spain; I believe you will be glad to see it.

I have traveled for six months through Spain and Portugal, living among people who despise all others except the French, whom they honor with their hate.

Gravity is the most prominent characteristic of both these nations. It is manifest especially in two ways, by spectacles and by mustaches.

Spectacles demonstrate clearly that their wearer is an accomplished man of knowledge, so absorbed in profound reading that his eyesight has been weakened; every nose so adorned or so burdened can pass without question as the nose of a savant.

As for the mustache, it is intrinsically respectable, independent of results. Sometimes, however, it has been of great service to the prince and to the honor of the nation, as a famous Portuguese general in the Indies once well demonstrated. Finding himself in need of money, he cut off part of his mustache and demanded a loan of twenty thousand pistoles from the inhabitants of Goa on this collateral; the money was lent at once, and he later recovered his mustache honorably.[1]

One can readily imagine that grave and phlegmatic people such as these might also be vain, and so they are. They usually base their pride upon two entirely sufficient things. Those who live in continental Spain or Portugal feel extremely superior if they are what are called "Old Christians," that is, if they are not descended from those persuaded in the last centuries by the Inquisition to become Christians. Those who live in the Indies are no less flattered to consider that they have the sublime merit to be, as they say, white-skinned. Never in the seraglio of the greatest prince has there been a sultana so proud of her beauty as the oldest and ugliest rascal among them is proud of his pale olive complexion, as he sits, arms crossed, in his

---

1 Jean de Castro. [De Castro (1500-48) was viceroy of Portuguese India; the story has several variants, but it always bases the loan upon a few strands of hair as collateral.]

doorway in a Mexican town. A man of such consequence, a creature so perfect, would not work for all the wealth in the world, or persuade himself to compromise the honor and dignity of his skin by vile mechanical industry.

For it must be appreciated that when a man gains a certain merit in Spain—as, for example, when he can add to the qualities already mentioned that of owning a long sword, or of having learned from his father the art of playing a discordant guitar [2]—he no longer works. His honor consists in the repose of his limbs. He who sits down ten hours a day receives exactly twice the consideration given to another who rests only five, for nobility is acquired in chairs.

But although these invincible enemies of work make great show of philosophic tranquillity, in their hearts they are anything but that, for they are always in love. Of all men, these are unsurpassed in dying of languor under their mistresses' windows, and no Spaniard without a head cold can pass for a gallant.

They are, primarily, devout; and, secondly, jealous. They guard their wives carefully against exposure to the enterprises of a soldier riddled with wounds, or a decrepit magistrate; but they closet them with a fervent novice who lowers his eyes, or with a robust Franciscan who raises his.

They permit their wives to appear with exposed bosoms, but they let no one see their heels or be surprised by the sight of their toes.

They say that the rigors of love are cruel everywhere; this is especially true for Spaniards. Women cure them of their pains of love but only by giving them others in their place, and often there remains with them a long and disagreeable souvenir of an extinct passion.

They have little courtesies which in France would appear out of place. For example, a captain never strikes his soldier without asking his permission, and the Inquisition never burns a Jew without offering apologies.

Spaniards who are not burned seem so attached to the Inquisition that it would be spiteful to take it from them. I would like them only to establish another, not against heretics but for the heresiarchs, who attribute the same efficacy to insignificant monastic practices as

---

[2] [This translation follows the minority opinion here; most texts have *faire jurer une discordante guitare* ("make a discordant guitar talk") rather than *faire jouer* ("play").]

to the seven sacraments, who worship what they should only respect, and who are so zealous that they are hardly Christian.

You can find wit and good sense among the Spanish, but do not
look for it in their books. Look at one of their libraries, with romances on one side and scholastics on the other; you would say the
parts have been made and the whole assembled by some secret enemy
of human reason.

Their only good book is one which shows the absurdity of all the
others.[3]

They have made enormous discoveries in the New World, and yet
they do not know their own country; their rivers are not yet entirely
explored,[4] and their mountains hold nations unknown to them.[5]

They say that the sun rises and sets within their lands, but it
must also be said that, in making its course, the sun encounters only
a wasted and deserted countryside.

I would not be displeased, Usbek, to see a letter written to
Madrid by a Spaniard traveling in France; I believe he could
well avenge his country. What a vast field for a detached and
thoughtful man! I imagine he would begin a description of
Paris like this:

"There is a house here in which they put madmen; one
would at first suppose it to be the largest building in the city.
But no; the remedy is too slight for the disease, and no doubt
the French, held in low esteem by their neighbors, shut a few
madmen into this house, in order to convince the world that
those outside it are sane."

Here I leave my Spaniard. Farewell, my dear Usbek.

Paris, the 17th of the moon of Saphar, 1715

---

3 [Cervantes' *Don Quixote*.]

4 [Texts vary on this passage. Some have *il y a sur leurs rivières tel port
qui n'a pas encore été decouvert;* others have *pont* ("bridge") for *port*
("port"); the 1761 edition, followed in this translation, largely because
it is most general and seems to make the most sense, has *point* ("place,"
i.e., on the rivers).]

5 The Batuecas. [These are the wild mountains between Salamanca and
Estramadura; there is no evidence that they contained "nations unknown"
to the Spanish.]

LETTER LXXIX

The chief black eunuch to Usbek, at Paris

Yesterday some Armenians brought to the seraglio a young Circassian slave they wished to sell. I conducted her into the secret apartments, undressed her, and examined her with the eyes of a judge. The more I looked the more graces I found in her. A virginal shame seemed anxious to hide them from my view, and I saw how much it cost her to obey. She blushed at seeing herself naked—even before me, who am exempt of passions capable of alarming a sense of shame, am delivered from the dominion of sex, and am the minister of modesty even in the freest actions, looking as I do with chaste eyes and able only to inspire innocence.

As soon as I had deemed her worthy of you, I lowered my eyes, threw a scarlet cloak over her, put a gold ring on her finger, and prostrating myself at her feet, I adored her as the queen of your heart. I paid the Armenians and hid her from all eyes. Happy Usbek! You possess more beauties than are contained in all the palaces of the East. What pleasure for you, to find upon your return everything ravishing that Persia has to offer, and to see the graces reborn in your seraglio as fast as time and possession work to destroy them!

> *The seraglio at Fatima, the 1st of the moon of Rebiab I, 1715*

LETTER LXXX

Usbek to Rhedi, at Venice

Since I have been in Europe, my dear Rhedi, I have seen many forms of government; it is not like Asia, where the rules of politics are the same everywhere.

I have often asked myself what kind of government most conformed to reason. It has seemed to me that the most perfect is that which attains its goal with the least friction; thus that government is most perfect which leads men along paths most agreeable to their interests and inclinations.

If under a mild government the people are as submissive as under a severe one, the first is preferable, since it better accords with reason than does severity, which is a motive alien to rationality.

Remember, my dear Rhedi, that obedience to the laws of a state does not correspond with the greater or lesser degrees of cruelty in punishment. In countries where penalties are moderate, they are as much feared as those in which they are tyrannical and dreadful.

Whether government be gentle or cruel, punishment must always be scaled so that greater or lesser chastisement is inflicted for greater or lesser crimes. Our imagination adapts itself to the customs of the country in which we live, and eight days in prison or a slight fine impresses the mind of a European, raised in a mild-mannered country, as much as the loss of an arm intimidates the Asiatic. A certain degree of fear attaches to a certain degree of punishment, and each feels it in his own way. A Frenchman will be overcome with despair at the disgrace of a punishment that would not disturb a quarter-hour of a Turk's sleep.

Furthermore, I do not see that the police regulations or the principles of justice and equity are any better observed in Turkey, Persia, or in the lands of the Mogul, than in the republics of Holland and Venice, or even in England. I see no fewer crimes committed there, no evidence that men, intimidated by the magnitude of punishment, are more submissive to the laws.

On the contrary, I notice a source of injustice and vexation within these very states.

I find that even the prince, who is the law, is less a master there than anywhere else.

I see that in times of rigorous severity there are always

tumultuous and leaderless upheavals, and that once a violent authority becomes despised, nothing anyone can do will restore it;

That to deny all hope of pardon is to strengthen and enlarge the disorder;

That in such states a small revolt never occurs, and that no interval comes between grumbling and sedition;

That in them great events are not necessarily prepared by great causes; on the contrary, the slightest accident produces great revolutions, so often as unforeseen by those who make it as by those who suffer from it.

When Osman, emperor of the Turks, was deposed, none of those who committed the crime ever intended to do it. As suppliants, they merely asked that justice be done with regard to some complaint; but by chance an unknown voice was heard from the crowd, the name of Mustapha was pronounced, and suddenly Mustapha was emperor.[1]

Paris, the 2nd of the moon of Rebiab I, 1715

LETTER LXXXI

Nargum, Persian envoy in Muscovy,
to Usbek, at Paris

Of all the nations of the world, my dear Usbek, none has surpassed the Tartars in the glory or in the magnitude of conquest. This people is the veritable ruler of the earth. All others seem made to serve it; it is both founder and destroyer of empires; throughout history it has signified its prowess to the world, and it has been the scourge of nations in every age.

---

1 [Osman II was deposed and strangled in 1622. Mustapha I, who had been deposed by Osman in 1618, succeeded him in 1622, to be again deposed the following year, and strangled in 1639.]

The Tartars have twice conquered China and still hold it in obedience.

They rule the vast territories which comprise the Mogul's empire.

Masters of Persia, they sit upon the throne of Cyrus and Gustaspes.[1] They have subdued Muscovy. Under the name of Turks, they have made immense conquests in Europe, Asia, and Africa, and they dominate these three parts of the earth.

And to speak of more remote times, it was from them that sprung some of those peoples who overturned the Roman Empire.

What are the conquests of Alexander compared to those of Genghis Khan?

All this victorious nation has lacked are historians to celebrate the memory of its marvelous deeds.

How many immortal acts have been buried in oblivion! How many empires have they founded, of whose origin we are ignorant! This warlike people, solely occupied with present glory and sure of victory forever, never thought to win renown in the future by memorializing its past conquests.

Moscow, the 4th of the moon of Rebiab I, 1715

LETTER LXXXII

Rica to Ibben, at Smyrna

Although the French talk a great deal, there is nevertheless among them a kind of silent dervish called "Carthusians." It is said that they cut off their tongues upon entering the convent, and it would be most desirable if all the other dervishes would remove in the same way everything rendered useless by their profession.

---

1 [Cyrus reigned as king of Persia from 559 to 529 B.C. On Gustaspes, see above, p. 117, footnote 6.]

Speaking of these silent people, there are some even more strange than they, who have a truly extraordinary talent: they can talk without saying anything and carry on a two-hour conversation without your being able to understand, repeat, or retain a word they have said.

This sort of person is adored by women, though not so much as some others, who have a natural and amiable gift of smiling whenever it is appropriate—that is to say, constantly—and who spread the grace of joyous approbation on everything the ladies say.

But they reach the peak of wit when they learn to find subtle meanings and a thousand little ingenuities in the slightest banalities.

I know some others fortunate enough to be able to introduce inanimate things into conversation, and to make their brocaded clothes, white wig, snuffbox, cane, and gloves speak for them. It is well to begin attracting attention while still in the street, by making a great noise with your carriage and pounding loudly at the door. This prologue prepares the way for the rest of the discourse; and if it is well done, it makes supportable all the stupidities which follow, but which happily occur too late to be noticed.

I assure you that these petty talents, for which we have no use, here serve those very well who are fortunate enough to possess them, and that a man of good sense has no chance of shining in their presence.

Paris, the 6th of the moon of Rebiab II, 1715

LETTER LXXXIII

Usbek to Rhedi, at Venice

If there is a God, my dear Rhedi, he must necessarily be just; for if he were not, he would be the worst and most imperfect of all beings.

Justice is the proper relationship actually existing between two things. This relationship is always the same whoever contemplates it, whether God, or angel, or, finally, man.

It is true that men do not always perceive these relationships, and even when they do see them they often turn away, as their self-interest is always favored in their sight. Justice raises its voice but finds it can hardly make itself heard in the tumult of the passions.

Men can be unjust, because it is in their interest to act so, and they prefer their own satisfaction to that of others. They always act with themselves in mind. No one is gratuitously wicked; there must be a determining cause, and it is always one of self-interest.

But it is impossible for God to be in any way unjust. Assuming that he perceives justice, it is necessary that he follow it; for as he has need of nothing and is sufficient unto himself, he thus has no motive for wrongdoing and would be the wickedest of beings if he did wrong.

Therefore, even if there were no God, we ought to love justice always, which is to say, to try to resemble that being of whom we have such a beautiful idea, and who, if he existed, would necessarily be just. However free we might be from the yoke of religion, we would still be bound by that of justice.

For these reasons, Rhedi, I think that justice is eternal and independent of human conventions. Were it dependent on them, this would be such a terrible truth that we would have to hide it from ourselves.

We are surrounded by men stronger than ourselves, who can injure us in a thousand different ways, and with impunity three quarters of the time. Is it not comforting to us to know that in the hearts of all these men there is an innate principle which fights in our favor and shelters us from their plots?

Without that we would be in continual fear. We would walk in front of men as before lions and never for a moment be sure of our property, our honor, or our lives.

All these thoughts lead me to oppose those metaphysicians who represent God as a being who exercises his power tyrannically, who make him act in a way we would not wish to act ourselves for fear of offending him, who charge him with every imperfection he punishes in us, and who inconsistently represent him sometimes as an evil being and sometimes as a being who hates evil and punishes it.

How satisfying it is, when a man examines himself and finds a just heart! This pleasure, austere though it is, ought to ravish him, for he sees himself as equally superior both to those who have not such a heart, and to tigers and bears. Yes, Rhedi, if I were sure to follow, always and without violation, that justice I see before me, I would consider myself the best of men.

Paris, the 1st of the moon of Gemmadi I, 1715

LETTER LXXXIV

Rica to ——————

Yesterday I went to the Invalides; [1] if I were a prince I would rather have founded this place than have won three battles. The hand of a great monarch is everywhere apparent on it. I believe it more worthy of respect that any other institution in the world.

What a sight it is, to see assembled in this one place all those men who sacrificed themselves for their country, men who breathed only to defend it, and who now, feeling the same way but without the same strength, complain only that their impotence prohibits their again sacrificing themselves for it!

What nobler sight than to see these disabled warriors observing in their retirement a discipline as precise as if they

---

[1] [The Invalides, a home for army veterans built by Louis XIV, is a major military shrine in Paris; Turenne, Napoleon I, and Foch are among those buried in its chapel.]

were constrained by an enemy's presence, seeking their last satisfaction in this semblance of war, and dividing their hearts and minds between the duties of religion and their military profession!

I would have the names of those who die for their country preserved in the temples and inscribed in registers which would become the source of glory and nobility.

Paris, the 15th of the moon of Gemmadi I, 1715

Usbek to Mirza, at Ispahan

You know, Mirza, that certain ministers of Shah Soliman [1] formed the plan of requiring all Armenians in Persia either to leave the kingdom or become Mohammedans, thinking that our empire would remain polluted so long as it kept these infidels in its bosom.

That would have been the end of Persian greatness, had the counsels of blind devotion won out on that occasion.

It is not known how the project failed. Neither those who made the proposal, nor those who rejected it, realized the consequence of their decision; chance assumed the office of reason and policy and saved the empire from a peril greater than would have resulted from the loss of a battle and the capture of two cities.

By proscribing the Armenians, it is calculated that all the merchants and most of the country's artisans would have been wiped out in a single day. I am sure that the great Shah Abbas [2] would rather have cut off both his arms than sign such

---

1 [Soliman (Suleiman) reigned in Persia from 1666 to 1694.]

2 [Abbas I reigned in Persia from 1587 to 1628. The implied references in this letter, of course, are to Louis XIV's revocation (1685) of the Edict of Nantes (1598), which ended the toleration of Protestantism proclaimed by Abbas' French contemporary, Henry IV.]

an order; in exiling to the lands of the Mogul and the other Indian kings his most industrious subjects, he would have felt that he was giving them half of his realm.

The persecution of the Guebres by our zealous Mohammedans has forced them to leave in crowds for India [3] and has deprived Persia of a hardworking people which, by its labor alone, was close to victory over the sterility of our soil.

Yet there remained to fanaticism a second blow to strike, that against our industry. The result was that the empire fell from within, bringing down with it, as a necessary consequence, that very religion which the zealots wished to strengthen.

If unprejudiced discussion were possible, I am not sure, Mirza, that it would not be a good thing for a state to contain several religions.

It is noticed that members of tolerated religions usually render more service to their country than do those of the dominant religion, because, cut off from the customary honors, they can distinguish themselves only by an opulence and wealth acquired by their labor alone, and often in the most difficult professions.

Furthermore, since all religions contain precepts that are socially useful, it is well that they be zealously observed; and what is better able to animate that zeal than a multiplicity of religions?

They are rivals who pardon nothing, and their jealousy extends to individuals. Each holds himself on guard, fearful of doing something which might dishonor his sect and expose it to the scorn and unpardonable censures of the other group.

Also, it is often observed that the introduction of a new sect into a state is the surest way to correct abuses in the old.

It is vain to say that it is not in the prince's interest to tolerate various religions in his realm. All the sects of the world assembled together would bring him no harm, for there is not

---

[3] [The Parsees emigrated from Persia and settled around Bombay. See above, p. 112, footnote 1.]

one of them that does not prescribe obedience and preach submission.

I admit that history is filled with religious wars, but let us be careful here, for it is not the multiplicity of religions which has produced these wars, but the spirit of intolerance stirring those who believed themselves to be in a dominant position.

This is the proselytizing spirit which the Jews caught from the Egyptians, and which has passed from them, like a common epidemic disease, to the Mohammedans and Christians.

It is, in short, a kind of madness, the progress of which can be regarded only as a total eclipse of human reason.

Finally, even if it were not inhumane to afflict another's conscience, and even if there did not result from such an act those bad effects which spring up by the thousands, it would still be foolish to advise it. Whoever would have me change my religion doubtlessly acts as he does because he would not change his, however he was forced; yet he finds it strange that I will not do something which he would not do himself, perhaps for the entire world.

Paris, the 26th of the moon of Gemmadi I, 1715

LETTER LXXXVI

Rica to ———

It seems that every individual in a family here is self-governing. The authority of a husband over his wife, the father over his children, and the master over his slaves is only a shadow. The law interferes in all their disputes, and you may be sure that it is always against the jealous husband, the sorrowing father, and the aggravated master.

The other day, I went to a place where justice is administered. Before getting there, you must run a gauntlet of a swarm of young shopgirls, who call to you in seductive tones.[1] At first this is a spectacle sufficiently amusing, but it becomes lugubrious when you enter the great halls, where you see only people whose clothing is even more solemn than their expressions. Finally, you reach those sacred precincts where all family secrets are revealed, and where the most hidden actions are brought to light.

Here a modest girl appears to confess the torments she has suffered from her too-long guarded virginity, her struggles, and her painful resistance. She is so little proud of her victory that she is constantly menaced by imminent defeat; and so that her father will no longer be ignorant of her needs, she exposes them to everyone.

Next a shameless woman comes forward to proclaim the ways she has outraged her husband as a reason for separation from him.

With similar modesty, another woman comes to announce that she is tired of being called a wife without enjoying her wifely rights. She reveals all the hidden mysteries of the marriage night and requests examination by the best experts so that all the rights of viriginity may be restored to her by proclamation. There are even some women who dare to challenge their husbands and who demand a public inquiry of them, which is made most difficult by the presence of witnesses and is as disgraceful for the wife who succeeds in it as for the husband who does not.[2]

A multitude of ravished or seduced girls make the men out to be much worse than they are. This court is a cacophony of love; one only hears of irritated fathers, abused girls, faithless lovers, and aggrieved husbands.

---

1 [The galleries of the law court in Paris were filled with small shops.]

2 [Technically an anachronism: the *parlement* of Paris had prohibited the ordeal *du congrès* in 1677. However, in 1714 the Marquise de Gèvres did legally accuse her husband of impotence; the testimony was printed in Holland in two large volumes, which served to enlarge the scandal considerably.]

By the law observed here, every child born during marriage is considered the husband's. It is useless for him to have good reasons for believing otherwise; the law believes it for him and relieves him of the need for inquiry or scruples.

Majority rule obtains in this court, but it is said that experience teaches that it would be better to follow the minority. This is natural enough, for while there are very few just minds, everyone agrees that there are unbalanced ones in abundance.

Paris, the 1st of the moon of Gemmadi II, 1715

LETTER LXXXVII

Rica to ———

Man is said to be a social animal. If this is the case, it seems to me that a Frenchman is more a man than anyone else; he is man in essence, for he appears to be made solely for society.

But I have noticed some among them who are not only sociable, but are society itself. They multiply in every corner and in no time populate the four quarters of a city; a hundred of this species suggests greater abundance than two thousand citizens, and they could cause a foreigner to think that the ravages of a pestilence or famine were repaired. The question is asked in the schools whether a body can be in several places at the same time; these people are proof of what the philosophers question.

They are always in a hurry, because theirs is the important business of asking everyone they meet where they are going and from where they have come.

No one can drive out of their heads the notion that it is properly polite to make a daily visit to each individual in society. By the rules of their etiquette they do not count those visits made in places of large public assembly, since such affairs are considered to be too brief.

Their knocking puts more strain on the doors of houses than do wind and storm. If all the porters' lists were examined, their names would be found every day, mutilated in a thousand ways in Swiss writing.[1] They pass their lives in attending funerals, in the rituals of condolences, or in marriage congratulations. The king never grants a favor without it costing these people the price of a rented carriage so they can ride to manifest their joy to the honored subject. Finally they return home, worn out, to regain in sleep the energy to carry them through the next day's arduous functions.

One of them died the other day of exhaustion; they put this epitaph on his tomb:

Here rests he who never rested. He attended five hundred and thirty funerals. He rejoiced at the birth of two thousand six hundred and eighty children. He congratulated his friends, and always in different terms, on pensions worth two million six hundred thousand livres. He covered nine thousand six hundred furlongs of city streets and thirty-six in the country. His conversation was amusing: he had a ready-made stock of three hundred and sixty-five stories and, dating from his youth, one hundred and eighteen maxims taken from ancient authors, which he employed on special occasions. At last he died in his sixtieth year. I say no more, traveler, for how could I ever finish telling you what he has done and seen?

Paris, the 3rd of the moon of Gemmadi II, 1715

LETTER LXXXVIII

Usbek to Rhedi, at Venice

Liberty and equality reign in Paris. Neither birth, nor virtue, nor even military distinction, however brilliant it may be, save a man from being confounded with the crowd. Jealousy be-

---

1 [The keepers of the gates of many Parisian town houses were Swiss.]

tween ranks is unknown. It is said that the leader of Paris is
the one who has the best horses drawing his carriage.

A great noble is a man who sees the king, speaks to ministers, and has ancestors, debts, and pensions. If, in addition to
this, he can conceal his indolence under a busy appearance or
by a feigned attachment to pleasure, he considers himself the
happiest of men.

In Persia the only nobles are those to whom the monarch
has delegated some part in the government. Here there are
people great in their birth but without such distinction. The
kings are like those skilled craftsmen who always employ the
simplest tools in their work.

Favor is the great French goddess, and the minister is the
high priest who offers up her many victims. Those surrounding her are not dressed in white, for as they sometimes make
the sacrifices and sometimes are themselves sacrificed, they
offer themselves up to their idol along with all the rest of the
people.

Paris, the 9th of the moon of Gemmadi II, 1715

LETTER LXXXIX

Usbek to Ibben, at Smyrna

The desire for glory does not differ from the instinct in all
animals for self-preservation. It seems we enlarge our existence when we can project it into another's memory; we acquire a new life, which becomes as precious to us as the one we
received from heaven.

But just as men are not equally attached to life, so are they
not equally sensitive to glory. That noble passion is always
deeply engraved in their hearts, but imagination and education modify it in a thousand ways.

This difference, found among individuals, is even more apparent among nations.

One can state it as a maxim: in each state the desire for glory increases and diminishes with the liberty of the subjects; glory never accompanies servitude.

The other day a sensible man said to me: "In many respects one is more free in France than in Persia, and thus we are more in love with glory. This fortunate illusion makes a Frenchman do things with pleasure and desire which your sultan exacts from his subjects only by constantly displaying rewards and punishments before them.

"Also, among us the prince is jealous of the honor of the meanest of his subjects. There are respected tribunals which maintain this honor, which is the sacred treasure of the nation and the only one not controlled by the sovereign, since to do so would defeat his own interests. Thus, if a subject discovers that his honor is hurt by the prince, whether by some preference or by the slightest mark of contempt, he immediately leaves his court, employment, and service and retires to his own estates.

"The difference between French troops and yours is this: yours, composed of slaves who are natural cowards, surmount fear of death only by fear of punishment, which produces in their soul a new kind of terror which stupifies it; ours, on the other hand, present themselves to combat with delight and banish fear by the superior feeling of satisfaction.

"But the sanctuary of honor, of reputation and virtue, seems to be established in republics and in lands where one dares to pronounce the word 'fatherland.' In Rome, Athens, and Sparta honor was the sole payment for the most distinguished services. An oak or laurel crown, a statue, or a eulogy, was immense reward for a victorious battle or a captured city.

"There a man felt himself sufficiently recompensed for a fine act by the act itself. He could not see another of his countrymen without pleasurably feeling that he was his benefactor; he reckoned the number of his services by the number of his fellow citizens. Every man is able to do a good deed for an-

other man; but to contribute to the happiness of a whole society is to approach the gods.

"Now, must not this noble emulation be entirely extinct
in the hearts of you Persians, whose employments and honors
are only the products of the sovereign's whim? There reputation and virtue are regarded as illusory unless accompanied
by the prince's favor, which controls their beginning and end.
A man enjoying public esteem is never sure that tomorrow he
will not be dishonored. Today a general of an army, tomorrow
the prince may decide to make him his cook and so leave
him with no hope of praise other than that of having made a
good ragout."

Paris, the 15th of the moon of Gemmadi II, 1715

Usbek to the same, at Smyrna

From the general passion of the French for glory, there has
developed in the minds of individuals a certain something
called "the point of honor," which is properly characteristic
of every profession but especially noticeable in military men;
theirs is the point of honor par excellence. It would be very
hard for me to explain this to you, for we have no idea quite
like it.

Formerly the French, and above all the nobles, followed no
other laws than those of this point of honor. The entire conduct of their lives was regulated by them, and they were so
severe that even to elude one of their most trivial commands—
I say nothing of infringing them—brought penalties more
cruel than death itself.

When questions arose on settling differences, only one
method of decision was prescribed: the duel, which resolved

all difficulties. But it had one drawback: the trial often took place between parties other than those directly interested.

However slightly one man might know another, he was obliged to enter the quarrel and pay with his person, as if he were himself angered. He always felt himself honored by such a choice and flattered by preference; and he who would not willingly give four pistoles to save a man and his entire family from the gallows would nonetheless risk his life for him a thousand times without complaint.

This method of decision was, of course, badly conceived; for it did not follow, just because one man was more skillful or stronger than another, that he had more right on his side.

Accordingly, kings have forbidden dueling under very strict penalties, but in vain; wishing always to rule, honor revolts and ignores the laws.

And so the French remain in a state of violence, for the laws of honor require a gentleman to avenge himself if insulted; but justice, on the other hand, punishes him cruelly for his vengeance. If you follow the laws of honor, you perish on the scaffold; but to follow the laws of justice means perpetual banishment from the society of men. There is, then, only this harsh alternative: to die or to be unworthy of life.

Paris, the 18th of the moon of Gemmadi II, 1715

LETTER XCI

Usbek to Rustan, at Ispahan

A person has appeared here who burlesques the role of a Persian ambassador and makes insolent sport of the two greatest kings on earth. He brings to the French monarch gifts which ours would not dream of offering to a king of Irimetta or Georgia, and by his mean avarice he has dishonored the majesty of two empires.[1]

He has made himself ridiculous before a people who pretend to be the most polished in Europe; and he has caused it to be said in the West that the king of kings only rules over barbarians.

He has received honors which he seemed eager to refuse; and, as if the French court had Persian majesty more at heart than he, it forced him to appear with dignity before a people who despise him.

Say nothing of this in Ispahan; spare the head of this unfortunate being. I do not want our ministers to punish him for their imprudence in making such an unworthy choice.

Paris, the last day of the moon of Gemmadi II, 1715

LETTER XCII

Usbek to Rhedi, at Venice

The monarch who reigned for so long is no more.[1] He made people talk much about him during his life; everyone is silent at his death. Firm and courageous in his last moment, he appeared to submit only to destiny. So too died the great Shah Abbas, after having filled the entire earth with his name.

Do not think that this great event has occasioned only moral reflections. Everyone has considered his own affairs and how to take advantage of the change. As the king, the great-grand-

---

1 [The Mohammedan adventurer Riza Bey was in Paris in 1715 on commission of Shah Husein. He made such a bad impression that some refused to credit him as an official ambassador, believing that the whole affair had been concocted at the French court as a joke.]

1 He died September 1, 1715.

son of the defunct monarch is only five years old, a prince, his uncle, has been declared regent of the realm.[2]

The late king had made a will which restricted the power of the regent, but this adroit prince has appeared before the *parlement,* and presenting there all the rights to which his birth entitles him, he has broken the will of the monarch who, wishing to survive himself, seemed to claim the rule even after his death.[3]

The *parlements* resemble those ruins which are trampled underfoot but are reminiscent always of some temple famed in the antique religion of the people. They now interest themselves only in judicial questions, and their authority will continue to weaken unless something unforeseen rejuvenates them. These great bodies have followed the destiny of all things human: they have yielded to time, which destroys all, to moral corruption, which enfeebles, and to supreme authority, which overthrows everything.

However, the regent, who wishes to make himself agreeable to the people, has so far appeared to respect this shadow of public liberty. As if he intended to rebuild the temple and the idol, he has decreed that they may be regarded as the support of the monarch and the base of all legitimate authority.

Paris, the 4th of the moon of Rhegeb, 1715

---

[2] [Louis XV succeeded his great-grandfather under a regency council headed by Philippe, Duc d'Orléans.]

[3] [Orléans, wanting full powers as regent and suspicious of the Duc du Maine, Louis XIV's legitimized bastard son, petitioned the Paris *parlement* to set aside the old king's will, which had created a regency council and thus divided the authority. The *parlement* complied, with the understanding that Orléans in turn would grant to it wider power in the formulation of law and policy. On September 15, 1715, he returned to the *parlement* the *droit de rémonstrance,* which permitted parliamentary objection to any royal edict; this right had been removed by Louis XIV.]

LETTER XCIII

Usbek to his brother, santon [1] at the monastary of Casbin

I humble and prostrate myself before you, holy santon; your footprints are to me as the pupils of my eyes. Your sanctity is so great that you seem to have the heart of our sacred Prophet; your austerities astonish heaven itself; the angels have watched you from the summit of glory and have said, "How is it that he is still on earth, since his soul is with us, flying about the throne borne up by the clouds?"

How should I not honor you, I who have learned from our doctors that dervishes, even if they are infidels, always possess a character of holiness which makes them venerable to true believers, and that God has chosen from all regions of the earth some souls more pure than others, whom he has separated from the impious world, that their mortifications and fervent prayers might hold in suspense his anger, ready to fall upon the rebellious multitudes?

The Christians tell of the miracles of their early santons, thousands of whom sought refuge in the fearful Theban deserts under the leadership of Paul, Anthony, and Pachomius.[2] If what is said of them is true, their lives were as full of prodigies as those of our most sacred imans. Ten entire years sometimes passed without their seeing a single man, but day and night they lived with demons and were ceaselessly tormented

---

1 [A santon is a Mohammedan monk.]

2 [Paul the Hermit, or Paul of Thebes, a historically shadowy figure much burdened with legend, was supposed to have fled to the Egyptian desert during the Decian persecutions (249-51) and there to have become the first of the Christian hermit monks. Anthony (born *c.* 250 and reputedly living for 105 years) has a better documented claim as the first Christian hermit and is known to have inspired many disciples. Pachomius (*c.* 292-346) organized many of the eremitical monks into a cenobitic community, and wrote a very influential monastic rule.]

by malignant spirits who sought them out in bed and at table; no asylum from them was possible. If all this is true, venerable santon, it must be admitted that no one ever lived in worse company.

Sensible Christians regard these stories as a very natural allegory, which can serve to make us aware of the wretchedness of the human condition. In vain do we seek tranquillity in the desert; temptations follow us always, and our passions, symbolized by the demons, never entirely leave us. These monstrosities of the heart, these mental illusions, these vain phantoms of error and falsehood are always present to seduce us, to attack us even in our fasts and hair shirts, that is to say, even in our greatest strength.

As for me, venerable santon, I know that God's messenger has chained Satan and hurled him into the abyss. He has purged the earth of Satan's power and made it worthy of the dwellings of angels and prophets.

Paris, the 9th of the moon of Chahban, 1715

LETTER XCIV

Usbek to Rhedi, at Venice

I have never heard a discussion of public law which was not preceded by a careful inquiry into the origins of society. This appears absurd to me. If men did not form into society, if they avoided and fled from one another, then it would be necessary to find the reasons why they kept apart. But they are born dependent upon each other. The son comes into the world beside his father and stays there, and this is both the definition and the cause of society.

International law is better understood in Europe than in Asia; however, it may be said that the passions of princes, the

patience of their subjects, and the flattery of writers have corrupted all its principles.

This law as it stands today is a science which teaches princes
how far they can violate justice without injuring their own
interests. What a design, Rhedi—to harden the conscience by
trying to reduce iniquity to a system, by prescribing rules for
it, by shaping its principles and deducing its consequences!

The unlimited power of our sublime sultans, which is a
law unto itself, does not produce more monsters than this infamous art, which undertakes to make pliant the inflexibility
of justice.

One would say, Rhedi, that there are two entirely different
kinds of justice: the one which regulates the affairs of individuals and reigns in civil law, the other which regulates differences between nations and tyrannizes over international
law—as if international law were not itself a civil law, not, to
be sure, of one country, but of the world.

I will explain in another letter my thoughts on this subject.

Paris, the 1st of the moon of Zilhage, 1716

LETTER XCV

Usbek to the same

Magistrates ought to administer justice between citizen and
citizen; and each nation ought to do the same between itself
and other nations. In this second administration of justice
only maxims applicable to the first can be used.

There is rarely a need for a third party to arbitrate between
two nations, because the subjects disputed are almost always
clear and easy to decide. The interests of two nations are usually so distinct that one need only love justice to find it, for
here one can hardly be prejudiced in his own cause.

It is not the same with the differences that arise between individuals. As they live together in society, their interests are so mixed and confused, and so varied, that a third party is required to clear up what the cupidities of the other two try to make obscure.

There are only two kinds of just wars: those undertaken in self-defense and those which aid an attacked ally.

There would be no justice in making war for the private quarrels of a prince, unless the crime were so grave as to warrant the death of the prince or of the people committing it. Thus a prince cannot make war because someone has refused an honor due to him, or because someone treats his ambassadors without proper respect, or any similar reason; no more could an individual kill someone refusing him precedence. The reason for this is that a declaration of war ought to be a just act in which the punishment is always in proportion to the crime; thus it must be determined whether he upon whom war is declared merits death, for to make war against someone is to will a death penalty.

In international law war is the most severe act of justice, since it may have the effect of destroying society.

Reprisals are second in severity. To measure the penalty by the crime is a law which tribunals have not been able to avoid.

A third act of justice is to deprive a prince of the advantages he might otherwise derive from us, always scaling the penalty to the offense.

The fourth act of justice, which ought to be the most frequent, is the renunciation of an alliance with a people against whom there is cause of complaint. Such a punishment corresponds to that of banishment imposed by the courts to remove criminals from society. Thus a prince, whose alliance is renounced, is cut off from our community and is no longer a member of it.

No greater affront can be given a prince than to renounce his alliance, and no greater honor can be given him than to contract with him. Nothing seems so honorable or so useful to men as to see others continually attentive to their preservation.

But, for an alliance to bind us, it must be just; thus an alliance made between two nations for the oppression of a third is not legitimate and may be violated without guilt.

It is not consistent with the honor and dignity of a prince to ally himself with a tyrant. It is told that a king of Egypt objected to the cruelty and tyranny of the king of Samos and summoned him to correct his ways; as he did not do so, he was advised that his friendship and his alliance were renounced.[1]

Conquest in itself does not establish right. As long as a people subsist, conquest is a pledge of peace and the reparation of wrong; but if the people are destroyed or dispersed, it is a monument of tyranny.

Treaties of peace are so sacred among men that they seem to be the voice of nature reclaiming her rights. They are all legitimate when the conditions are such that the two nations can preserve themselves; if this is not the case, that nation in danger of perishing, deprived by peace of its natural defense, may seek it in war.

For nature, although she has established different degrees of strength and weakness in men, has also frequently made weakness equal to strength by adding despair to it.

This, my dear Rhedi, is what I call international law, the law of nations, or rather, the law of reason.

Paris, the 4th of the moon of Zilhage, 1716

---

1 [According to Diodorus of Sicily (I. 95), King Ahmose of Egypt broke his alliance with Polycrates, the ruler of Samos, for such reasons.]

LETTER XCVI

The chief eunuch to Usbek, at Paris

There have arrived here a great number of yellow-skinned women from the kingdom of Visapour.[1] I bought one of them for your brother, the governor of Mazanderan,[2] who a month ago sent me his sublime command along with a hundred tomans.

I am skilled at judging women, particularly so because they cannot deceive me, since my eyes are not disturbed by the workings of my heart.

I have never seen such regular and perfect beauty; her dazzling eyes enliven her face and set off a glowing complexion which would eclipse all the charms of Circassia.[3]

The chief eunuch of an Ispahan merchant bid against me; but she disdainfully cast aside his attention and seemed to seek mine, as if she wished to tell me that a common merchant was unworthy of her and that she was destined for a more illustrious husband.

I confess to you that a secret joy stirs within me when I think of the charms of this beautiful person. I imagine that I see her entering your brother's seraglio, and I am delighted to predict the astonishment of all his wives: the haughty grief of some, the mute but even sadder affliction of others, the maliciously consoling pleasure of those who no longer have hopeful expectations, and the enraged ambition of those who still do hope.

I am about to travel from one end of the kingdom to the other to change the entire aspect of the seraglio. Such passions

---

[1] [Until 1686, Visapour (Bijapur) was an independent kingdom in India. It is now within the state of Mysore.]

[2] [Mazanderan is an Iranian province south of the Caspian Sea.]

[3] [The Circassians are tribes of the northern Caucasus; they are a characteristically tall people, oval-faced, brown-eyed, and noted for their physical beauty.]

will I provoke! So many fears and punishments am I preparing!

Yet, for all this internal turmoil, outward tranquillity will be undisturbed. Great revolutions will be hidden deep within the heart; griefs will be devoured and joys contained; obedience will be no less exact or the rules less flexible; and the sweet manners, always required, will spring even from the depths of despair.

We have noticed that the more women we have to watch, the less trouble they give us. A greater necessity to please, less opportunity for conspiracy, more examples of submission: all this forges their chains. They are constantly watchful of each other's deportment, and it seems that, in concert with us, they work to make themselves more dependent; they become an accessory to our work and open our eyes when we close them. What do I say? They ceaselessly excite their master against their rivals and do not see how close they put themselves to the punishment they incite against others.

But all this, magnificent lord, all this is nothing without the master's presence. What can we do with this vain phantom of an authority which is never entirely delegated to us? We can feebly represent only half of you; we can only show them an odious severity. You temper fear with hope; you are more absolute when you caress than when you menace.

Return then, magnificent lord, return and bring to this place the mark of your authority. Come to ease despairing passions; come to remove every pretext for weakness; come to pacify complaining love, and to make duty itself agreeable; return, finally, to relieve your faithful eunuchs of a burden which grows heavier every day.

> *The seraglio at Ispahan, the 8th of the moon of Zilhage, 1716*

Usbek to Hassein, dervish of the mountain of Jaron [1]

O wise dervish, whose inquisitive mind glitters with so much knowledge, hear what I have to say.

There are philosophers here who, it is true, have not yet attained the heights of Oriental wisdom. They have not yet been transported to the luminous throne; they have neither heard the ineffable words of the angelic choirs nor sensed the formidable presence of divine frenzy. Left to themselves and deprived of holy miracles, they silently follow the trail of human reason instead.

You would not believe where this trail has led them. They have cleared up chaos and explained in simple mechanical terms the principles of the divine architecture. The Creator of nature has put matter in motion: nothing further is required to produce the unbelievable variety of effects that we perceive in the universe.

Ordinary legislators propose laws to regulate human society, laws as subject to change as the minds proposing them or the people obeying them. These others speak only of immutable and eternal general laws which manifest themselves without exceptions and with order, regularity, and infinite speed in the immensities of space.

And what, O holy man, do you suppose these laws might be? Perhaps you may imagine that, entering the counsel of the eternal, you will be astounded by the sublimity of mystery and abandon in advance any hope of understanding and expect only to admire.

But you will soon change your opinion. These laws do not dazzle us by pretended profundity; rather, their simplicity has kept them a long time misunderstood, and only after much

---

1 [Jaron (Djaroun) is a town in Persia, hard against a steep mountain and described by Chardin.]

reflection have people seen in them all their fecundity and generality.

The first is that every body in motion tends to describe a straight line unless turned aside by contact with some obstacle. The second, which is only a consequence of the first, is that every body revolving about a center tends to fly from it, because the farther away it is, the more nearly the line it describes approaches a straight line.[2]

There, sublime dervish, is the key to nature. These are the fruitful principles from which may be drawn consequences beyond our power to see.

The knowledge of five or six truths has made their philosophy full of miracles and has enabled them to perform almost as many prodigies and marvels as those told of our sacred prophets.

For, in short, I am persuaded that there is not one of our doctors who would not be embarrassed if he were asked to weigh in a balance all the air surrounding the earth, or to measure all the water which annually falls upon its surface; not one who, without much thought, could say how many leagues sound travels in an hour, or how long it takes for a ray of light to come to us from the sun, or how many fathoms

---

2 [Usbek here refers to Descartes' famous first laws of motion, but somewhat carelessly in the case of the second law. As stated in Descartes' *Principles of Philosophy* (Part II, Principle 37) the first law is: "Every reality . . . always remains in the same condition as far as it can, and never changes except through external causes. . . . [Therefore] a moving body, so far as it can, goes on moving." The second law is: "Any given piece of matter considered by itself tends to go on moving, not in any oblique path, but only in straight lines. . . . The reason . . . is the immutability and simplicity of the operation by which God preserves motion in matter" (*Ibid.*, Principle 39).

Usbek does not exaggerate the importance of these principles to science. Descartes' laws, which flatly contradicted the Aristotelian concept of motion as a "violent" state in a universe in which rest was the more "natural" condition, formed the basis on which the classical physics of the seventeenth and eighteenth centuries was erected.]

it is from here to Saturn, or what a ship's lines ought to be to make it sail in the best possible way.

Perhaps if some holy man had embellished the works of these philosophers with lofty and sublime words, if he had introduced bold figures and mysterious allegories, he might have made a fine work, second only to our sacred Koran.

However, if I must tell you what I think, I do not much care for a figurative style. In our Koran there are a number of things which always seem petty to me, however they are enhanced by forceful and vital expression. It seems, at first thought, that inspired books are those in which divine ideas are turned into human language; in our Koran, on the other hand, one often finds God's language and human ideas—as if by some remarkable caprice God had spoken the words and man had furnished the ideas.

You may perhaps say I speak too freely of what is most sacred to us; you will believe that such is the product of the independence of this country. But no. Thanks to heaven, my mind has not corrupted my heart, and Hali will be my prophet for as long as I live.

Paris, the 15th of the moon of Chahban, 1716

LETTER XCVIII

Usbek to Ibben, at Smyrna

There is no country in the world where fortune is as inconstant as here. Every ten years a revolution occurs, casting the rich into dire poverty and swiftly winging the poor to the heights of wealth. They are both astonished: the one at his poverty, the other at his affluence. The newly wealthy marvel at the wisdom of providence; the poor, at the blind fatality of destiny.

Those who collect taxes swim in treasure, and there are few Tantaluses among them.[1] Yet it is crushing poverty that drives them into this trade. While they remain poor, they are despised like mud; but as they are sufficiently esteemed when rich, they neglect nothing to gain that esteem.

At present they are in a dreadful situation. A chamber of justice, so-called because its intent is to strip them of all their wealth, has just been established. They can neither transfer nor hide their property, for they are obliged to make an exact declaration of it, under penalty of death; thus, they are forced to pass through the narrow strait defined, so to speak, by their life and their money.[2] To crown their misfortune, there is a minister well known for his wit, who honors them with his jokes and makes fun of all the council's deliberations.[3] As ministers disposed to making people laugh are not found every day, they ought to be grateful to him for trying.

The class of lackeys is more respectable in France than anywhere else; it is a seminary for great lords and fills up the vacancies in the other ranks. Those who compose it take the places of unfortunate nobility, ruined magistrates, and gentlemen killed in the fury of war; and when they are unable to do so themselves, they re-establish all the great families by means of their daughters, who are a kind of manure which fertilizes barren and mountainous soil.

I find, Ibben, that providence is wonderful in the way it distributes riches. If wealth fell only to good people, we might easily have identified it with virtue, and thus its worthlessness

---

1 [Tantalus, in Greek mythology a son of Zeus and a wealthy king guilty of great crimes, was punished in the afterworld by being forced to stand in waters that came to his chin but receded whenever he tried to drink, while above him hung rich fruits which were drawn out of his reach.]

2 [This chamber of justice was established by an edict of March of 1716; it was intended to prosecute abuses in the tax-farming system, but its accomplishments were few and it was abolished a year later.]

3 [Adrien-Maurice, Duc de Noailles, from 1715 to 1718 *Président* of the Council of Finance.]

would not have been clearly appreciated. But when we see what kind of people have the most money, our contempt for the rich will turn before long into a contempt for riches.

Paris, the 26th of the moon of Maharram, 1717

Rica to Rhedi, at Venice

I find the caprices of fashion among the French astonishing. They have forgotten how they were dressed last summer and have even less idea of how they will be dressed this winter; but the truly unbelievable thing is the cost to a husband of maintaining his wife in fashion.

What would be the use of my describing to you their dress and ornaments? A new fashion would come along and destroy all my work and that of their workmen; before you received my letter, everything would be changed.

A woman leaving Paris for six months in the country returns as old-fashioned as if she had disappeared for thirty years. The son does not recognize the portrait of his mother, so alien to him are the clothes in which she is painted; he supposes the picture is of some American, or that the painter has indulged one of his fantasies.

Sometimes coiffures go up gradually, to be lowered all at once by a style revolution. At one time their immense height put the woman's face in her middle. At another, her feet are there, with her pedestal heels holding them high in the air. Who would believe it? Architects have often been obliged to raise, lower, and enlarge their doors according to the exigencies of dress style, which the rules of their art must be bent to serve. Sometimes you see an immense number of beauty patches on a face; the next day they are all gone. Formerly women had figures and teeth; today they are of no importance.

In this changeable nation, whatever the jokers may say, daughters are made differently from their mothers.

As with style in dress, so it is with customs and fashions of living: the French change their manners with the age of the king. The monarch could even make this nation serious if he tried to do so. The prince impresses his characteristics on the court, the court upon the city, and the city upon the provinces. The soul of the sovereign is a mold which forms all the others.

Paris, the 8th of the moon of Saphar, 1717

LETTER C

Rica to the same

The other day I told you of the amazing inconstancy of the French in their fashions. Yet, it is unbelievable how obstinate they are about them. Fashion determines everything; according to its rules they judge everything done in other countries, and what is foreign seems ridiculous to them. I confess I hardly know how to reconcile this passionate attachment to their customs and the inconstancy which changes them daily.

When I say they scorn everything foreign, I am speaking only of trifles, for in important things they are so diffident that they almost degrade themselves. They will readily admit that other people are wiser, provided you concede that they are better dressed. They are willing to subordinate themselves to the laws of a foreign power if only French wigmakers are allowed to legislate on the shape of foreign wigs. Nothing seems more splendid to them than to see the taste of their cooks dominating from north to south, and the dictates of their hairdressers commanding every European toilette. With such splendid advantages, what does it matter to them that good sense is imported, and that they have borrowed from their neighbors everything concerning political and civil government?

Who would think that the oldest and most powerful kingdom in Europe would be governed, for more than ten centuries, by laws not designed for it? If the French had been conquered, it would not be difficult to comprehend; but they are the conquerors.

They have abandoned the old laws made by their first kings in general assemblies of the nation, and strange as it seems, they have substituted Roman laws, which were in part made and in part codified by emperors contemporary with their own lawmakers.

And so that the acquisition would be complete and all wisdom might come from outside, they have adopted all the papal constitutions and have made them a new part of their law, that is, a new form of servitude.

It is true that they have more recently drawn up some city and provincial statutes; but they too are mostly taken from Roman law.

The abundance of these adopted and, so to speak, naturalized laws is so great that it overwhelms both justice and the judges. But these volumes of law are nothing by comparison with the appalling army of glossarists, commentators, and compilers, people as feeble in wisdom and justice as they are strong in numbers.

This is not all. These foreign laws have introduced formalities which, in excess, are the shame of human reason. It would indeed be difficult to decide whether formalism is more pernicious in jurisprudence or in medicine, whether its ravages are greater under the robe of a jurist or under the wide hat of the physician, and whether the one has ruined more people than the other has killed.

Paris, the 17th of the moon of Saphar, 1717

LETTER CI

Usbek to ———

The constant topic of conversation here is the *Constitution*.[1] The other day I went to a house where the first person I saw was a fat, red-faced man who told me in a loud voice: "I have issued my charge; I will not respond to anything you say, but read my charge, and you will see I have resolved all your doubts. I really sweated over it," he continued, wiping his hand across his forehead. "I needed all my doctrinal learning and had to read many Latin authors." "I believe it," said a man next to him, "for it is a fine work, and I defy even that Jesuit, who so often visits you, to make a better one." "Read it then," he said, "and in a quarter-hour you will be better instructed on these matters than if I talked all day to you." In this way he evaded conversation and a display of his incompetence. But when he was pressed hard, he had to leave his entrenchments and began to utter great theological stupidities, sustained by a dervish who listened with great respect. When two other men present denied any one of his precepts, he immediately said, "It is certain, for we have so judged it, and we are infallible judges." "And how is it," I finally said, "that you are infallible judges?" "Can't you see," he replied, "that the Holy Spirit enlightens us?" "That is fortunate," I answered, "for considering the way you have spoken today, I see you are in great need of enlightenment."

Paris, the 18th of the moon of Rebiab I, 1717

---

1 [The papal bull *Unigenitus*. See above, p. 43, footnote 3.]

Usbek to Ibben, at Smyrna

The most powerful states in Europe are those of the emperor and those of the kings of France, Spain, and England. Italy and a large part of Germany are divided into an infinity of little states, whose princes are, properly speaking, martyrs to sovereignty. Our glorious sultans have more wives than some of these princes have subjects. Those of Italy, being less united, are the more pitiful: their states lie as open caravansaries in which they are obliged to lodge firstcomers. They must, therefore, attach themselves to great princes and share with them their fear rather than their friendship.

Most European governments are monarchies, or rather, are called such—for I am not sure there has ever been a true monarchy, and in any case they have not long been able to remain so in purity. It is a violent state, invariably degenerating into either despotism or a republic. Power can never be equally divided between people and prince, and as equilibrium is too difficult to maintain, power must diminish on one side as it is augmented on the other. The advantage, however, is usually with the prince who commands the armies.

Accordingly, the power of the kings of Europe is very great; indeed, as great as they could wish. However, they do not exercise it as extensively as do our sultans, because, first, they do not wish to shock the manners and religion of the people, and second, because such extreme usage is not in their interest.

Nothing brings our princes closer to the condition of their subjects than the immense power they wield over them; nothing makes them more susceptible to the reversals and whims of fortune.

Their custom of putting to death all who displease them even slightly upsets the proper relationship between crimes and punishments; and as that relationship, which is vital to the existence of states and the harmony of empires, is scrupulously maintained by Christian princes, they have a great advantage over our sultans.

A Persian who, by imprudence or misfortune, attracts the displeasure of the prince is sure to die; the slightest fault or the smallest irregularity puts him under that necessity. But should he make an attempt on the sovereign's life or seek to betray fortifications to the enemy, his life is equally forfeit; thus he runs no greater risk in the latter actions than in the former.

So, seeing death as certain in the slightest disgrace and seeing nothing worse, he is naturally led to disturbing the state and conspiring against the sovereign, as this is the only resource left open to him.

It is not like this with the nobility of Europe, from whom disgrace removes only royal favor and good will. They retire from the court and content themselves with the enjoyments of a peaceful life and the privileges of their birth. Since they can be killed only for crimes of high treason, they fear such commitment, as they know how much there is in it for them to lose and how little to gain. Consequently, there are few revolts, and few princes die violently.

If our princes, with their unlimited authority, did not take great precautions for their safety, they would not survive a single day; and if they had not in their pay numberless troops to tyrannize their other subjects, their rule would not last a month.

It was only four or five centuries ago that a French king levied guards, contrary to the custom of the time, to protect himself from the assassins which a petty Asian prince had sent to kill him; until then kings had lived peacefully among their subjects, as fathers amidst their children.[1]

---

1 [Philip II, "Augustus," (1165-1223) built up a considerable force of mercenary guards; one of the reasons credited at the time was the rumor

Far from the kings of France being able, on their own account, to take the lives of their subjects, as do our sultans, they instead always carry with them mercy for all criminals. For a man to be once again worthy of life, it is sufficient only that he be fortunate enough to behold the august countenance of his prince; for these monarchs are like the sun, bringing warmth and life everywhere.

Paris, the 8th of the moon of Rebiab II, 1717

LETTER CIII

Usbek to the same

Following up the subject of my last letter, here is substantially what a rather sensible European told me the other day:

"The worst course Asian princes could have adopted is to secret themselves as they do. They hope to make themselves more respected, but they create respect for royalty and not for the king himself; they cause the minds of their subjects to become attached to a particular throne, not to a particular person.

"That invisible governing power is always the same for the people. Although ten kings, known to them only by name, might successively have their throats cut, the people sense no difference; it is as if they were governed by successive ghosts.

"If that detestable parricide of our great king, Henry IV,[1]

---

that Richard I ("the Lionhearted") of England had hired members of the Persian Ismailian sect called the Assassins to kill him. The "petty Asian prince" is the Assassin leader, called by the Christian Crusaders "The Old Man of the Mountain." The dreaded Assassin sect was destroyed by the Mongols in the thirteenth century.]

[1] [Henry IV was assassinated in 1610 by François Ravaillac.]

had directed his blow against a king of the Indies, he would have become master of the royal seal and of the vast treasure apparently amassed for him and would peacefully have taken up the reins of authority, without a single man thinking to inquire after the king, his relatives, and his children.

"We are astonished that there is almost no change in the government of Eastern princes. Can the cause of this be other than the fact that they inspire fear and are tyrannical?

"Changes can be made only by the prince or the people; but in Asia the princes are careful to change nothing, because their power is as absolute as it can be, and they could change something only to their disadvantage.

"As for the subjects, should one of them conceive some plan, he is unable to put it into effect in the state, for it would be necessary that he suddenly counterbalance a redoubtable and unitary power, and for this both time and means are lacking. However, he has only to go to the source of that power, and then he needs nothing but an arm and an instant.

"The murderer mounts the throne as the monarch descends from it, falling to die at his feet.

"In Europe a malcontent dreams of spying, of going over to the enemy camp, of seizing fortifications, or of exciting foolish complaints among the subjects. In Asia a malcontent goes directly to the prince, surprises, strikes, and overthrows; he destroys even the memory of a prior existence, for in an instant the slave becomes master, and the usurper is legitimatized.

"Unhappy the king who has only one head! All power is united in it, apparently only to show to the first ambitious man the place where that power may be found entire."

Paris, the 17th of the moon of Rebiab II, 1717

LETTER CIV

Usbek to the same

All the nations of Europe are not equally submissive to their princes; the impatient temper of the English, for instance, leaves little time for the king to impose his authority. Submission and obedience are virtues for which they little flatter themselves. On this subject they say the most extraordinary things. According to them gratitude is the only bond between men: a husband and wife, a father and son are united only by the love they have for each other, or by the benefits they mutually receive; and these great motives of gratitude are the origin of all kingdoms and all societies.

But if a prince, instead of making his subjects happy, tries to oppress and destroy them, the obligation of obedience ceases; nothing binds or attaches them to him, and they return to their natural liberty. They maintain that no absolute power can be legitimate, because it could never have had a legitimate origin. "For we cannot," they say, "give to another more power over us than we have ourselves. Now we have not absolute power over ourselves; for example, we cannot take our own lives. Therefore," they conclude, "no one on earth has such power."

The crime of high treason is, according to them, nothing other than the crime committed by the weaker against the stronger; it is simply an act of disobedience, whatever form it may take. Thus the people of England, finding themselves stronger than one of their kings, declared it a crime of high treason for a prince to make war against his subjects.[1] They have, therefore, good reason to say that the precept of their Koran, which orders submission to the powers that be, is not difficult to follow; it is impossible for them not to observe it,

---

[1] [In 1649, opening the trial of Charles I, the House of Commons declared it possible for a king to be guilty of *lèse-majesté* toward the people.]

as they are obliged to submit not to the most virtuous, but to the strongest.

The English tell of one of their kings who, having defeated and imprisoned a prince who disputed the crown with him, began to reproach him for infidelity and treachery. "It was decided only a moment ago," said the unfortunate prince, "which of us was the traitor." [2]

A usurper declares rebellious all those who have not oppressed the country as he did; and, believing no law exists when he sees no judges, he causes the caprices of chance and fortune to be revered like the ordinances of heaven.

Paris, the 20th of the moon of Rebiab II, 1717

LETTER CV

Rhedi to Usbek, at Paris

In one of your letters you have said much of the sciences and arts cultivated in the West. You may regard me as a barbarian, but I am not convinced that the utility drawn from them compensates men for the evil purpose to which they are continually put.

I have heard it said that the invention of bombs alone deprived all the European nations of freedom. Princes, unable any longer to trust the defense of their towns to citizens, who would surrender after the first bomb, have made this a pretext for enrolling large bodies of regular troops, whom they have subsequently used to oppress their subjects.

You know that since the invention of gunpowder there have been no impregnable places; and this is to say, Usbek, that

---

2 [The reference is to the story told of the Lancastrian Prince Edward, son of Henry VI, who was captured and killed by the Yorkist Edward IV at the Battle of Tewkesbury (1471).]

there is no longer an asylum from injustice and violence anywhere on the earth.

I am in constant terror that ultimately someone will succeed in discovering some secret which will furnish an even more efficient way to kill men, by destroying whole peoples and entire nations.

You have read the historians; give them your careful attention. Almost all monarchies have been founded on ignorance of the arts and have been destroyed only when they became excessively cultivated. The ancient empire of Persia can furnish us with an example near at hand.[1]

I have not been in Europe long, but I have heard much from sensible people about the ravages of chemistry. It seems to be a fourth plague, ruining men and destroying them one by one, but continually, while war, pestilence, and famine annihilate great numbers, but only at intervals.

What have we gained by the invention of the mariner's compass and the discovery of so many people who have contributed disease rather than wealth to us?[2] Gold and silver have been established by general consent as the means of purchase and as a gauge of the value of goods, because these metals are rare and otherwise useless. Of what significance is it to us, then, that they have become more abundant, and that we now indicate the value of a commodity by two or three signs instead of one? This is only more inconvenient.

Moreover, that invention has been most harmful to the

---

1 [Perhaps a reference to the story recounted by Herodotus (IX. 122) of Cyrus the Great (king of Persia, 550-29 B.C.), who resisted counsel to move to a gentler land, arguing that "soft countries gave birth to soft men" and that "there was no region which produced very delightful fruits and, at the same time, men of warlike spirit." It was the Persians' departure from this policy in their later imperialism, Herodotus implies, which brought their downfall.]

2 [The discovery of the Americas was largely credited, in the eighteenth century, to the invention and use of the mariner's compass. Exploration of America was seen as productive of two important results for Europe: an increase in the quantity of precious metals, and the introduction of venereal disease.]

countries discovered. Whole nations have been destroyed, and those who escaped death have been reduced to a slavery so harsh that the account of it makes even Mussulmans shudder.

Happy in their ignorance are the children of Mohammed! Amiable simplicity, so cherished by our holy Prophet: you remind me always of the naïveté of earlier times and of the tranquillity which reigned in the hearts of our ancestors.

Venice, the 5th of the moon of Rhamazan, 1717

LETTER CVI

Usbek to Rhedi, at Venice

Either you do not think as you say, or you act better than you think. You have left your country to learn, and you despise all learning. You come for instruction to a country where the fine arts are cultivated, and you regard them as pernicious. May I say it, Rhedi? I am more in accord with you than you are with yourself.

Have you really reflected upon the barbarous and unhappy state into which we would be plunged by loss of the arts? It is not necessary to imagine it, for it may be seen. There are still people on the earth among whom a passably trained ape might live with honor. He would find himself almost on a level with the other inhabitants; they would find neither his attitude unusual nor his character bizarre, and he would pass well among them, distinguished, in fact, by his gracefulness.

You say that the founders of empires have almost all been ignorant of the arts. I do not deny that barbarous nations have spread over the earth like impetuous floods, covering the most civilized nations with their ferocious armies. But note: they have either learned the arts or forced the conquered peoples to practice them, and without that their power would have vanished like the noise of thunder and tempests.

You claim to fear that someone may invent a method of destruction more cruel than those in use. No, if such a fatal invention were discovered, it would soon be prohibited by the law of nations and suppressed by unanimous consent. It is not in the interest of princes to make conquests by such means, for they seek subjects, not territories.

You complain of the invention of gunpowder and bombs; you find it strange that there are no longer impregnable places. This is to say that you find it strange that wars today should be terminated more quickly than they were formerly.

You should have noticed in reading history that since the invention of gunpowder battles are much less bloody than they once were, because there is almost no hand-to-hand fighting.

Furthermore, even though one might find a particular instance where an art is injurious, should one on that account reject it? Do you think, Rhedi, that the religion brought from heaven by our sacred Prophet is harmful because it will someday serve to confound the perfidious Christians?

You believe that the arts weaken the people and consequently are the cause of the collapse of empires. You speak of the ruin of the ancient Persians, which was the effect of their softness; but this example is hardly decisive, since the Greeks, who defeated them so often and subjugated them, cultivated the arts with infinitely greater care.

When one says that the arts make men effeminate, one at least does not speak of the people working at them, for they are never lazy, and of all the vices this is the one which most weakens courage.

Thus it is only a question of those who enjoy the products of the arts. However, in a civilized country those who enjoy the benefits of one art must work at another or see themselves reduced to shameful poverty; so it follows that laziness and effeminacy are incompatible with the arts.

Paris is perhaps the most sensual city in the world, and its pleasures are the most refined; yet perhaps in no other city is life so arduous. For one man to live elegantly, a hundred must labor ceaselessly. A woman gets it into her head that she should

appear at a ball in a certain dress, and from that moment
fifty artisans can sleep no more nor find the leisure to drink
and eat; she commands and is more promptly obeyed than our
monarch would be, because self-interest is the greatest monarch on earth.

This ardor for work, this passion for gain, passes from one
class to another, from artisans to nobles. No one likes to be
poorer than those he sees immediately below him. In Paris
you see a man who has enough to live on until Judgment
Day, working constantly and at the risk of shortening his days
to amass, as he says, the necessities of life.

The same spirit prevails throughout the nation; one sees
only work and industry. Where, then, is that effeminate people
of which you speak so much?

I suppose, Rhedi, that one might allow in a kingdom only
the arts absolutely necessary for cultivation of the earth—
these are numerous, by the way—and one might banish everyone serving only luxury or fancy; yet I maintain that that
country would be one of the most miserable on earth.

Though the inhabitants might have enough courage to dispense with so many things their needs require, yet they would
rapidly decay, and the state would become so feeble that any
petty power could conquer it.

It would be easy to detail this and to show you that the
incomes of individuals would stop almost completely, as consequently would those of the prince. There would be almost
no exchange of services among the citizens, and that circulation of wealth and increase of income which comes from
the interdependence of the arts would stop. Each individual
would live on his own land and take from it only what was exactly needed to avoid starvation. But as this is sometimes not
the twentieth part of the state's revenues, it would follow that
the number of inhabitants would diminish proportionately
until only the twentieth part remained.

Pay close attention to the amount of the revenues of industry. Land produces annually for its owner only a twentieth
part of its value, but with some colored paints worth one

pistole an artist will make a picture which will bring him fifty. One can say the same of the goldsmiths, wool and silk workers, and all kinds of artisans.

From all of this one should conclude, Rhedi, that for a prince to be powerful his subjects must live in luxury, and that he must work to procure for them every kind of superfluity as attentively as he works to provide for the necessities of life.

Paris, the 14th of the moon of Chalval, 1717

<hr>

LETTER CVII

Rica to Ibben, at Smyrna

I have seen the young monarch. His life is most precious to his subjects; it is no less so for the whole of Europe because of the great troubles his death might produce.[1] But kings are like gods, and while they live they must be considered immortal. His face is majestic, but charming; in him good education seems to combine with a happy disposition, and already there is promise of a great prince.

It is said that the character of Western kings can never be known until they have passed the two great tests: selection of their mistress and their confessor. We will soon see both work to capture the mind of this one, and the struggles will be great. For under a young prince these two powers are always rivals, though they become reconciled and allies under an old man. Under a young prince the dervish has a very difficult role to play; the king's strength is his weakness, but the mistress triumphs equally in his weakness and his strength.

<hr>

1 [Other than Louis XV, seven years old in 1717 and in apparently fragile health, there was no French Bourbon in immediate line of succession to the throne; his death without a male heir, therefore, might precipitate a major European war of succession, as the Spanish Bourbons had never renounced their claims to France.]

When I arrived in France, I found the late king entirely governed by women, although at his age I think no monarch on earth had less need of them. One day I heard a woman say: "Something must be done for this young colonel. I know his worth; I will speak to the minister about it." Another said: "It is remarkable that this young abbé should have been forgotten. He ought to be a bishop; he is of good family, and I can speak for his morals." You must not suppose that women speaking in this way were favorites of the prince; they had spoken to him perhaps not twice in their lives, though it is easy to approach European princes. But there is no one employed in any way at the court, in Paris, or in the provinces who does not have a woman through whose hands pass all the favors, and sometimes the injustices, that he can give. These women are all in contact with each other; they form a kind of republic, whose members are continually active in mutual aid and service. It is like a state within a state; and anyone at court, in Paris, or in the provinces who observes the action of the ministers, magistrates, and prelates, unless he knows the women who govern them, is like a man watching a machine work without knowing about the springs that drive it.

Do you think, Ibben, that a women decides to become a minister's mistress so she may sleep with him? What a thought! Her purpose is to be able to submit five or six petitions to him every morning; and the natural goodness of these women shows itself in their eagerness to do favors for a host of unfortunate people, who in turn procure for them incomes of one hundred thousand livres.

In Persia people complain that the kingdom is governed by two or three women. It is even worse in France, where women generally rule and, not content with the wholesale capture of authority, even retail it among themselves.

Paris, the last day of the moon of Chalval, 1717

LETTER CVIII

Usbek to ————

There is a kind of book, unknown to us in Persia, which seems to be very fashionable here—the journals. Idleness is flattered by reading them; one is enchanted to be able to run through thirty volumes in a quarter-hour.[1]

In most books the author has scarcely made his usual compliments before the readers are in despair and are forced, half dead, to enter a subject drowned under a sea of words. This one hopes to immortalize himself by a duodecimo, that one by a quarto, another, with the most expansive expectation, by a folio. The subject of his book must, of course, be enlarged proportionately; this he does mercilessly with no consideration of the poor reader, who kills himself trying to reduce what the author has taken such pains to amplify.

I do not know, ————, what merit there is in making such works; if I wanted to ruin both my health and a publisher, I could do as well myself.

The greatest mistake the journalists make is to speak only of new books, as if truth were forever new. It seems to me that until a man has read all the old books, he has no reason to prefer the new.

Moreover, when they impose upon themselves the rule to speak only of books still hot from the presses, they impose another: to be very tiresome. Whatever their reasons for it, they refrain from criticizing the books from which they extract; indeed, where is the man foolhardy enough to want to make ten or twelve enemies every month?

Most authors are like poets who will suffer a heavy caning without complaint, but who, however careless they are of their

---

[1] [The eighteenth-century French journal was a literary periodical largely devoted to condensations and reviews of current books, with only an occasional original article.]

shoulders, are so jealous of their work that they cannot bear the slightest criticism of it. One must, then, be very careful not to strike them in such a sensitive spot. The journalists know this well and consequently do the very opposite: they begin with praise for the subject treated—the first stupidity—and proceed to lauding the author. Forced praise all of it; for they are dealing with people still living, always insistent on justice for themselves, but ready to annihilate a bold journalist with their pens.

Paris, the 5th of the moon of Zilcade, 1718

LETTER CIX

Rica to ———

The University of Paris is the eldest daughter of the kings of France, and the very eldest indeed: she is more than nine hundred years old, and so she dotes now and then.

I have been told that some time ago she had a great quarrel with certain doctors over the letter *q*, which she wanted pronounced as a *k*.[1] The dispute was so hot that some people were despoiled of their property because of it, and the *parlement* had to settle the difference by granting permission in a solemn proclamation to all subjects of the king of France to pronounce the letter as they liked. It was a great sight to see two of the most respected bodies in Europe occupied in deciding the fate of one letter of the alphabet!

It seems, my dear ———, that the heads of the greatest men grow smaller when they are brought together, and that wher-

---

[1] He means the quarrel with Ramus. [Pierre la Ramée (1515-72), latinized as Ramus, argued in his *Scholae grammaticae* (1559) that the *q* should be followed by the *u* sound. The Sorbonne opposed the pronunciation and stripped a cleric of his benefice for adopting it; the cleric appealed his case to the *parlement* and won.]

ever you have the greatest number of wise men, you have the least wisdom. Large groups always get so attached to minutiae and petty procedures that the essentials are set aside until later. I have heard of a king of Aragon,[2] who assembled the estates of Aragon and Catalonia, the first sessions of which were devoted to deciding what language should be used for the deliberations. The dispute was lively, and the estates would have been split a thousand times, had there not been devised the expedient of having questions put in the Catalan language and the answers in Aragonese.[3]

Paris, the 25th of the moon of Zilhage, 1718

LETTER CX

Rica to ————

The role of a pretty woman is much more serious than one might suppose. Nothing is more important than what happens each morning at her toilette, surrounded by her servants; a general of an army pays no less attention to the placement of his right flank or his reserve than she does to the location of a beauty patch, which can fail, but from which she hopes or predicts success.

What anxiety and care to be constantly conciliating the interests of two rival suitors, to appear neutral to both while she is surrendering to each, and to mediate all the subjects of complaint of which she is the cause!

What a task it is to make one party after another a success and to anticipate all the accidents that might disturb them!

---

[2] It was in 1610.

[3] [According to Carcassonne, Montesquieu drew this incident, which is of dubious historical accuracy and of illusive source, from material he received from Père Desmolets.]

To all this add the greatest difficulty, which is to appear amused when one is not. Bore the ladies as much as you please, and they will forgive you, provided that they are able to make you believe they have had a gay time.

The other day I was at a country supper given by some ladies who, on the way there, kept saying, "At least, we ought to be highly amused."

We found ourselves rather badly matched and consequently quite dull and serious. "I must say we are having a diverting time," said one of the women; "in the whole of Paris there cannot be a party today as gay as ours." As boredom overwhelmed me, another woman shook me and said, "My, aren't we in high spirits?" "Certainly," I replied, yawning, "I am about to be split from laughing." Melancholy finally triumphed, however, and as for me, I was conducted from yawn to yawn into a lethargic sleep that ended all my pleasures.

Paris, the 11th of the moon of Maharram, 1718

Usbek to ———

The reign of the late king was so long that the end of it had caused the beginning to be forgotten. It has now become the fashion, however, to be interested only in the events of his minority, and only memoirs from that period are read.[1]

---

1 [The interest in the period of Louis XIV's minority (1643-61) was much stimulated by the publication in 1717 of the memoirs of the Cardinal de Retz, a major figure in the politics and intrigue of the time. Louis' chief minister during this period was Cardinal Mazarin, who victoriously directed the forces of royal absolutism against those of the nobility and *parlements* in the confused civil war called the *Fronde* (1648-53).]

Here is a speech which one of the generals of the city of Paris delivered in a council of war; I confess I do not understand much of it.

Gentlemen, although our troops have been repulsed with losses, I think it will be easy for us to repair this defeat. I have six couplets of a song all ready to be published, which I am sure will re-establish equilibrium. I have selected several very clear voices which, issuing from the cavities of as many powerful chests, will agitate the people marvelously. These couplets are set to a melody which has always been most effective.

If this is not sufficient, we can circulate a print showing Mazarin hanged.

Fortunately for us, he does not speak good French, and because he so mutilates the language, his fortunes must decline. We have not failed to keep the people well reminded of the ridiculous accents of his pronunciation. Some days ago we pointed out a grammatical fault so gross that it has become a joke in every street.[2]

I hope that within a week the people will make the name of Mazarin a generic word for all beasts of burden.

Since our defeat our songs about his original sin have so much annoyed him that, to keep his partisans from dwindling to half, he has had to dismiss all his pages.[3]

Therefore, rouse yourselves, take courage, and be sure that with our hisses we will soon drive him back over the mountains.

Paris, the 4th of the moon of Chahban, 1718

---

[2] Cardinal Mazarin, an Italian, wishing to say *arrêt d'union* ["decree of alliance"] before the deputies of the *parlement,* actually said *arrêt d'oignon* [*oignon* meaning "onion"]; the people made many a joke about this. [Montesquieu's note in the 1721 and 1722 editions.]

[3] [Despite the strong opposition of many powerful elements in the state, Mazarin controlled the government during Louis XIV's minority. This was at least partly explainable by his well-known intimacy ("his original sin") with the regent, Anne of Austria, to whom he may have been secretly married. Though a cardinal, Mazarin never took orders as a priest.]

Rhedi to Usbek, at Paris

While in Europe I am reading the ancient and modern historians. I compare all epochs, pleased to have them, so to
speak, pass in review before me; and my attention is especially
fixed upon the great changes which have made one age so different from another and the earth so unlike what it once was.

Perhaps you have not noticed something which continually
surprises me. How is it that the earth is so sparsely populated,
compared to what it was formerly? How has nature come to
lose that prodigious fertility of the earliest times? Can it be
that she is already in old age and slipping into decline?

I have been more than a year in Italy where I have seen [1]
only the debris of the old and formerly great Italy. Although
everyone lives in the towns, they are quite deserted and depopulated; they seem to exist only to mark the place where
those powerful and storied cities of history once stood.

Some people maintain that the single city of Rome once
contained more people than today live in a large European
kingdom. There were some Roman citizens who had ten or
even twenty thousand slaves without counting those who
worked in their country houses; and as there were calculated
to be four or five hundred thousand citizens, one's imagination
staggers at the task of reckoning the total number of inhabitants.

In Sicily there once were powerful kingdoms and large
populations, which have since disappeared; the island now has
nothing more remarkable than volcanoes.

Greece is so empty that it contains not the hundredth part
of its old population.

---

1 [Most texts have the verbs in this sentence in the simple past tense.
Considering, however, that Rhedi is still in Italy (Venice) as he writes,
this construction, which appears in the 1761 edition, seems more correct.]

Spain, formerly so crowded, today shows only an uninhabited countryside; and France is nothing compared to the
ancient Gaul described by Caesar.²

The northern countries are much thinned out; no longer is
it necessary, as it once was, for their people to leave in swarms,
in colonies, and entire nations to seek other domiciles.

Poland and European Turkey have almost no people in
them.

We cannot find in America the fiftieth part of the men who
once formed great empires there.

Nor is Asia in any better condition. Asia Minor, which contained so many powerful monarchies and a wonderful number
of large cities, now has only two or three. As for Greater Asia,
the land under Turkish control is not any more densely populated; and as for that under the dominion of our kings, if we
compare it to the flourishing state it once was, we will see that
it has but a tiny part of the numberless inhabitants it had in
the times of Xerxes and Darius.³

And as for the little states surrounding these great empires,
they are really deserts: witness the kingdoms of Irimetta, Circassia, and Guriel.⁴ These princes, with their vast estates, count
scarcely fifty thousand subjects.

Egypt is no less deficient than the other lands.

In short, I travel the entire earth and find only decay, which
I think I see as the result of the ravages of pestilence and
famine.

Africa has always been so little known that one cannot speak
of it as precisely as of the other parts of the world; but to
consider only the Mediterranean coast, which has always been

---

2 [In *Commentarii de bello Gallico,* Julius Caesar's account of his
Gallic campaigns down to 52 B.C.]

3 [Darius the Great, the son of Hyataspes, was for thirty-six years ruler
of the Persian Empire; he died in 486 B.C. and was succeeded by his son
Xerxes, best known for his unsuccessful invasion of Greece (480-79 B.C.).
Xerxes died in 465 B.C.]

4 [Irimetta (Imeretia), Circassia, and Guriel (Guria) were petty principalities in the Caucasus, and are now within the Soviet Union.]

known, it is clear that it has declined radically from what it was under the Carthaginians and Romans. Its princes are to-day so weak that they are the most insignificant powers on earth.

After a calculation as exact as is possible in such matters, I have found that hardly one-tenth as many people are now on the earth as there were in ancient times. What is more astonishing is that this depopulation goes on daily, and if it continues, the earth will be a desert in a thousand years.

This, my dear Usbek, is the greatest catastrophe the world has ever known. But it is hardly perceived, because it has happened gradually and over many centuries; it is the symptom of an internal defect, a secret and hidden poison, a corrupting disease afflicting human nature itself.

Venice, the 10th of the moon of Rhegeb, 1718

LETTER CXIII

Usbek to Rhedi, at Venice

The earth, my dear Rhedi, is not incorruptible. Even the heavens are not: astronomers are eyewitnesses of their changes, which are the perfectly natural effects of the universal motion of matter.

The earth, like the other planets, is subject to the laws of motion; she suffers an internal and perpetual struggle between her elements: the sea and land masses seem to be at eternal war; each instant produces new combinations.

In an abode so subject to change men are in a similarly un-certain state; a hundred thousand causes can act to destroy them and, more easily, to augment or diminish their number.

I will not speak of those particular catastrophes, so common in history, which have destroyed cities and entire kingdoms;

there are general calamities which have often brought mankind within an inch of annihilation.

History is full of these universal plagues which have consecutively desolated the world. It tells of one that was so virulent it destroyed even the roots of plants and was felt throughout the known world, even to the empire of Cathay. One more degree of corruption and it would have destroyed all of mankind, perhaps in a single day.[1]

Not two centuries ago the most shameful of all diseases appeared in Europe, Asia, and Africa; in a very short time it had unbelievable effect, and had it continued its progress with the same fury, the human race would have been finished.[2] Riddled by disease from birth, incapable of maintaining the burdens of societal obligations, all men would have perished miserably.

What would have happened had the poison been a bit stronger, as doubtless it would have become, if a remedy[3] as powerful as any yet discovered had not fortunately been found? Perhaps that disease, which attacks the organs of generation, would have attacked generation itself.

But why speak of destruction which might have come to mankind? Has it not in fact happened? Did not the Deluge reduce the race to a single family?

There are philosophers who distinguish two creations: that of things and that of men. They cannot believe that matter and created things are only six thousand years old, or that God postponed his work for an eternity and used his creative power only yesterday. Was it because he was unable, or because he was unwilling? But if he were not able at one time, he could not be able at another. Thus it must be that he was

---

[1] [Montesquieu refers to the plague, or Black Death, which reached its virulent peak in Europe in 1348.]

[2] [Venereal disease was widely believed to have been native only in the Americas, and imported into Europe by returning explorers. See above, p. 175, footnote 2.]

[3] [Mercury.]

unwilling; but since for God there cannot be succession in time, if it is granted that he willed something once, then he has willed it always and from the beginning.

However, all historians speak of a first father; they show us human nature at birth. Is it not natural to think that Adam was saved from some widespread calamity, as Noah was from the flood, and that such great occurrences have been frequent on the earth since the creation of the universe?

But all destruction is not violent. We observe that several parts of the earth tire of furnishing subsistence to man; how do we know that the entire earth has not within it some general, slow, and imperceptible causes of exhaustion?

I am pleased to give you these broad ideas before responding more particularly to your letter on the diminishing population of the past seventeen or eighteen centuries. I will show you in a subsequent letter that, independent of these physical causes, there are also moral ones which have produced this effect.

Paris, the 8th of the moon of Chahban, 1718

LETTER CXIV

Usbek to the same

You seek the reason why the earth is less populous than it once was; if you study the matter carefully, you will see that the chief cause is to be found in a change of customs.

Things have much altered since the Christian and Mohammedan religions divided the Roman world; for these two religions are not nearly as favorable to the propagation of the species as was that of those masters of the world.

In Roman morality polygamy was forbidden, which gave it a large advantage over the Mohammedan religion; and divorce was permitted, which gave it a no less considerable advantage over the Christian.

I find nothing more contradictory than the plurality of wives permitted by the sacred Koran and the order, given in the same book, to satisfy them all. "Visit your wives," the Prophet said, "because you are as necessary to them as their clothing, and they are as necessary to you as yours." [1] Now this is a precept which makes the life of a true Mussulman most arduous. He who has the four wives established by law, and only as many concubines or slaves—must he not be overburdened by so much clothing?

"Your wives are your fields," the Prophet said further; "approach them then, labor for the good of your souls, and you will gain your reward." [2]

I see the good Mussulman as an athlete, destined to compete without letup, but who, overburdened and weakened by his first efforts, languishes even on the field of victory and finds himself, so to speak, buried under his own triumphs.

Nature always works slowly and, as it were, economically. Her operations are never violent, and even in creation she requires temperance; she never moves but by rule and measure, and if she is made to hurry, she soon tires, employs all her remaining strength for self-preservation, and loses all her productive ability and generative power.

We are put into this state of weakness by this great number of women, who are better able to exhaust than to satisfy us. Among us it is common to see a man, in a huge seraglio, with but a very small number of children; moreover, these children usually are feeble and in poor health and share their father's languor.

---

[1] ["You are allowed on the night of the fast to approach your wives; they are your garment and you are their garment" (Koran, sura 2, 183).]

[2] ["Your wives are your field: go in, therefore, to your field as you will; but do first some act for your soul's good: and fear you God, and know that you must meet him; and bear these good tidings to the faithful" (Koran, sura 2, 223).]

And that is not all. These women, forced to be continent, need people to guard them and these can only be eunuchs, for religion, jealousy, and reason itself forbid all others to approach them. And these guardians must be numerous, both to maintain peace within the seraglio, amid the ceaseless wars of the women, and to prevent attempts from without. Thus a man with ten wives or concubines needs at least as many eunuchs to guard them. But what a loss to society is this great number of men who are dead from birth! What a depopulation must follow!

The female slaves, who with the eunuchs serve the many women in the seraglio, almost always grow old there in distressed virginity; for while they stay they cannot marry, and once accustomed to them, their mistresses almost never release them.

So you see how one man employs for his pleasure many persons of both sexes, making them as good as dead to the state and useless for the propagation of the race.

Constantinople and Ispahan are the capitals of the two greatest empires in the world. To them everything ought to turn; people, attracted for a thousand reasons, ought to flock to them from every direction. Yet they are decaying internally and would long since have perished, had not their sovereigns in almost every century caused entire new nations to enter and repopulate them. I will continue this subject in another letter.

Paris, the 13th of the moon of Chahban, 1718

LETTER CXV

Usbek to the same

The Romans did not have fewer slaves than we; indeed, they had more, but they made better use of them.

Far from preventing the multiplication of their slaves by

forcible means, they instead favored it in every way possible;
they united them in marriages of a sort, and in this way they
filled their houses with servants of both sexes and every age,
and the state with innumerable people.

These children, who were eventually to become the wealth
of their master, were born around him in countless numbers;
for as he alone was charged with their nurture and education,
the fathers, freed of that burden, followed their natural inclination and multiplied without fear of an overly large family.

I have told you that, among us, all the slaves are occupied
in guarding our wives and in nothing else; that with regard
to the state they are in perpetual lethargy, so that the cultivation of the arts and agriculture is restricted to a few free men
and heads of families, and even they exert themselves as little
as possible.

It was not like this among the Romans. The republic used
its slave population to vast advantage. Each one of them had
his own savings, possessed under terms imposed by the master,
but which he put to work in whatever manner he chose. One
became a banker, another turned to shipping; one sold goods
at retail, another applied himself in some mechanical art or
even went into farming. Not one of them failed to try with all
his power to increase his hoard; this served at the same time
to make his present slavery more comfortable and to give him
hope of future liberty. All of this created a hard-working people and encouraged industry and the arts.

Having grown wealthy by their thrift and labor, these slaves
bought their freedom and became citizens; thus the republic
was continually built up, receiving unto itself new families as
the old ones died out.

Perhaps in a future letter I will have occasion to prove to
you that commerce flourishes in proportion to an increase of
men in a state; I will prove as easily that the number of men
augments according to the increase in commerce, for these two
things necessarily aid and favor each other.

If this is so, how large must this great number of constantly
industrious slaves have grown? Industry and abundance caused

them to be born; they in turn served to create industry and abundance.

Paris, the 16th of the moon of Chahban, 1718

Usbek to the same

So far we have spoken only of Mohammedan countries, in seeking the reason why they are less populous than those which were under Roman domination. Let us now inquire into what has produced the same effect among the Christians.

Divorce was permitted in the pagan religion and forbidden to the Christians. This change, which at first appears to be of such slight consequence, gradually produced effects so terrible that one can hardly believe them.

This not only removed all sweetness from marriage but put its very purpose under attack. The desire to tighten the knots loosened them instead; and rather than uniting hearts, as was pretended, they were separated forever instead.

Into a free act in which the heart ought to have so large a part, there were introduced constraint, necessity, and the fatality of destiny itself. Counted for nothing were the dislikes, the whims, the incompatibilities of temper; the heart, and that is to say the most variable and inconstant thing in nature, was fixed; and people, however weary of one another and almost always poorly matched, were joined together without hope or possibility of change, just as tyrants used to join living men to dead bodies.

Nothing contributed more to mutual attachment than easy divorce. Husband and wife were encouraged to support domestic troubles patiently, knowing that it was in their power to end them; they often retained this power throughout their lives but were restrained from using it by the single thought that they were free to do so.

It is not the same with the Christians, whose present difficulties make them despair of the future. They see only that the disagreements of marriage are lasting or, in a manner of speaking, eternal. Hence arise disgust, discord, scorn, and a loss to posterity. After scarcely three years of marriage the partners neglect to do what is essential to it. Together they pass thirty cold years, privately separated in a way as complete, and perhaps more harmful, than if it were made public; each lives alone, all to the prejudice of future generations. A man, disgusted with one everlasting woman, soon turns to prostitutes—a shameful commerce and harmful to society, which does not fufill the aim of marriage and at best only counterfeits its pleasures.

Of two persons so joined, if one is not properly suited by nature for propagation of the species, whether by temperament or age, that one similarly enslaves the other and renders both equally useless.

Thus it is not suprising to see so many Christian marriages produce such a small number of citizens. Divorce is abolished; bad marriages cannot be rectified; women no longer successively pass, as they did among the Romans, into the hands of several husbands, who consecutively made the best possible use of them.

I hazard to say that in a republic like Sparta, where the citizens were constantly restrained by unusual and subtle laws and where the state was the only family, if it had been decreed that husbands could change wives every year, an innumerable people would have been born.

It is quite difficult to understand clearly what reason led the Christians to abolish divorce. Marriage, in every nation on earth, is a contract sensitive to all conventions, and from it should be abolished only what could enfeeble its intended purpose. But the Christians do not regard it from this point of view, and they go to considerable trouble to explain their attitude. Marriage to them does not consist in sensual pleasure; on the contrary, as I have already told you, it seems they wish to banish that element from it as much as possible. Rather, it is to them an image, a symbol, and something mysteriously more, which I do not understand.

Paris, the 19th of the moon of Chahban, 1718

LETTER CXVII

Usbek to the same

The prohibition of divorce is not the only cause of the depopulation of Christian countries; of no less importance is the great number of eunuchs among them.

I am referring to those priests and dervishes of both sexes who are sworn to perpetual chastity. Among Christians this is the supreme virtue, which I find hard to comprehend, since I do not see how something which produces nothing can be a virtue.

I find their theologians manifestly in contradiction when they say that marriage is sacred and that its opposite, celibacy, is even more so. They fail to consider that precepts and fundamental doctrines should conclude that what is useful is always the best.

The number of these people professing celibacy is enormous. Formerly, fathers condemned their children to it while still in the cradle; now they commit themselves at the age of fourteen, which amounts to the same thing.

This vocation of chastity has annihilated more men than plagues and the bloodiest wars. Each religious house is an eternal family, to which no one is ever born, and which depends upon others for its maintenance. These houses are always open, like so many pits in which to bury future generations.

Such a policy is much opposed to that of the Romans, who established legal penalties against those who refused to marry and wished to enjoy a liberty so contrary to the public good.[1]

I refer here only to Catholic countries. In the Protestant religion everyone has the right to have children; it tolerates neither priests nor dervishes; and if, in the establishment of that religion, which restored everything to the early order, its founders had not been constantly accused of incontinence, there can be no doubt that, having made the institution of marriage universal, they would further have eased the yoke and ended by entirely destroying the barrier which, on this point, separates the Nazarene and Mohammed.

But however that may be, it is certain that religion gives to the Protestants an infinite advantage over the Catholics.

I dare to say that, given the present condition of Europe, the Catholic religion cannot possibly last more than five hundred years.

Prior to the decline of Spanish power, the Catholics were much stronger than the Protestants. The latter, however, have gradually achieved an equality, and the Protestants will become richer and more powerful, the Catholics weaker.

Protestant countries ought to be, and in fact are, more populous than the Catholic. From this it follows, in the first place, that their income from taxation is larger, since this increases in proportion to the number who pay; secondly, that their lands are better cultivated; finally, that their commerce is more prosperous, because there are more people who have a fortune to make, and because there are more needs and, consequently, more resources employed to satisfy them. When there are only enough people to cultivate the earth, commerce necessarily perishes, just as the earth is poorly cultivated when there are only enough people to sustain commerce; this is to

---

[1] [In *L'Esprit des lois* (Bk. XXIII, chap. 21), Montesquieu discusses at some length Augustus' decree (*Julia et Papia Poppaea*), which rewarded married men who had numerous children, and established penalties, chiefly regarding inheritance, on the unmarried and childless.]

say that both fall together, because devotion to one can only be at the expense of the other.

As for the Catholic countries, not only is agriculture abandoned, but industry itself is pernicious, consisting only of learning five or six words of a dead language. As soon as a man has made that provision for himself, he need no longer fret about his fortune; in the cloister he finds a tranquil life, which in the outside world would have cost him much sweat and toil.

This is not all. The dervishes hold in their hands most of the state's wealth; and they are an avaricious lot, always taking and never giving, constantly hoarding their revenue so as to acquire capital. All this wealth becomes paralyzed, so to speak, thus putting an end to the flow of currency, to business, the arts, and industry.

There is no Protestant prince who does not levy heavier taxes on his people than the pope does on his; yet the latter are poor while the others live in opulence. Commerce vitalizes everything in the one society; monasticism spreads death in the other.

Paris, the 26th of the moon of Chahban, 1718

LETTER CXVIII

Usbek to the same

We have nothing more to say of Asia and Europe; let us pass on to Africa. One can speak only of its coasts, as the interior is unknown.

The Barbary coasts, where Mohammedanism is established, are not as populous as they were in Roman times, for the reasons I have already given. As for the Guinea coasts, they must be dreadfully stripped, since for two hundred years the petty kings or village chiefs have sold their subjects to the princes of Europe, who in turn had them taken to their American colonies.

What is strange is that America, which annually received so many new inhabitants, is itself deserted, gaining not at all from Africa's continual losses. These slaves, transported to another climate, perished there by the thousands. In addition, the work in the mines, in which both the natives of the country and foreigners are employed, the poisonous vapors issuing from them, and the quicksilver, which must constantly be used, utterly destroy them.

Nothing is more extravagant than to cause countless men to perish in extracting gold and silver from the depths of the earth, metals in themselves absolutely useless, and which constitute wealth only because we have chosen them as symbols for it.

Paris, the last of the moon of Chahban, 1718

LETTER CXIX

Usbek to the same

The fertility of a people sometimes depends upon the most trifling circumstances in the world, so that often only a new direction to their imagination is required for their numbers to increase considerably.

The Jews, who are constantly exterminated but forever rising again, have repaired their continual losses and destructions by the single hope, held by every family, that from one of them will be born a powerful king who will become master of the earth.

The ancient kings of Persia had so many thousands of subjects only because of that dogma in the religion of the Magi which held that the human acts most agreeable to God were the creation of a child, the tilling of a field, and the planting of a tree.

If China contains such a huge population, it derives only from a certain manner of thinking; for, since children regard their fathers as gods, they respect them as such in this life and honor them after death by sacrifices, which they believe will enable the soul, absorbed into the *t'ien*,[1] to take up a new life; each man, therefore, is disposed to augment a family which is so submissive in this life and so necessary in the next.

On the other hand, Mohammedan countries become more deserted daily, because of an opinion which, holy though it is, can only have very bad effects when it becomes rooted in the mind. We consider ourselves as travelers, who ought only to think of another land; hard and useful work, concern about an assured fortune for our children, all projects which carry beyond a short and fleeting life, seem somehow absurd to us. Tranquil in the present, free from worry about the future, we cannot be bothered to repair the public buildings, to reclaim wasteland, or to cultivate those which are ready for our care; we live in a kind of general insensitivity, and leave everything to providence.

It is a spirit of vanity which established in Europe the unjust law of primogeniture, so unfavorable to propagation in that it turns the father's attention to but one of his children and away from all the others, in that it forces him to make a solid fortune for one by forbidding the establishment of several, and, finally, in that it destroys equality, which is the source of wealth, among the citizens.

Paris, the 4th of the moon of Rhamazan, 1718

---

1 [*T'ien* was the name given by the Chinese to both the afterlife and the supreme deity; as the Christian missionaries eventually discovered, it did not exactly signify the Christian concepts either of heaven or of God.]

LETTER CXX

Usbek to the same

Lands inhabited by savages are ordinarily sparsely populated, because of the alienation of almost all of them from work and cultivation of the soil. This unfortunate aversion is so strong that when they make a curse against an enemy, they ask only that he be reduced to labor in the fields, believing that only hunting and fishing are occupations worthy of themselves.

But since there are often years when hunting and fishing produce little, they are ravaged by frequent famines, without considering that no land is so abundant in game and fish that it can support a large people, because animals always flee from thickly settled places.

Furthermore, the savage villages, numbering two or three thousand inhabitants, separated from one another, and with interests as diverse as two empires, cannot sustain themselves, because they lack the resources of large states, in which all parts are in accord and render mutual assistance.

Among savages there is another custom, no less harmful than the first: this is the cruel habit the women have of aborting themselves, so that their pregnancy will not make them disagreeable to their husbands.[1]

Here there are laws against this crime, which are so dreadful that they approach madness. Every unmarried girl who does not declare her pregnancy to a magistrate is punished by death if her offspring dies; neither modesty, shame, nor even accidents excuse her.[2]

Paris, the 9th of the moon of Rhamazan, 1718

---

[1] [Carcassonne identifies Montesquieu's probable source as Flacourt's *Histoire de la grande île Madagascar* (Paris, 1658; Vol. I, pp. 91-93), where, however, the custom is attributed only to unmarried women.]

[2] [A law passed in the reign (1547-59) of Henry II provided for such a penalty. Montesquieu mentions it in *L'Esprit des lois* (Bk. XXVI, chap. 3) as an example of a civil law contrary to the natural law of self-defense.]

LETTER CXXI

Usbek to the same

The usual effect of colonization is to weaken the home country without populating the colony.

Men ought to stay where they are. Various diseases come from changes of bad and good air; others appear simply from the fact of change itself.

The air, like plants, is loaded with particles of the soil of each country, and it acts upon us in such a way that our temperament is fixed by it. When we are transported to another country, we become ill; for as our fluids are accustomed to a certain consistency, our solids to a certain order, and both to a certain degree of motion, they cannot tolerate other new arrangements, and they resist.

When a country is deserted, it may be assumed that there is some natural fault in its soil or climate; consequently, when men are moved from fortunate regions and sent to such a country, the outcome is exactly contrary to what is intended.

The Romans knew this by experience: they relegated all criminals to Sardinia and also sent the Jews there. For this loss they found it very easy to console themselves, since they held these unfortunates in great contempt.

The great Shah Abbas, wishing to deprive the Turks of the means of maintaining large armies on their frontiers, transported almost all of the Armenians from their country and sent more than twenty thousand families into the province of Guilan,[1] where almost all perished within a very short time.

None of the transportations of people to Constantinople has ever succeeded.[2]

---

1 [Guilan (Gilan) is a Persian province bordering on the Caspian Sea and west of Mazanderan.]

2 [Constantinople was seriously depopulated by the Turkish conquest in 1453 and by an earthquake in 1509. The Ottoman rulers, determined to make the city great again, undertook a vigorous policy of resettlement

The enormous numbers of Negroes, of whom we have spoken, have not begun to fill America.

Since the destruction of the Jews under Hadrian, Palestine has been uninhabited.[3]

It must thus be admitted that great destructions are practically irreparable, because a people, once brought to a certain low point, remains there; if, by chance, it is to recover, centuries are necessary.

But if in this state of decay there occurs even the slightest of the circumstances I have mentioned, a people will not only not rejuvenate itself but will decline daily and approach annihilation.

The expulsion of the Moors from Spain is still felt as acutely as on the first day it happened; the void, far from being filled in, grows greater every day.

Since the devastation of America the Spaniards, who have taken the place of the original inhabitants, have not been able to repopulate it; on the contrary, by a fatality which I would rather call divine justice, the destroyers constantly destroy and consume each other.

Princes, therefore, ought not to dream of populating great countries by colonization. I do not say that they will not sometimes succeed: there are some climates so favorable that the race multiplies constantly, as witness those islands[4] settled by the sick cast off from passing vessels, who there immediately recovered their health.[5]

---

with peoples from various parts of Anatolia, Thrace, and the neighboring islands. The policy was in fact much more successful than Montesquieu indicates.]

[3] [Hadrian, Roman emperor from A.D. 117 to 138, provoked the last survivors of long-persecuted Palestinian Jewry to a bitterly fought but hopeless revolt from 132 to 135; after the Roman victory, Jerusalem was prohibited to the Jews. The scattering of the Palestinian Jews (the Diaspora), though it did not begin with this event, was much accelerated by it.]

[4] Perhaps the author means the Isle of Bourbon.

[5] [Flacourt, in his *Histoire de la grande ile Madagascar* (Vol. II, p. 434). mentions a French ship which put in at the Isle of Bourbon (now Ré-

However, even when colonies succeed, they divide rather than increase power, unless they are very tiny, such as those places occupied for commercial reasons.

The Carthaginians, like the Spaniards, discovered America, or at least some large islands with which they carried on a vast commerce; but when it was noticed that the number of inhabitants was declining, that wise republic prohibited further commerce and navigation to its subjects.

I venture to say that if, instead of sending Spaniards to the Indies, the Indians and half-breeds had been brought to Spain, if that monarchy had reunited all its dispersed peoples, and if only half of its great colonies had survived, Spain would have become the most formidable power in Europe.

Empires may be compared to a tree in which the overly extended branches deprive the trunk of all its sap and are useful only to make shade.

Nothing is better suited to cure the madness of princes for distant conquest than the example of the Portuguese and Spanish.

These two nations conquered immense kingdoms with unbelievable rapidity; then, more astonished by their victories than were the conquered peoples by their defeat, they considered means to conserve their gains. Each chose a different way.

The Spanish, despairing of keeping these vanquished nations faithful to themselves, decided to exterminate them and to send out loyal people from Spain to take their place. Never was a horrible plan more punctually executed. A people, as numerous as the entire population of Europe, was seen to disappear from the earth at the approach of these barbarians who, in discovering the Indies, seemed only to have thought of disclosing to mankind the final degree of cruelty.

By such barbarism they retained that land under their dominion. From this you may judge how disastrous conquests

---

union) in the Indian Ocean for water and repairs; the sick crewmen were left on the island and quickly recovered their health.]

are, since they have such effects; for, in fact, this frightful remedy was the only one possible. How could they have held so many million men in obedience? How could they have sustained a civil war at such a distance? What would have become of them, had they given these people time to recover from their amazement at the arrival of these new gods, and from the fear of their guns?

As for the Portuguese, they chose an entirely opposite method. They employed no cruelties, and they were also soon driven from every land they had discovered. The Dutch encouraged the people to rebel and profited from it.

What prince would envy the lot of these conquerors? Who would want conquests under these conditions? One was soon driven away, the other made deserts not only of the conquered lands but of the home country.

It is the fate of heroes to ruin themselves either by conquering lands they soon lose or by subduing nations they are themselves obliged to destroy. They are like that madman who was consumed with a desire to buy statues to throw into the sea and glass to break.

Paris, the 18th of the moon of Rhamazan, 1718

LETTER CXXII

Usbek to the same

Benign government contributes marvelously to the propagation of the species. All the republics are constant proof of this, and especially Switzerland and Holland, which are the two worst countries in Europe with respect to terrain and yet are the most heavily populated.

Nothing attracts foreigners more than liberty and the wealth which always follows from it. The one is sought for itself, and our needs direct us to countries where we may find the other.

Mankind increases in a land where abundance provides for the children without any reduction in the parents' living.

The very equality of the citizens, which normally results in an equality of wealth, brings abundance and life into all parts of the body politic and spreads them everywhere.

It is not the same in countries under an arbitrary power, where the prince, the courtiers, and a few other individuals possess all the wealth, while all the rest groan under a crushing poverty.

If a man is not well off and feels that his children would be poorer than he, he either will not marry, or, if he does, he will fear having too many children, who might complete the ruin of his fortune and sink even lower than their father's level.

I admit that the rustic or peasant, once married, will produce children regardless of his wealth or poverty. He is unaffected by that consideration, for he always has a safe inheritance to leave his children—his plow—and nothing prevents him from blindly following his natural instincts.

But of what use to a state are these crowds of children, languishing in misery? They die almost at the rate they are born. They never prosper; feeble and debilitated, they perish individually from a thousand causes and are carried off in the mass by those frequent and common diseases which misery and malnutrition invariably induce; those who escape attain adulthood without any of its vigor and waste away for the rest of their lives.

Men are like plants and never flourish unless well cultivated. Among poverty-stricken people the race falters and sometimes even degenerates.

France can provide a good example of all this. In the recent wars the fear that all young men of good family had of being drafted into the militia led them all to marry at too young an age, and in the clutch of poverty. From so many marriages many children were born who are not now to be found in France, as poverty, famine, and disease have carried them off.

If such remarks can be made in a climate as favorable and in a kingdom as well governed as France, what is to be said of the other states?

Paris, the 23rd of the moon of Rhamazan, 1718

LETTER CXXIII

Usbek to the mollah Mohammed Ali, guardian of the three tombs, at Cum

Of what use to us are the fasts of the imans and the hair shirts of mollahs? The hand of God has twice fallen heavy upon the children of the law. The sun hides itself and seems to shine only upon their defeats. Their armies gather to be scattered like dust.

The Osmanli empire is shaken by the two greatest defeats it has ever received. A Christian mufti supports it only with difficulty; the grand vizier of Germany is the scourge of God, sent to punish the followers of Omar. He carries everywhere the wrath of a heaven aroused against their rebellion and treachery.[1]

---

1 [Prince Eugene of Savoy, fighting for Austria and the Empire, captured Timisoara in 1716 and Belgrade in 1717, and was to conclude the Treaty of Passarowitz, disastrous for the Turks (the "followers of Omar"; see above, p. 14, footnote 2) in 1718. The "Christian mufti" supporting the Turks is Cardinal Giulio Alberoni (1664-1752), after 1715 the prime minister of Spain. Alberoni, the favorite of Queen Elizabeth Farnese of Spain, was charged with the execution of an ambitious policy to win the Italian principalities of Parma and Piacenza for herself. As Austria controlled Italy after the Treaty of Utrecht (1713), and as Alberoni's policies could succeed only if the forces of Austria and the Empire were dissipated on other fronts (e. g., the Turkish), this logically made Spain an ally of the Turks. The general Spanish attempts to undo the Treaty of Utrecht kept the Mediterranean in diplomatic and military turmoil until England, France, Austria, and Holland allied to force upon Spain a compromise

Holy spirit of the imans, thou weepest day and night over the children of the Prophet whom the detestable Omar has misled; thy bowels are moved at the sight of their calamities; thou desirest their conversion, not their destruction; thou wouldst see them reunited under Hali's standard by the tears of the saints, not dispersed over mountains and deserts by their terror of the infidels.

Paris, the 1st of the moon of Chalval, 1718

LETTER CXXIV

Usbek to Rhedi, at Venice

What can be the motive behind these enormous liberalities that princes shower upon their courtiers? Is it to gain their attachment? But they already practically own them; and besides, while they may acquire some subjects by buying them, by doing so they lose a multitude of others by impoverishing them.

When I consider the condition of princes, constantly surrounded by greedy and insatiable men, I can only pity them; and I pity them the more when they lack the strength to resist demands for things which they, who desire nothing, find tiresome.

Every time I hear their liberalities, favors, and pensions discussed, a thousand thoughts occur to me; a swarm of ideas crowds my mind; I seem to hear this ordinance proclaimed:

The indefatigable courage of some of our subjects in demanding pensions having continually taxed our royal munificence, we have finally ceded to the multitude of requests which have been made of us, and which hitherto have been the chief concern of the throne.

settlement (1720) which was not to the Queen's liking, and Alberoni, disgraced, returned to his native Italy.]

Some have represented to us that since our accession to the crown they have never missed one of our levées, that in our passage we have always seen them as motionless as posts, that they contemplate our serenity only by raising themselves high on the shoulders of the very tallest. We have even received several requests on behalf of persons of the fair sex, begging us to note that they are notoriously difficult to maintain. Others, antiquated and with quavering heads, have prayed us to recall that they ornamented the courts of the kings preceding us, and that if the generals of the armies made the state formidable by their military feats, they made it no less celebrated by their intrigues. Therefore, desiring to treat all supplicants with generosity, and to grant all their requests, we have decreed as follows:

That every laborer having five children shall daily reduce by a fifth the bread which he gives them. Fathers are enjoined to make this reduction equitably, insofar as this is possible.

It is expressly forbidden to all who cultivate their estates, or who rent them as farms, to make any improvements upon them of whatever kind.

All persons employed in the mean and mechanical trades, who have never attended a levée of Our Majesty, are ordered henceforth to purchase clothes, whether for themselves, their wives, or their children, only once in four years. Also strictly forbidden are the little celebrations which they have been accustomed to hold within their families on the principal holidays of the year.

And as we are advised that most of the citizens of our good towns are solely occupied in providing establishments for their daughters, whose only claim to the state's attention is a melancholy and tedious modesty, we decree that fathers wait to marry them off until, having attained the age stipulated by ordinance, they [the daughters] can insist upon it. We forbid our magistrates to provide for the education of their children.

Paris, the 1st of the moon of Chalval, 1718

LETTER CXXV

Rica to ———

In any religion one is embarrassed to give some idea of the pleasures awaiting those who have lived well. It is easy to terrify the wicked with long accounts of the torments menacing them, but one hardly knows what to promise the virtuous. The essence of pleasure, it seems, is its short duration, and the imagination is hard put to represent it otherwise.

I have seen descriptions of paradise that would have made any sensible person reject it. Some would have the joyous shades play incessantly upon the flute; others would condemn them to the torture of an eternal promenade; others, who would have them dream on high of their mistresses down below, have assumed that even in a hundred million years they will not lose their taste for such uneasy affairs.

In this connection I recall a story I once heard from a man who had visited the lands of the Mogul; it shows that Indian priests are as sterile as any others in their ideas of the pleasures of paradise.

A woman who had just lost her husband went with due ceremony to the governor of the city to demand permission to burn herself; but since, in lands ruled by Mohammedans, that cruel custom has been abolished wherever possible, he categorically refused.

When she saw that her prayers were useless, she flew into a great rage. "See," she said, "how we are oppressed! A poor woman is not even allowed to burn herself if she likes! Have you ever seen anything like it? My mother, my aunt, and my sister were all properly burned. But when I come to request permission from this wretched governor, he becomes angry and shouts like a madman."

A young bonze [1] happened to be there. "Infidel," the gover-

---

[1] [A bonze is a Buddhist priest; Montesquieu evidently confuses the distinction between bonze (Buddhist) and Brahman (Hindu).]

nor said to him, "is it you who have so deranged this woman's mind?" "No," he said, "I have never spoken to her. But if she believes as I do, she will consummate her sacrifice, for the act will be agreeable to the god Brahma, and she will also be well rewarded by meeting her husband again in the other world and beginning a second marriage with him." "What are you saying?" asked the surprised woman. "I will find my husband again? Ah! Then I will not sacrifice myself. He was jealous, irritable, and also so old that, unless the god Brahma has somehow improved him, he surely has no need of me. Burn myself for him! . . . Not even the end of my finger, even to pull him from the bottom of hell. Those two old bonzes who misled me, knowing of my life with him, took care not to tell me that; if Brahma has only this present to make me, I renounce such beatitude. Your Honor, I will turn Mohammedan. And as for you," she said, looking at the bonze, "you may, if you like, go and tell my husband that I am doing very well."

Paris, the 2nd of the moon of Chalval, 1718

LETTER CXXVI

Rica to Usbek, at ————

I expect you here tomorrow; nonetheless I am sending you your letters from Ispahan. Mine carry the news that the ambassador of the Great Mogul has been ordered to leave the kingdom. They add that the prince, the king's uncle who is entrusted with his education, has been arrested, taken to a castle, and there strictly guarded and stripped of all honors.[1] I am moved by the lot of this prince, and I pity him.

---

1 [The allusions here are to the so-called Cellamare conspiracy of 1718. Antoine de Cellamare ("the ambassador of the Great Mogul") was Spanish ambassador to France; in concert with the Duc and Duchesse du Maine, he undertook negotiations with Spain which would, the conspirators

I confess, Usbek, that I have never seen anyone's tears without being touched. The humanity within me feels for the unfortunates, as if their misfortune alone made them men; even the great, whom I regard with a hard heart while they are exalted, I love as soon as they fall.

Indeed, what need have the great of useless affection while they are prosperous? It implies too much equality; they much prefer respect, which demands no reciprocation. But once fallen from their lofty place, it can be recalled to them only by our laments.

I find something truly innocent and even great in the words of a prince about to fall into the hands of his enemies, who said to the weeping courtiers who stood around him, "By your tears, I see I am still your king." [2]

Paris, the 3rd of the moon of Chalval, 1718

LETTER CXXVII

Rica to Ibben, at Smyrna

You have heard much talk of the famous king of Sweden. He was besieging a place in a kingdom called Norway, and while he was visiting the trenches with his engineer, he received a shot in the head and died from it. His prime minister was immediately arrested, and the assembled estates have condemned him to lose his head.[1]

---

hoped, weaken the position of Orléans in the regency and strengthen the power and claims of the Spanish Bourbons in France. Discovered, Cellamare was ordered to leave France, and du Maine was arrested and imprisoned.]

[2] [Perhaps a reference to the story told by Darius III, king of Persia, after his disastrous defeat by Alexander at Arbella (330 B.C.).]

[1] [Charles XII of Sweden was killed at Frederikshald on November 30, 1718. His first minister, Baron von Goertz, was tried and executed (1719)

He was accused of a great crime: that of slandering the nation and of causing the king to lose confidence in it—a crime which, in my opinion, merits a thousand deaths.

For if it is an evil act to blacken the character of the meanest subject in the prince's mind, what must it be to blacken the entire nation and to deprive it of the goodwill of him whom providence has ordained to effect its happiness?

I would have men speak to kings as the angels spoke to our holy Prophet.

You know that in those sacred banquets, when the king of kings descends from the most sublime throne on earth to communicate with his slaves, I make it a severe rule to control a loose tongue; and no one has ever heard me utter a single word which could be injurious even to the least significant of his subjects. And when I was obliged to abandon discretion, I never ceased to be a gentleman; in that proof of our fidelity, I risked my life but never my virtue.

I do not know why, but there has never been a prince so bad that his minister was not worse; whatever evil act he does, it has almost always been suggested to him. Hence the ambition of the prince is never so dangerous as his counselor's servility. But can you understand how a man, who came into the ministry only yesterday and may be out of it tomorrow, can become in a moment the enemy of himself, his family, his country, and of all those people yet to be born of those he seeks now to oppress?

A prince has passions; the minister rouses them, and in this manner he directs his ministry. He has no other end in mind and wishes to hear of no other. Courtiers seduce by praise; ministers flatter more dangerously by their counsels, by the designs they inspire, and by the maxims they propose.

Paris, the 25th of the moon of Saphar, 1719

---

for, among other alleged crimes, weakening the confidence of the king in his people.]

Rica to Usbek, at ———

As I was crossing the Pont-Neuf [1] with one of my friends the other day, he recognized an acquaintance who was, he told me, a geometer. And everything about him suggested it; he was in profound meditation, and my friend had to tug at his sleeve and shake him for some time before he descended to earth, so occupied was he with a curve which had tormented him for perhaps more than a week. They much complimented each other and exchanged some literary news. The conversation continued up to the door of a café, which I entered with them.

I noticed that our geometer was cordially received there by everyone, and that the café waiters were more attentive to him than to the two musketeers seated in a corner. As for him, he seemed to find the place agreeable, for he relaxed his face a bit and began to smile as if there was nothing of the geometer in him.

Yet his precise mind measured everything said in the conversation. He resembled a man in a garden who cuts off with his sword the head of every flower which rises above the others. A martyr to his own precision, he was as much offended by a witty remark as weak eyes are offended by too strong a light. Nothing was indifferent to him, provided it were true; accordingly, his conversation was remarkable. That day he had come from the country with a man who had seen a superb château and its magnificent gardens; he, however, had seen only a structure sixty feet long and thirty-five feet wide, and a ten-acre [2] park in the form of a parallelogram. He would rather

---

1 [The Pont-Neuf (finished in 1604) is the oldest of the extant Paris bridges; it joins the right and left banks of the city across the downstream tip of the Île de la Cité.]

2 [The measures given in the text are in arpents (1 arpent = 30 to 50 ares, depending on local custom; in modern measure 1 are = 100 square

have it that the rules of perspective had been so observed that the avenues would all have appeared to be of equal width, and for the purpose he would have supplied an infallible method. He was very pleased to show us a very curiously constructed dial he had discovered there, and he became very angry with a scholar seated near me, who unfortunately asked him if this dial marked the Babylonian hours. A newsmonger spoke of the bombardment of the castle of Fontarabia; [3] the geometer then quickly gave us the properties of the line that the bombs described in the air, and, charmed with this knowledge, he showed no interest whatsoever in their success. A man complained of having been ruined by a flood during the winter before. "What you tell me is most gratifying," the geometer said, "for I see that I am not mistaken in my observation that at least two inches more rain fell this year than last."

A moment later he left and we followed. As he walked rapidly and neglected to look before him, he ran straight into another man; they collided violently, and each rebounded from the blow in reciprocal proportion to their speed and masses. When they had somewhat recovered from their dizziness, this man, hand on forehead, said to the geometer, "I am delighted you ran into me, for I have great news to tell you. I have just finished my Horace." "But what's this?" said the geometer. "He was published two thousand years ago!" "You do not understand me," the other replied. "It is a translation of that ancient author which I am bringing out. For twenty years I have been busy with translations."

"What, sir?" said the geometer. "For twenty years you have not thought? You speak for others, and they think for you?" "Sir," said the scholar, "don't you believe I have done the

meters). This translation has arbitrarily made arpents and acres equivalent.]

3 [Fontarabia (Fuenterrabia) is a small Spanish city on the French border, which the Duke of Berwick bombarded and took for France on July 18, 1719. France and England had allied against Spain in 1719, largely to force Spanish acceptance of a negotiated settlement of the confused Italian question. See above, p. 207, footnote 1.]

public a great service by familiarizing them with good authors?" "That was not exactly my point; I esteem as much as
anyone those sublime geniuses you misrepresent. But you
don't resemble them at all, for were you to translate forever,
no one will ever translate you.

"Translations are like copper coins which have the same
value as a piece of gold: they are even of greater use to the
people, but they are always light and of poor alloy.

"According to you, your intention is to revive in our midst
those illustrious dead, and I concede that you do indeed give
them a body. But you do not impart life; a soul is always
lacking to animate them.

"Why not apply yourself instead to the search for the many
beautiful truths which we discover every day by simple calculation?" Following this bit of advice they separated, each, I believe, most discontented with the other.

Paris, the last day of the moon of Rebiab II, 1719

LETTER CXXIX [1]

Usbek to Rhedi, at Venice

Most legislators have been limited men, made leaders by
chance, who relied for the most part only upon their prejudices
and fancies.

It seems they have misconceived the greatness and dignity of
their work; they have amused themselves with devising childish institutions, which, to be sure, are congenial enough to
petty minds but disgraceful to people of good sense.

They plunge into useless details and concern themselves
with particulars—which is the mark of a narrow mind, able to
see things only in pieces and with no general vision.

---

[1] [In early editions and in some translations, this letter is placed earlier
in the text, with appropriate adjustment in the numbering of the letters.]

Some of them have even affected to use a language other than the vernacular, absurd though this is for a maker of laws; for how can they be obeyed if they are not understood?

They have frequently and needlessly abolished laws they found already established, which is to say, they have thrown the people into the disorders which are inseparable from change.

It is true that, because of peculiarities found more in man's nature than in his mind, it is occasionally necessary to change certain laws. But such cases are rare, and when they occur, the law must be treated with trembling hands; so many solemnities ought to be observed, and so many precautions taken, that the people will naturally conclude that the laws are indeed sacred, since so many formalities are needed to abrogate them.

Often the laws are made too subtly, according to logical ideas rather than a natural equity. Consequently they are found to be too strict, and the principles of justice require that they be set aside; but such a remedy is really a new ill. Whatever the laws may be, they must always be obeyed as the expression of the public conscience, to which individuals ought to conform without exception.

Yet it must be admitted that, in one matter, some lawmakers have shown great wisdom: they have given fathers wide authority over their children. Nothing serves as well as this to free the magistrates, to clear the courts, and, in sum, to spread peace throughout the state; for morality always makes better citizens than the laws.

Of all powers, this one is abused the least. It is the most revered of all magistracies, for it is the only one which depends on no conventions and in fact precedes them all.

It is noteworthy that the best regulated families are in countries where rewards and punishments are put into paternal hands; for fathers are the image of the creator of the universe, who can direct men by his love but does not neglect to attach them still more closely to him by motives of hope and fear.

I cannot end this letter without remarking upon a peculiarity in the French mind. They say they have retained from the

Roman laws a multitude of worthless things, and even worse;
yet they have not taken from them the principle of paternal
power, which the Romans established as the primary legitimate authority.

Paris the 4th of the moon of Gemmadi II, 1719

LETTER CXXX

Rica to ————

In this letter I will tell you of a certain tribe called the quid-
nuncs,[1] who gather in a magnificent garden, where their indolence is kept constantly busy. They are entirely useless to
the state, and fifty years of their conversation has had the same
effect as would have been produced by an equal period of
silence; however, they consider themselves important, because
they entertain splendid projects and discuss great interests.

The basis of their conversations is a frivolous and absurd
curiosity. There is no place, however secret, they effect not to
have penetrated. They do not admit ignorance of anything;
they know how many wives our august sultan has, how many
children he fathers each year; and though they expend nothing for spies, they are instructed in the measures he is taking
to humiliate the Turkish and Mogul emperors.

Scarcely have they exhausted the present when they rush
into the future, and marching in advance of providence they

---

1 [Montesquieu's word is *nouvellistes,* which has elsewhere been translated, in a slightly different context, as "newsmongers" (Letter CXXVIII).
There is no exact contemporary English equivalent, but quidnunc (Latin,
quid nunc, "what now?") seems to convey reasonably well the sense of
gossipy irrelevance that Montesquieu intended. In a country where official
news was very incomplete, the *nouvellistes* were actually better informed
and of more significance than Montesquieu realized. The garden where the
"tribe" gathered is the Tuileries.]

anticipate its workings in the affairs of men. They lead a general by the hand, and having praised him for a thousand follies he has not committed, they prepare for him a thousand others which he will not commit.

They make armies fly like cranes and bring down walls like cards; they have bridges over every river, secret routes through all the mountains, immense arsenals in burning deserts. They lack nothing but good sense.

A man with whom I lodge received this letter from a quidnunc: since it struck me as unusual I kept it. Here it is:

Sir:

I am seldom mistaken in my conjectures on the affairs of the day. On the first of January, 1711, I predicted that the Emperor Joseph would die in the course of the year. It is true that, as he was in excellent health, I felt I would invite mockery if I explained myself too clearly, and so I employed somewhat enigmatic terms; but really rational people understood me. On the 17th of April in that same year he died of smallpox.

As soon as war was declared between the emperor and the Turks,[2] I sought out our group from every corner of the Tuileries, assembled them near the fountain, and predicted to them that Belgrade would be besieged and taken. I was fortunate enough to have my prediction fulfilled. It is true that towards the middle of the siege I bet one hundred pistoles that it would be taken on August 18,[3] and it was not taken till the next day; but can one lose any more closely?

When I saw that the Spanish fleet was landing troops in Sardinia, I judged that they would conquer it; I said so and was proved right. Elated by this success, I added that the victorious fleet would land at Finale [4] to conquer the Milanese. Since I found this idea met with resistance, I decided to vindicate it gloriously and bet fifty pistoles— and lost again, for that devil Alberoni,[5] violating the trust in

---

[2] [Austria went to war with the Ottoman Empire in 1716 as the ally of the Venetians, who had been at war with the Turks since 1714; the campaign was fought chiefly in Hungary.]

[3] 1717.

[4] [Finale Ligure, a small city on the Italian coast near Genoa.]

[5] [See above, p. 207, footnote 1.]

treaties, sent his fleet to Sicily and at once fooled two great states-
men: the Duke of Savoy and me.[6]

All this has so upset me, sir, that I have resolved to continue
predicting but never to bet. Formerly, we at the Tuileries knew
nothing of the custom of betting, and the late Count of L.[7] would
hardly have tolerated it; but since a crowd of lesser lights has mixed
in with us, we no longer know where we are. We hardly open our
mouths to announce a bit of news, when one of these youngsters
offers to bet the contrary.

The other day, as I was opening my manuscript and adjusting
my spectacles on my nose, one of these braggarts, seizing exactly the
interval between the first and second word, said to me, "I bet one
hundred pistoles against it." I pretended not to have noticed this
vulgarity, and beginning again in a louder voice, I said, "The Mar-
shal of ———, having learned. . . ." "That is false," he said; "you
always exaggerate the news; there is no common sense in any of it."
I beg you, sir, to favor me with a loan of thirty pistoles, for I confess to you that these bets have much embarrassed me. I am sending
you copies of two letters I have written to the minister. I am, etc.

LETTERS OF A QUIDNUNC TO THE MINISTER

My Lord:

I am the most zealous subject the king has ever had. It is I who insisted that one of my friends execute the project I had formed for a
book, showing that Louis the Great was the greatest of all the princes
who have merited the name of "Great." Since then I have labored
long on another work, which will bring even greater honor to our
nation, if Your Excellency will grant me a privilege. My plan is to
prove that, since the founding of the monarchy, the French have
never been defeated, and that everything told of our defeats by
previous historians is simple fabrication. I am obliged to correct
them on many occasions, and I flatter myself that I am especially
brilliant as a critic. I am, my lord, etc.

---

6 [Spain landed troops in Sardinia in August of 1717, and eleven months
later invaded Sicily. Victor-Amadeus II, Duke of Savoy, was compelled
to exchange Sicily for Sardinia, becoming king of Sardinia, in the eventual
settlement of the Italian problem (1720).]

7 [The Comte de Lionne, who died in 1716; he reputedly was a good
friend and patron of the *nouvellistes*.]

My Lord:

Since we have sustained the loss of the Count of L., we pray you to have the goodness to permit us to elect a president. Our meetings have fallen into disorder; affairs of state are not discussed in the same depth as in the past; our young people have absolutely no regard for their elders, and no discipline; it is exactly like the council of Rehoboam, where youth imposed itself on age.[8] In vain do we point out to them that we were in peaceable possession of the Tuileries twenty years before they were born; I believe they will eventually drive us away, and that we, obliged to leave those places where we have so often evoked the spirits of our French heroes, will be forced to hold our meetings in the Jardin du Roi,[9] or some even more remote place. I am, etc.

Paris, the 7th of the moon of Gemmadi II, 1719

LETTER CXXXI

Rhedi to Rica, at Paris

One of the things that has most piqued my curiosity since arriving in Europe is the history and origin of republics. You know that most Asiatics not only have no idea of this form of government, but their imagination is unable even to conceive of there being any form on earth other than despotism.

The first governments of which we have knowledge were monarchies; only by chance, and after the passage of many centuries, were republics created.

---

[8] [In I Kings 12: 6-11, King Rehoboam, son of Solomon, was petitioned by the people to lighten the load of his yoke upon them. Taking counsel, Rehoboam listened to the old men who recommended leniency, but followed the contrary advice of his young contemporaries.]

[9] [The *Jardin royal des herbes médicinales* was founded in the early seventeenth century; now called the *Jardin des plantes*, and much expanded, it comprises both a botanical and zoological collection of great significance. It is in Paris on the left bank, and in the early eighteenth century was on the southeastern edge of the city.]

Greece, having been destroyed by a flood, came to be populated by new inhabitants; almost all of these colonists came
from Egypt and closely neighboring countries in Asia, and
since these lands were governed by kings, the people leaving
them were similarly ruled. But, the tyranny of these princes
becoming too harsh, their yoke was thrown off, and from the
debris of so many monarchies there arose the republics which
made Greece, the only civilized country in the midst of barbarism, flourish so splendidly.

Love of liberty and hatred of kings preserved Greece in independence for a long time and far extended the republican
form of government. Greek cities found allies in Asia Minor,
and they sent colonies there as free as themselves, which served
them as ramparts against the schemes of the Persian kings.
And that is not all: Greece populated Italy; and Italy in turn
populated Spain and perhaps the Gauls. We know that the
great Hesperia, so famous among the ancients, was at first
Greece, which was regarded by all its neighbors as the abode of
felicity.[1] Greeks who could not find that happy land in their
own country went to seek it in Italy; those in Italy, to Spain;
those in Spain, to Baetica[2] or Portugal—so that all those regions bore the name [of Hesperia] among the ancients. These
Greek colonists carried with them a spirit of liberty from that
fortunate country; hence almost nothing is seen of monarchy,
in those remote times, in Italy, Spain, or the Gauls. You will
shortly see that the northern and Germanic peoples were no
less free, and if one finds indications of monarchy among
them, it is because chiefs of armies or republics have errone-
ously been considered kings.

All this took place in Europe, for Asia and Africa have always been crushed under despotism, with the exception of the
few cities in Asia Minor already referred to and the republic
of Carthage in Africa.

---

1 [In Greek mythology the Hesperides were nymphs, daughters of
Hesperus, who guarded the place where golden apples grew, in the Isles
of the Blest, at the western extremity of the earth.]

2 [Roman name for present-day Andalusia, Spain.]

The world was divided between the two powerful republics of Rome and Carthage. Nothing is so well known as the founding of the Roman Republic; nothing so little known as the origin of Carthage. We are totally ignorant of the succession of African princes following Dido and how they lost their power. The astounding aggrandizement of the Roman Republic would have been a great blessing to the world, if it had not involved the unjust distinction between Roman citizens and conquered peoples, if the provincial governors had been given less sweeping authority, if the laws, which righteously forbade their tyranny, had been observed, and if the governors had not employed, to silence the laws, the very treasures which their injustice had amassed.

Caesar crushed the Roman Republic and subjected it to an absolute power.

For a long time Europe groaned under a violent military government, and Roman benevolence was changed to cruel oppression.

However, a multitude of unknown tribes issued from the north, spread like a flood through the Roman provinces, and finding conquest as easy as pillage, dismembered the Empire and founded kingdoms. These people were free, and they so firmly restricted the authority of their kings that they in fact were only chieftains or generals. Thus these kingdoms, though founded by force, felt no conqueror's yoke. When the peoples of Asia, such as the Turks or Tartars, made conquests, they thought only of gaining new subjects for the one man to whose will they were subject, and establishing by arms his forceful sway; but the northern peoples, free in their own land, mastered the Roman provinces and yet gave no great power to their chiefs. Indeed, some of these peoples, like the Vandals in Africa and the Goths in Spain, deposed their kings whenever they were not satisfactory; among other peoples, the authority of princes was limited in a thousand different ways: a large number of nobles shared it with them, wars were undertaken only with their consent, spoils were divided between leader and soldiers, no imposts favored the prince, and laws

were made in the assemblies of the nation. That is the fundamental principle on which all those states, formed out of the
wreckage of the Roman Empire, were founded.

Venice, the 20th of the moon of Rhegeb, 1719

Rica to ———

Five or six months ago I was in a café and observed a rather
well-dressed gentleman who had everyone's attention. He
spoke of the pleasure of living in Paris and deplored the situation that required him to waste away in the country. "I
have," he said, "fifteen thousand livres in land rents, and I
would be happier if I had a quarter of it, but in money and
movable goods. It does me no good to squeeze my tenants and
load them with the expenses of lawsuits; I only make them
more insolvent than ever. I have never seen a hundred pistoles
at one time, and if I owed ten thousand frances, all my lands
would be seized and I would be in the poorhouse."

I left without having paid careful attention to all this talk,
but finding myself yesterday in the neighborhood I entered
the same café, where I saw a solemn man with a long pale
face, sad and pensive in the midst of five or six gossipers, until
he suddenly broke into the talk. "Yes, gentlemen," he said in a
rising voice, "I am ruined. I have nothing to live on, for at
home I have two hundred thousand livres in bank notes and
one hundred thousand *écus* in silver. My condition is frightful: I thought I was rich, and here I am at the poorhouse. If
only I had a little land to which I could retire, at least I would
be sure of a living; but I have less land than this hat would
hold." [1]

---

[1] [The references here are to the financial manipulations of John Law
and their consequences. Law (1671-1729) was an honest, clever, and en-
thusiastic Scot, with some essentially sound but, for his time, unusual

By chance I turned my head in another direction and saw a man grimacing as if possessed. "Who can be trusted any more?" he shouted. "A traitor, whom I so strongly believed was my friend that I lent him my money, has returned it to me! What horrible treachery! No matter what he ever does, in my mind he will be forever disgraced." [2]

Close by was a very poorly dressed man who said, lifting his eyes to heaven: "May God bless our ministers' projects! May I see the shares go to two thousand, and every lackey in Paris richer than his master!" I was curious and asked his name. "He is an extremely poor man," someone told me, "and

---

ideas on national fiscal policy. His "system," intricate beyond the limits of a note to describe completely, involved a paper currency regulated in quantity by the government according to demand rather than specie support, the creation of a national bank, the incorporation of all French-chartered trading companies into one great company which would assume the entire debt of France and dominate its foreign trade, and the promotion and public sale of shares in this company, which Law hoped would prosper by exploitation of the undeveloped French colonies, particularly Louisiana. Shares promised annual interest of four per cent, and as they were the equivalent of government preferred bonds they appeared to be excellent securities. Orléans, beset as were most French monarchs with desperate financial difficulties, eagerly supported Law, and the reorganization of the French finances began on a large scale in 1718.

The public's expectation of the potential of the *Compagnie des Indes,* however, was driven to absurd heights in 1719 and early 1720, abetted by Law's publicity and not scrupulously ethical promotion; at the height of the boom shares sold for many times their face value and true worth. The speculative "bubble" burst in 1720, ruining many, leaving some who sold in time very wealthy, and adversely affecting the honest and sensible investors in that their four per cent return was now paid in inflated currency.

While stock prices generally rose in 1719, there were brief but intense reversals, and with each rise and fall the prices of land fluctuated accordingly. Montesquieu here specifically refers to a temporary break in stock values late in 1719, which raised land prices precipitously.]

2 [As Law's "system" neared its ultimate collapse, the government attempted to stabilize the paper bank notes by withdrawing specie from circulation and making the inflated notes legal tender; debtors, of course, hastened to pay their obligations in the depreciated notes, and the panic intensified. This was in 1720; Montesquieu apparently errs in dating this letter 1719.]

he has a poor trade: he is a genealogist, and he hopes that if present trends continue, all the newly rich will need him to improve upon their names, to polish up their ancestors, and adorn their coaches. He fancies that he is about to make as many people of quality as he wishes, and he quivers with joy at the prospect of his business expanding."

Finally, I saw an old, pale, and withered man enter, whom I recognized as a quidnunc before he sat down. He was not one of those whose self-assurance triumphs over all reverses, and who is always predicting victories and trophies; on the contrary, he was one of the fearful sort, who have only bad news. "Things are going very poorly in Spain," he said; "we have no cavalry on the frontier, and it is feared that Prince Pio, who has a large force, may put all Languedoc under contribution." [3] Directly across from me was a philosopher, appropriately ill-clothed, who contemptuously shrugged his shoulders in proportion as the quidnunc raised his voice. I went close to him, and he whispered to me: "Look at that fool, worrying us for an hour with his fears about Languedoc. And I, I who last evening saw a sunspot which, if it gets bigger, may bring all of nature to stagnation, I have not said a single word."

Paris, the 17th of the moon of Rhamazan, 1719

Rica to ———

The other day I went to see a large library in a convent of dervishes, who guard it but are required to admit the public at certain hours. [1]

---

3 [Prince Pio de Savoia y Corte Real was commanding the Spanish forces in the French war with Spain in 1719.]

1 [The library of St. Victor Abbey in Paris was made available to the public in 1707.]

Upon entering, I saw a serious-looking man walking among the innumerable volumes surrounding him. I went to him and asked about certain of these books which I saw were better bound than the others. "Sir," he replied, "I am in a foreign country here and know no one. Many people ask me such questions, but you surely understand that I am not going to read all these books to satisfy them. My librarian will give you satisfaction, however; he does nothing day or night but decipher all these things. He is good for nothing and a great burden to us, because he doesn't work for the convent. But I hear the refectory bell, and those who are leaders in a community, like me, ought to be first at all its exercises." So saying, the monk pushed me out, closed the door, and like a shot disappeared from sight.

Paris, the 21st of the moon of Rhamazan, 1719

<hr>

LETTER CXXXIV

Rica to the same

I returned to the library the next day, where I found a man entirely different from the one I had first met. He had a simple air about him, an intelligent face, and a very agreeable way of greeting. As soon as I had made known my curiosity, he dutifully undertook to satisfy it and, as I was a foreigner, to instruct me further.

"Father," I said, "what are those fat volumes which fill the whole side of the library?" "Those," he replied, "are interpretations of Scripture." "There are certainly many of them," I answered. "The Scripture must have been most obscure once, but very clear now. Do any doubts remain? Can there still be any contested points?" "Can there? Good heavens! Can there! There are about as many doubts as there are lines." "Indeed?"

I said, "then what have all these authors done?" "These authors," he rejoined, "have not searched Scripture for what must be believed but for what they believed themselves. They have seen it not as a book containing dogmas they were bound to accept, but as a book which could give authority to their particular ideas. It is for this reason that they have corrupted its meaning and submitted every passage to torture. It is a land upon which men of every sect descend and pillage at will; it is a battlefield where enemy tribes clash in combat, attacking and skirmishing in every possible manner.

"Right next to those, you see the ascetic or devotional books; next, books on morality, somewhat more useful; then theology, doubly unintelligible, because of the subject matter and the way it is treated; then the works of the mystics, which is to say, devotees with passionate hearts." "Ah, Father!" I said, "wait a moment; not so fast. Tell me about these mystics." "Sir," he said, "devotion heats a heart disposed to passion and sends impulses to the brain which also heat it, and from this come ecstasies and raptures. This is the delirious state of devotion. It often is perfected or, rather, corrupted into quietism; you are aware that a quietist is nothing other than a man at once mad, devout, and a libertine.

"You see there the casuists, who bring into daylight all of the secrets of the night, who form in their imagination all the monsters which the demon of love can produce, who gather and compare them and make them the constant object of their thoughts. Fortunate are they indeed if their hearts are not involved in all this, and if they do not themselves become accomplices to all the irregularities they describe so naïvely and paint so darkly!

"You see, sir, that I think freely and talk with you candidly. I am naturally artless, and more so with you who are a foreigner and curious about things as they are in fact. If I wished, I could speak of all this only with admiration. I could say endlessly, 'This is divine; that is respectable; there is the marvelous.' And one of two things would happen: either I would deceive you, or I would dishonor myself in your mind."

We left it at that, for the dervish had some business which interrupted our conversation until the next day.

Paris, the 23rd of the moon of Rhamazan, 1719

LETTER CXXXV

Rica to the same

I returned at the appointed time, and my man began at precisely the point where we had left off. "Here," he said, "are the grammarians, the glossarists, and the commentators." "Father," I asked, "have all these people been able to dispense with good sense?" "Yes," he said, "they have, and indeed it never appears; yet these works are not the worse for the lack, which is very convenient for them." "True," I said, "and I know a number of philosophers who would do well to apply themselves to studies of this sort."

"Over there," he continued, "are the orators, who have the talent of persuading regardless of their reasoning, and the geometers, who persuade a man in spite of himself and overwhelm him by sheer force.

"And here are books on metaphysics, treating of enormous subjects in which infinity is met everywhere; and books on physics, which find the economy of the vast universe no more amazing than the simplest contrivances of our artisans.

"Books on medicine: monuments to the fragility of nature and to the power of art, they cause us to tremble even when speaking of trifling maladies, because they dwell so much upon imminent death, but make us as secure as if we were immortal, when they talk of remedies.

"Next to them are books on anatomy, containing much less about the parts of the human body than of the barbarous names given to them—and so cure neither the patient of his disease nor the doctor of his ignorance.

"Here are the alchemists, who end up either in the poor-house or the insane asylum, both places equally suited to them.

"And here are the books on occult science or, rather, on occult ignorance, such as those smacking of witchcraft—abominable, according to most people; pitiful, in my opinion. Such also are the books on judicial astrology." "What, Father? Books on judicial astrology!" I retorted heatedly. "But we in Persia make the most of them: they regulate every action of our lives and determine our every enterprise. Astrologers, properly speaking, are our counselors, and even more, for they influence the affairs of state." "In that case," he said, "you live under a yoke even more harsh than that of reason. Yours is the strangest of all sovereignties; I much pity a family, even more a nation, which allows itself to be ruled by the planets." "We make use of astrology," I replied, "as you use algebra. Every nation has its science, according to which its policies are determined. All our astrologers together have not committed as many follies in Persia as one of your algebraists has made here. Don't you believe that the fortuitous concurrence of stars is as sure a guide as the neat speculations of your builder of systems?[1] Take a vote on this in France and in Persia, and astrology would easily triumph. You would see the schemers properly humbled, and from that, what a destructive corollary might be adduced against them!"[2]

Our dispute was interrupted, and we had to stop.

Paris, the 26th of the moon of Rhamazan, 1719

---

[1] [John Law. See above, p. 224, footnote 1.]

[2] [A popular vote against them and for astrology would perhaps humble the "schemers" (John Law and his followers), but it is not clear what "destructive corollary" could be drawn from their downfall. Perhaps Montesquieu means that Law's system is nothing but astrology in a new guise; or especially poor astrology; or that a public humiliation would show how little faith the "schemers" really had in their own system. At best, the logic is elusive.]

LETTER CXXXVI

Rica to the same

In our next interview my scholar led me into another room. "Here are books on modern history," he told me. "First notice the historians of the Church and the popes, books which I read to be edified but which often have a contrary effect.

"There are those who have written on the decline of the great Roman Empire, itself formed out of the debris of many monarchies, and from which as many others were formed after its fall. An infinite throng of barbarian peoples, as unknown as the lands they inhabited, appeared suddenly, overran and ravaged the Empire, cut it into pieces, and founded every kingdom you now find in Europe. These people were not exactly barbarians, because they were free; but they became barbarous, since most of them submitted to absolute power and lost that sweet liberty which is so consonant with reason, humanity, and nature.

"You see there the historians of the Germanic Empire. It is only a shadow of the first Empire, but I believe it is the only power ever on earth not to be weakened by divisions; the only one, I further believe, strengthened in proportion as it loses land, and which, slow though it is to profit by success, becomes invincible in defeat.

"Here are the historians of France, in which you may see the original power of the monarchy form, die twice, come to life again, languish for several centuries, and then, strengthened by the imperceptible addition of forces from every direction, enter its most recent period. It is like those rivers which lose their water, or run underground, and then reappear swollen by streams emptying into them, to draw rapidly along with them everything that blocks their passage.

"There you see the Spanish nation springing from the mountains, the Mohammedan princes as slowly subjugated as they had rapidly conquered, many principalities joined into a vast monarchy which almost became the only one, until, overwhelmed by her own grandeur and specious opulence, she lost her strength and even her reputation, and retained of earlier power only her pride.

"These, here, are the English historians, who show liberty endlessly issuing from the fires of discord and sedition, the prince always tottering on an immovable throne. You see an impatient nation, wise even in anger, and, becoming mistress of the seas (a thing unheard of before), combining trade with empire.

"Right next to them are the historians of that other queen of the seas, the republic of Holland, respected in Europe and formidable in Asia, where her merchants behold numbers of kings prostrate before them.

"The historians of Italy show you a nation once supreme in the world, but today a slave to all others, with its princes divided and feeble, and with no attribute of sovereignty other than a vain statecraft.

"There are the historians of the republics of Switzerland, the image of liberty, and Venice, with only economic resources, and Genoa, great only for its buildings.

"Here are those of the North, among them Poland, who makes such bad use of her liberty and her right to depose kings that it seems she wishes by her actions to console her neighbors, who have lost both liberty and right."

Thereupon, we separated until the next day.

Paris, the 2nd of the moon of Chalval, 1719

LETTER CXXXVII

Rica to the same

The next day he led me into yet another room. "Here are the poets," he told me, "which is to say, authors whose trade it is to shackle common sense and to crush reason with embellishment, as women were once buried under ornaments and jewelry. You know them, for they are not rare in the Orient, where a more intense sun seems to heat even the imagination.

"These are epic poems." "Ah! And what are epic poems?" "To be truthful," he said, "I don't know. Connoisseurs say that there are only two of them,[1] and that all others so-called are not. About this, too, I know nothing. Moreover, they say that it is impossible ever to write a new one, which is even more surprising.

"Here are the dramatic poets, in my opinion the best of poets and masters of the passions. There are two types: the comic, who stir our feelings very gently, and the tragic, who shake us violently.

"These are the lyric poets, whom I despise as much as I admire the others, and whose art consists of harmonious extravagances.

"Next we see the authors of idyls and pastorals; they please even the people at court by giving them a sense of tranquillity which they themselves lack but which is to be found among shepherds.

"Of all the authors we have seen, these here are the most dangerous: the makers of epigrams—little, sharp darts which make deep and incurable wounds.

"You see here the romances, whose authors are poets of a sort, and who equally outrage the language of the mind as well as that of the heart. They spend their lives seeking the natural and always miss it: their heroes are as unnatural as winged dragons and hippogriffs."

"I have seen some of your romances," I told him, "and if you could see ours you would be even more disgusted. They are similarly unnatural, and our customs further make them extremely dull: ten passionate years must pass before a lover may see even the face of his mistress. Yet authors are forced to keep their readers' interest through all these tiresome preliminaries, and since it is impossible to vary the incidents, they have recourse to a device worse than the evil they seek

---

[1] [Probably the *Iliad* and the *Odyssey*.]

to cure: prodigies. I am sure you would hardly approve of a sorceress calling forth an army from the underworld, or of a single hero destroying an army of a hundred thousand men. Yet such are our romances: cold and often repetitious adventures which bore us, and extravagant prodigies which disgust."

Paris, the 6th of the moon of Chalval, 1719

LETTER CXXXVIII

Rica to Ibben, at Smyrna

Ministers here succeed and destroy each other like the seasons; in three years I have seen the financial system change four times. Taxes are levied in Turkey and Persia today just as they were when the empires were founded; this is certainly not the case here. It is true that we do not dwell on the matter as much as Occidentals do. We believe that there is no more difference between the administration of the prince's revenues and those of a private person than there is in counting a hundred thousand tomans or counting one hundred; but here the matter is considered much more delicate and mysterious. The great minds must work day and night; they must endlessly and painfully give birth to new projects; they must hear the advice of a multitude of people who, unasked, work for them; they must retire and live in the recesses of a room which is inaccessible to the great, and sacred to the small; they must keep their heads constantly filled with important secrets, amazing plans, and new systems; and, absorbed in their thoughts, they must deprive themselves of speech and sometimes even of politeness.

As soon as the late king had closed his eyes, the establishment of a new administration was considered. It was felt that things were going badly, but no one knew how to improve them. The unlimited authority of preceding ministers was not believed desirable; hence, they sought to divide power. To this end six or seven councils were created, and this ministry governed France with more good sense than any previous one had shown. Its duration was short, as was the good it produced.[1]

France, at the time of the late king's death, was a body afflicted with a thousand ills. N——[2] took the knife in hand, cut off the useless flesh, and applied some specific remedies. But there always remained the interior disease to cure. A foreigner[3] arrived to undertake the cure; after many violent remedies, he believed he had made the patient healthfully plump, when in fact she was only obese.

Everyone who was rich six months ago is now poor, and those who then did not even have bread are now gorged with wealth. Never have these two extremities come so close to touching. This foreigner has turned the state inside out as a tailor turns a coat; what was below he put on top, and what was above he put below. Such unexpected fortunes, unbelievable even to those who made them! God creates men out of nothing with no greater rapidity. How many valets are now served by their comrades, and perhaps tomorrow by their masters!

All this often produces queer things. Lackeys who made their fortune under the last regime today boast of their birth. They unload upon those who have just doffed their livery in a certain street[4] all the contempt that was directed at them six months ago. They shout with all their strength: "The nobility is ruined! The state is disordered! Ranks are confused!

---

1 [The Duc d'Orléans, unable and unwilling to rule as regent as Louis XIV had absolutely ruled as king, instituted government by council. The plan was not as popular with most people as with Montesquieu, and it was abandoned in 1718.]

2 [The Duc de Noailles, *Président* of the Council of Finance until January, 1718.]

3 [John Law.]

4 [The rue Quincampoix, where John Law's headquarters were located, and the center of the speculative frenzy.]

Now only nobodies are making fortunes!" I assure you that the latter will also have their revenge on those coming after them; in thirty years these people of quality will in turn make a considerable noise in the world.

Paris, the first of the moon of Zilcade, 1720

LETTER CXXXIX

Rica to the same

Here is a fine example of conjugal affection, not only in a woman, but in a queen. The queen of Sweden, having firmly resolved that her husband the prince should share the throne, has sent a declaration to the estates, which is intended to remove all difficulties by her promising to resign her rule if he is elected.[1]

It was some sixty years ago that another queen named Christina abdicated the throne so as to give herself entirely to philosophy.[2] I do not know which of these two examples we ought to admire more.

Although I emphatically agree that each person should stay fixed in the position where nature has placed him, and while I cannot praise the weakness of those who feel themselves inferior to their position and leave or practically desert it, yet I am struck by the greatness of soul in these two princesses, in whom the mind of the one and the heart of the other rise superior to their fortunes. Christina dreamed of knowledge at

---

1 [Queen Ulrika Eleonora, sister of Charles XII, overwhelmed with the duties of her office, abdicated in 1720 in favor of her consort, Frederick of Hesse-Castel.]

2 [Queen Christina, daughter of Gustavus Adolphus, abdicated in 1654. She had earlier invited Descartes to Sweden to instruct her in philosophy; he died in Stockholm in 1650.]

an age when others dreamed only of enjoyment; and the other wishes enjoyment only if her entire happiness is put in the hands of her august husband.

Paris, the 27th of the moon of Maharram, 1720

LETTER CXL

Rica to Usbek, at ———

The *parlement* of Paris has just been banished to a little town called Pontoise.[1] The council ordered it to register or approve a declaration which would have dishonored it, and it registered it in a way which dishonored the council.

Some other *parlements* of the realm are threatened with similar treatment.

These assemblies are always hateful, for they approach kings only to tell them unwelcome truths; and while a crowd of courtiers forever represents to their kings that the people are happy under their government, the *parlements* come to give the lie to flattery and to carry to the foot of the throne the laments and the tears with which they have been entrusted.

Truth is a heavy burden, my dear Usbek, when it must be carried even to princes! Therefore it always ought to be remembered that those who do so are constrained to it, and that they would never have decided to take a step so unfortunate for themselves in its consequences, were they not forced to it by their duty, their respect, and even their love.

Paris, the 21st of the moon of Gemmadi I, 1720

---

[1] [The *parlement*, conservative in financial matters and sensitive as always about its prerogatives, refused to register a decree retiring two hundred million francs in bank notes, and was exiled in July of 1720. The decree was carried out despite the opposition, and the *parlement* was permitted to return to Paris in December of the same year.]

LETTER CXLI

Rica to the same

I will come to see you at the end of the week. How agreeably the days will pass in your company!

Some days ago I was presented to a lady of the court, whose whim it was to see my foreign appearance. I found her lovely, even worthy of the attention of our monarch and deserving a high place in the sacred precincts of his heart.

She asked me a thousand questions about Persian customs and the way of life led by Persian women. It seemed to me that life in a seraglio was not to her taste, and she found it repugnant that one man was shared by ten or twelve women; she was envious of the happiness of the one and could only pity the condition of the others. Since she enjoys reading, and especially the works of the poets and novelists, she asked that I tell her about ours. What I said redoubled her curiosity, and she begged me to have translated a fragment from one of those I had with me. I did so, and some days later sent her a Persian tale. Perhaps you might enjoy seeing it in French guise:

In Persia in the days of Sheik Ali Khan, there lived a woman named Zulema. She knew the holy Koran by heart; no dervish understood better than she the traditions of the holy prophets; the Arab doctors had said nothing so mysterious that she did not completely understand it; and to this great knowledge she joined a gaiety of spirit that left those who listened to her in doubt as to whether she meant to amuse or to instruct them.

One day, when she was with her companions in one of the rooms of the seraglio, someone asked her what she thought of the next life, and whether she believed the old tradition among our learned men, that paradise was made only for men.

"That is the common opinion," she told them. "Nothing has been left undone to degrade our sex. There is even a nation spread all over Persia, called the Jews, who on the authority of their sacred books maintain that we have no souls.

"These insulting opinions have their origin only in the vanity of men, who wish to carry their superiority even beyond this life, not considering that on Judgment Day every creature will appear before God as nothing and shorn of every privilege except those which virtue has placed in them.

"God will not limit himself in his rewards; and just as men, who have lived wisely and used well the authority they hold over us here below, will enter a paradise filled with such celestial and ravishing beauties that, if a mortal had seen them, he would immediately kill himself in his impatience to enjoy them, so too will virtuous women go to a place of delights where they will be surfeited with a torrent of pleasures by divine men subservient to them. Each woman will have a seraglio in which the men will be kept, and eunuchs, more faithful than ours, to guard them.

"I have read in an Arab book," she added, "of an insupportably jealous man named Ibrahim. He had twelve most beautiful wives, whom he treated in the harshest possible manner. He no longer trusted them to his eunuchs or to the walls of the seraglio, but kept them almost constantly locked up in their rooms, so they could not see or talk to one another—for he was jealous even of innocent friendship. All his actions took on the mark of his natural brutality; never a gentle word left his mouth, and never was the slightest gesture made that did not add something to the rigor of their slavery.

"One day when he had them all assembled in a room of his seraglio, one woman, bolder than the others, reproached him for his bad nature. 'When one searches so hard for means to make himself feared,' she told him, 'he always finds means to make himself hated first. We are so unhappy that we cannot be prevented from wanting change. Others in my place might wish for your death; I desire nothing but my own. Since in this way only can I hope to be separated from you, death will be the sweeter for that reason.' This speech, which should have moved him, instead put him into a terrible rage, and drawing his dagger he plunged it into her breast. 'My dear friends,' she said in a failing voice, 'if heaven pities my virtue, you will be avenged.' With these words she departed this unfortunate life, to enter the bower of delight, where women who have lived a good life enjoy a happiness that is eternally renewed.

"First she saw a smiling meadow, whose verdure was enhanced by the most brilliantly colored flowers; a brook, with waters clearer than crystal, wound intricately through it. She then entered a charming grove, quiet save for the sweet songs of birds. Next she came upon magnificent gardens, which nature in all her glory and simplicity had adorned. Finally, she discovered a great palace prepared for her and filled with godlike men destined for her pleasure.

"Two of them came forward immediately to undress her; others put her in a bath and perfumed her with the most delicious essences. Next they offered her clothing infinitely richer than her own, and then they led her into a large room, where she found a fire of aromatic wood and a table covered with the most exquisite delicacies. Everything seemed to conspire to ravish her senses: on one side she heard music as divine as it was tender; on the other she saw these godlike men dancing solely to please her. All these pleasures, however, served only to lead her gradually to greater ones. She was led into a room, and having again undressed her, they placed her in a splendid bed, where two men of delightful beauty received her in their arms. By then in utter ecstasy, she was carried even beyond her desires. 'I am totally transported,' she told them. 'I would believe I were dying, were I not so certain of my immortality. It is too much! Leave me; I succumb to the violence of pleasure. Yes, now a little calm returns to my senses; I breathe again and come back to myself. Why have the torches been taken away? Why can't I still see your divine beauty? Why can't I see. . . ? But why see? You bring me back to my first raptures. O gods! How lovely this darkness is! I will be immortal, immortal with you! I will be. . . . No, grant me respite; for I see you are such men as never ask it for yourselves.'

"She was obeyed, but only after she had asked several times and had showed she meant it seriously. She rested languidly and slept in their arms. Two moments of sleep overcame her lassitude, and two kisses opened her eyes and immediately enflamed her. 'I am disturbed,' she said, 'for I fear you no longer love me.' Not wishing to remain long in such doubt, she soon had from them all the assurance she could desire. 'I see my mistake,' she cried. 'Pardon me, pardon; I am sure of you. You say nothing to me, but your proof is better than anything you could say. Yes, yes, I confess, no one has ever loved so much. But what is this? You quarrel over the honor of persuading me! Ah, if you contend with each other, if you join ambition to the pleasure of my defeat, then I am lost; you will both be conquerors, and I the only one vanquished. But I will sell the victory dearly to you!'

"All this was interrupted only at daybreak. Then her faithful and pleasant servants entered the room, bade the young men rise, and sent them with two old men to the place where they were guarded for her pleasure. She then arose, appeared to her adoring court first in the charm of simple undress, and then clothed in the most sumptuous raiment. The night had enhanced her beauty, given life to her complexion and animation to her charms. Throughout the day there were nothing but dances, concerts, feasts, games, and promenades; and it was remarked that Anaïs withdrew occasionally to fly to her two young heroes for a few precious moments of interview, and then to return, with a still more serene expression, to the crowd she had left. Finally, toward evening they lost her entirely; she had gone to shut herself up in the seraglio, where, she said, she wished to acquaint herself with those immortal captives who would live with her forever. She visited the most remote and exquisite apartments, where she counted fifty miraculously beautiful slaves; and all night she went from room to room, receiving everywhere homage which was always different and yet always the same.

"And so the immortal Anaïs spent her life, now in thrilling raptures, now in solitary pleasures; now admired by a brilliant throng, now embraced by an impassioned lover. Often she left the enchanted palace to wander through a sylvan grotto, where flowers seemed to be born that she might walk upon them, and delights crowded to present themselves before her.

"For more than a week in that blissful place she was so carried away that she had not a single thought; she had enjoyed her pleasure without contemplating it, without one of those tranquil moments when the passions are silent and the soul, so to speak, takes account and listens to itself.

"The blessed have such vivid pleasures that they seldom indulge this freedom of the spirit; absolutely attached to the things of the present, they entirely lose their memory of the past and have no concern for what they knew or loved in the other life.

"But Anaïs had a truly philosophical mind, having passed almost all her life in meditation, and having pushed her thoughts much further than one would expect of a woman left entirely to herself. Only this enjoyment had been left to her in that austere seclusion imposed by her husband.

"It was this strength of mind that made her scorn both the fear which paralyzed her companions and the death which was to end her pains and begin her happiness.

"Thus, gradually, she came out of the intoxication of pleasure and

shut herself alone in an apartment of her palace. She permitted
herself sweet reflections upon her past condition and present felicity,
but she could not help pitying her companions in their misery, for
one is sensitive to torment shared with others. Anaïs did not remain
within the mere limits of compassion; more tenderly inclined toward her unfortunate friends, she resolved to aid them.

"So she ordered one of her young men to assume the figure of her
husband, to enter his seraglio, master it, drive him out, and then
remain in his place until she recalled him.

"Execution was prompt. Cleaving the air, he arrived at the door
to the seraglio of Ibrahim, who was not in. He knocked, and everything was opened to him, the eunuchs falling at his feet. He flew
toward the apartments where Ibrahim's wives were imprisoned; on
his way he had taken the keys from the pocket of that jealous
grouch, to whom he was invisible. Entering, he first surprised them
by his gentle and agreeable manner; immediately thereafter, he surprised them even more by his eagerness and by the rapidity of his
enterprises. All of them had a part in the astonishment, and had it
not been so real, they would have taken it for a dream.

"While these new scenes were being played in the seraglio, Ibrahim was hurling himself at the door, storming and crying out his
name. After much difficulty he entered and threw the eunuchs into
extreme disorder. He strode forward grandly, but recoiled and fell
as if thunderstruck when he beheld the false Ibrahim, his very
image, in the fullest of the master's liberties. He cried for help, for
the eunuchs to aid him in killing the impostor; but they did not
obey. Only one feeble recourse remained: to submit the matter to
judgment by his wives. In an hour the false Ibrahim had corrupted
all the judges. The other was chased and dragged ignominiously from
the seraglio and would have died a thousand deaths had not his
rival ordered that his life be saved. Then the new Ibrahim, in possession of the battlefield, showed himself more and more worthy of the
choice and distinguished himself by miracles unknown until then.
'You are not like Ibrahim,' the women said. 'Say rather that that impostor is not like me,' said the triumphant Ibrahim. 'But what does
it take to be your husband, if what I do is not sufficient?'

" 'Oh, it is not for us to doubt,' said the women. 'If you are not
Ibrahim, it is enough for us that you have so well deserved to be;
you are more Ibrahim in one day than he has been in ten years.'
'You promise me, then,' he replied, 'that you declare yourselves for
me and against that impostor?' 'Never doubt it,' they said in unison.

'We swear eternal fidelity to you; we have been too long abused. That traitor did not question our virtue at all but only his own impotence. We see clearly that all men are not at all like him; no doubt it is you they resemble. If you knew how much you have made us hate him!' 'Ah, I will give you frequent new reasons to hate him,' responded the false Ibrahim. 'You do not yet know all the wrong he has done you.' 'We judge his injustice by the magnitude of your vengeance,' they replied. 'Yes, you are right,' said the divine man, 'I have fit the punishment to the crime, and I am pleased that you are content with my manner of punishment.' 'But,' said the women, 'if the impostor returns, then what do we do?' 'It would be difficult, I think, for him to deceive you,' he answered. 'While I am here near you, one could hardly succeed by trickery; and besides, I will send him so far away that you will never hear of him again. Henceforth, I myself will undertake to care for your happiness. I will not be jealous, for I know how to be sure of you and without restraining you. I have a sufficiently high opinion of my merit to believe that you will be faithful; and if you cannot be virtuous with me, then with whom would it be?' The conversation lasted for a long time between him and the women, who were more struck with the difference than with the similarity between the two Ibrahims, but never dreamed of asking for an explanation of all these marvels. At last, the desperate husband returned to trouble them again, but he found the entire household joyful and his wives more unbelieving than ever. It was not a place for a jealous man, and he left, furious. An instant later the false Ibrahim followed, seized him, carried him through the air, and left him two thousand leagues away.

"O gods, in what desolation the women found themselves while their beloved Ibrahim was gone! Already their eunuchs resumed their accustomed severity; the household was in tears. They sometimes imagined that all that had happened was only a dream; glancing from one to the other, they recounted the most insignificant episodes of their strange adventures. Finally, the heavenly Ibrahim returned, even more loving; it seemed to them that his journey had not been a tiring one. This new master's conduct was so opposed to the other's that all the neighbors were astounded. He dismissed all the eunuchs, opened his house to all, and would not even allow his wives to be veiled. It was a remarkable thing to see them among the men at the feasts, and as free as the men themselves. Ibrahim believed, and correctly, that the customs of the land were not made for citizens like him. However, he spared no expense and dissipated in great profusion all the wealth of the jealous husband, who, returning three years later from the distant land to which he had been transported, found nothing left but his wives and thirty-six children."

Paris, the 26th of the moon of Gemmadi I, 1720

LETTER CXLII

Rica to Usbek, at ———

Here is a letter I received yesterday from a scholar; you may find it remarkable:

Sir:

Six months ago I inherited five or six hundred livres and a superbly furnished house from a very rich uncle. It is a pleasure to have wealth when one knows how to make good use of it; but I have no ambition or taste for sensual delights, for I am almost always shut up in a tiny room, where I lead the life of a scholar. It is in such a place that the dedicated lover of antiquity is to be found.

When my uncle died, I much hoped to have him buried with the ceremonies observed by the ancient Greeks and Romans, but at that time I had no lacrymatories, urns, or antique lamps.

Since then, however, I have acquired a fine collection of these precious rarities. A few days ago I sold my silver plate in order to buy an earthen lamp which once served a Stoic philosopher. I have sold all the mirrors with which my uncle had covered almost every wall in his apartment, so that I might get a small and slightly cracked mirror once used by Virgil; I am delighted to see my face where once were reflected the features of the Swan of Mantua. And that is not all; for one hundred louis d'or I have bought five or six copper coins current two thousand years ago. As far as I know, I do not presently have any furniture in my house that was made after the decline of the Empire. I have a little cabinet full of the most precious and expensive manuscripts, and although I am ruining my eyesight by reading them, I much prefer them to the printed versions, which are not as correct, and which everyone has. Although I almost never go out, I do not fail to have a boundless passion to know all the old roads in use in Roman times. There is one near my house, made by a proconsul of Gaul about twelve hundred years ago; I invariably take it when I go from my house to the country. It is very inconvenient and takes me more than a league out of the way, but what really angers me is that wooden posts have been put along the road to mark the distance from town to town; I am in despair to see these miserable markers instead of the military columns that once were there. I expect to have them restored by my heirs, however, and will so stipulate in my will. If you, sir, have some Persian manuscript, you would give me great pleasure to let me have it. I will pay anything you ask, and beyond that, I will give you some of my work, which will show you that I am not a useless citizen of the republic of letters. Among others, you will notice a dissertation in which I prove that the triumphal crown of early times was of oak and not of laurel; you will admire another, in which I prove by scholarly deductions from the most authoritative Greek authors that Cambyses [1] was wounded in the left, not the right leg; and still another, where I demonstrate that a low forehead was a mark of extreme beauty among the Romans. Moreover, I will send you a quarto volume which explains òne verse in the sixth book of Virgil's *Aeneid*. You will receive all this in a few days. In the meantime, I am content to send you this fragment I discovered in the dust of a library; it is from an old Greek mythologist and has never been published. I leave you now for some important business I have underway: the restoration of a fine passage in Pliny the Naturalist,[2] which the fifth-century copyists have curiously disfigured. I am, etc.

FRAGMENT OF AN ANCIENT MYTHOLOGIST

On an island near the Orcades, a child was born whose father was Aeolus, god of the winds, and his mother a Caledonian nymph.[3] It is said of him that he learned to count on his fingers entirely by himself, and that by the time he was four he was so perfectly able

---

[1] [See above, p. 112, footnote 2.]

[2] [Gaius Plinius Secundus, or Pliny the Elder, was born in northern Italy in A.D. 23 or 24 and died at Pompeii in 79. A famous savant and prolific writer, he is chiefly remembered for his only extant work, the encyclopedic and often credulous *Historiae Naturalis*.]

[3] [This entire allegory is a thinly disguised satire on John Law and his reception in France; see above, p. 224, footnote 1. The Orcades is the Latin name for the Orkney Islands, off northern Scotland.]

to distinguish metals that when his mother tried to substitute a tin ring for his gold one, he recognized the trickery and threw it away.

When he had grown up, his father taught him the secret of capturing the wind in bags, which he then sold to travelers; but since this merchandise was not in much demand in his country, he left it to wander over the world, accompanied by the blind god of chance.

In his journeys he learned that in Baetica [4] gold glistened everywhere, and he hastened his steps there. He was very poorly received by Saturn, who was then reigning; [5] but when that god departed this earth, he decided to go to all the crossroads and shout incessantly in a hoarse voice: "People of Baetica, you believe you are rich because you have gold and silver. I pity your error. Believe in me, leave this land of base metals, enter the empire of the imagination; and I promise riches that will astonish you." He immediately opened a large number of the bags he carried and distributed his merchandise to all who desired it.

The next day he returned to the same crossroads and cried: "People of Baetica, do you want to be rich? Imagine, then, that I am very rich and that you are, too. Convince yourselves every morning that your fortune has doubled overnight. Then get up, and if you have creditors, go pay them with what you have imagined, and tell them to imagine likewise."

Some days later he reappeared and spoke thus: "People of Baetica, I see clearly that your imagination is not as lively as it was at first. Allow yourselves to follow mine: every morning I will present you with a bill, which will be a source of wealth for you; you will see on it only four words, [6] but very significant ones, for they will control the dowries of your wives, the fortunes of your children, and the number of your servants. And as for you," he said to the group nearest him, "as for you, my dear children (I can call you that, for you have received from me a second birth), my bill will decide upon the magnificence of your establishments, the sumptuousness of your feasts, and the number and the pensions of your mistresses."

Several days later he appeared at the crossroads, out of breath

---

4 [Baetica is part of ancient Spain, now Andalusia; here, of course, read "France."]

5 [Louis XIV. Law visited Paris in 1708, enjoyed amazing (and to some, suspicious) luck in gambling, and was requested to leave.]

6 [*Le cours des actions* ("the price of shares").]

and beside himself with anger, and shouted: "People of Baetica, I advised you to imagine, and I see you have not. All right, now I order you to do it." He then left abruptly but on second thought returned. "I understand that some of you are contemptible enough to hoard your gold and silver. I am willing to ignore the silver; but as for the gold . . . , for the gold. . . . Ah, that really angers me. . . . I swear by my sacred windbags that if those people do not bring it to me, I will punish them severely." [7] Then he added most persuasively: "Do you think it is to keep these miserable metals that I ask them of you? Was not my sincerity proven some days ago when you brought them to me, and I immediately gave half of them back to you?" [8]

The next day he kept himself rather aloof and addressed them in soft, flattering, and insinuating tones: "People of Baetica, I learn that you keep part of your wealth in foreign countries. I pray you to have it sent to me, and I will be pleased and forever grateful."

Aeolus' son was speaking to people hardly disposed to laughter, but they could not prevent it, and he turned away confused. Regaining his courage, however, he risked another little request. "I know that you have precious stones; in the name of Jupiter, give them up, for nothing will impoverish you as swiftly as things of this sort; get rid of them, I tell you. If you cannot do it yourselves, I will send you some excellent men for the purpose. What wealth will pour upon you if you do as I advise! Yes, I promise you the finest things in my bags."

Finally, he mounted on a platform and in a more assured voice said: "People of Baetica, I have compared your present happy state to that in which I found you when I arrived. I see you as the richest people on earth; but so that your fortune may be complete, permit me to take half of your property." With these words Aeolus' son disappeared on magic wings, leaving his audience in unutterable consternation. This caused him to return the next day to speak in this fashion: "I perceived yesterday that my talk displeased you greatly. Well, then, forget what I said. It is true, half is too much. There are other expedients to gain the goal I proposed. Let us assemble

---

[7] [The government demonetized gold as of May of 1720, and promised the same for silver in the following months.]

[8] [At the beginning of the boom in the sale of shares, all claims against the *Banque Royale* were paid half in specie and half in bank notes.]

our wealth all in the same place; [9] this we can do easily, since there is not much of it left." And immediately he made three-fourths of it disappear.

Paris, the 9th of the moon of Chahban, 1720

Rica to Nathaniel Levi, Jewish doctor, at Leghorn

You ask me what I think of the virtues of amulets and the power of talismans. Why do you address yourself to me? You are a Jew and I am a Mohammedan; that is to say, both quite credulous people.

I always carry with me more than two thousand passages of the holy Koran; I tie around my arms a little slip on which are written the names of more than two hundred dervishes; the names of Hali, of Fatima, and of all the Pure are hidden about my clothes in more than twenty places.

However, I do not at all disapprove of those who refuse to believe in the power attributed to the use of certain words. It is indeed more difficult for us to answer their reasoning, than for them to answer our experiences.

Through long habit I carry all these sacred trinkets to conform to universal practice. I believe that while they may have no more virtue than the rings and other ornaments with which we adorn ourselves, yet they have no less. But you—you place your entire confidence in certain mysterious letters, and without that safeguard you would be in a continual fright.

Men are truly unfortunate! They drift constantly between false hopes and absurd fears, and instead of depending upon reason, they manufacture intimidating monsters or seductive phantoms.

---

9 [The *Banque Royale*.]

What result do you expect from the arrangement of certain letters? What is it that their disarrangement can disturb? What relation have they with the winds, that they should calm the storm; with gunpowder, that they should overcome its effects; with what doctors call peccant humors and the morbific cause of disease, that they should be cured?

The extraordinary thing is that those who exhaust their reason in establishing connections between certain events and occult powers make no less an effort to prevent themselves from seeing the real cause.

You will tell me that certain charms have won battles; and I will say that you must be blind not to find that the lay of the land, the number or courage of the soldiers, or the experience of the captains are sufficient for the effect whose cause you choose to ignore.

I will grant you, for the moment, that there may be charms; in turn, grant me for a moment that there may not be—for this is not impossible. What you concede does not prevent two armies from engaging in battle; in this case, would you have it that neither side could be victorious?

Do you believe that the outcome will remain uncertain until an invisible power comes to determine it; that all blows will be wasted, all prudence vain, and all courage useless?

Do you think that on such occasions the presence of death in a thousand guises could not produce in men's minds those panic terrors which you find so difficult to explain? Do you suppose that in an army of one hundred thousand men there could not be one timid man? Do you believe that his cowardice could not produce cowardice in another, and that the second man, having abandoned a third, would not encourage him immediately to abandon a fourth? Nothing more is needed for a defeatist spirit suddenly to seize an entire army, and the larger the army the more easily this happens.

Everyone knows and feels that men, like all creatures with an instinct for self-preservation, passionately love life. This is generally understood; why, then, on a particular occasion, seek further to explain their fear of losing it?

Although the sacred books of every people are full of these panic or supernatural terrors, I cannot imagine anything more frivolous; because to be certain that an effect, which can be produced by a hundred thousand natural causes, is really supernatural, one must first have determined that none of these causes has acted—and that is impossible to do.

I will say nothing more, Nathaniel, for it seems to me that the subject does not deserve such serious treatment.

Paris, the 20th of the moon of Chahban, 1720

P.S. As I was finishing, I heard them shouting in the streets advertising a letter from a physician in the provinces to a physician in Paris (for here every bagatelle is printed, published, and purchased). I thought I might send it to you, since it bears on our subject. [There are many things in it that I do not comprehend, but you, who are a physician, ought to understand the language of your colleagues.] ¹

LETTER FROM A PHYSICIAN IN THE PROVINCES
TO A PHYSICIAN IN PARIS

We had in our town a patient who had not slept for thirty-five days. His physician prescribed opium, but he could not make up his mind to take it, and with the cup in his hand he was more undecided than ever. Finally he said to his physician: "Sir, I ask your indulgence just until tomorrow. I know a man who does not practice medicine, but who has in his house countless remedies for insomnia; let me send for him, and if I do not sleep tonight, I promise I will come back to you." With the doctor gone, the sick man drew the curtains and told his page, "Go to M. Anis, and ask him to come

---

¹ [In his final corrections for the 1754 edition of *The Persian Letters,* Montesquieu first directed the publisher to delete all of Letter CXLIII, but he later changed his mind and omitted from the main text only a part of it. The material Montesquieu wished excluded (or placed in notes) includes this sentence, the final paragraph of the following "Letter from a Physician," and all the subsequent prescriptions; all this material is here enclosed in brackets. It is included, either in the text or in notes, in almost every edition of *The Persian Letters.*]

to me." M. Anis arrived. "My dear M. Anis, I am dying for lack of sleep. Have you not in your shop *The C. of G.* or, better, some devotional book written by an R. P. J., which you have not been able to sell? [2] For often the remedies longest in stock are the best." "Sir," said the bookseller, "I have at your service Father Caussin's *The Holy Court,* in six volumes; [3] I will send it to you and hope that you find it good. If you would like the works of the Reverend Father Rodriguez, the Spanish Jesuit,[4] don't hesitate to ask. But, believe me, you had better stick to Father Caussin. With God's help, I believe that one sentence from Father Caussin will do you as much good as an entire page of *The C. of G.*" With this M. Anis left, hastening to seek the remedy in his shop. *The Holy Court* arrived, was dusted off, and the sick man's son, a young student, began to read it aloud. He was the first to feel its effects, and by the second page he was articulating poorly, the entire company was weakening, and a moment later everyone was snoring except the sick man, who held out for a long time, but finally succumbed.

The physician arrived early the next morning. "Well, did he take my opium?" No one said anything, but the wife, daughter, and little boy, all beside themselves with joy, pointed to Father Caussin. He asked what it was. They answered, "Long live Father Caussin! We must send him to be bound. Who would have thought it? Who would have believed it? It is a miracle. There, sir, behold Father Caussin, the volume which has put my father to sleep." And they explained to him the thing as it had happened.

[The physician was a subtle man, versed in the mysteries of the cabala and in the power of words and spirits; he was struck by all this, and after some reflection, resolved to change his manner of practice entirely. "This is a very singular fact," he said. "I must push the experiment further. Why shouldn't a mind be able to transmit to his work the same qualities he has himself? Don't we see this happening every day? At least, it is worth the trouble of a trial. I am tired of apothecaries; their syrups, potions, and Galenic drugs

---

[2] [*The C. of G.* is probably *La Connoissance du globe;* R. P. J. is *Révérend Père Jésuite.*]

[3] [Nicolas Caussin (1583-1651) was the confessor of Louis XIII and was later exiled by Richelieu for conspiracy. The book is *La cour sainte ou institution chrétienne des grands* (1627).]

[4] [Alfonso Rodriguez (1526-1616), author of the ascetic, mystical, and widely translated *Exercicio de perfection i virtutes religiosas.*]

ruin patients and their health as well. Let us change the method and test the virtue of minds." On this idea he set up a new pharmacy, as you may see from the following description of the principal remedies he put into practice.

PURGATIVE DECOCTION

Take three leaves of Aristotle's *Logic*, in Greek; two leaves of the most acute treatise on Scholastic theology, as, for example, that of the subtle Scotus; four of Paracelsus; one of Avicenna; six of Averroës; three of Porphyry; as many of Plotinus; as many of Iamblicus.[5] Infuse the whole for twenty-four hours and take four times daily.

A STRONGER PURGATIVE

Take ten *A—— of the C——* concerning the *B—— and the C—— of the I——;*[6] distill them in a water bath; dilute the acrid and pungent drop which is produced in a glass of water and swallow it confidently.

---

[5] [The "subtle Scotus" is John Duns Scotus (*c.* 1265-1308), Scottish Franciscan philosopher, best known for his critique of Thomistic innovations in Scholasticism. Paracelsus (Theophrastus Bombast von Hohenheim, *c.* 1490-1541) was a noisily opinionated German physician, whose chief contributions to science were a lofty vision of the future of medicine, a contempt for all traditional authorities, and a practical method. Avicenna (Abu-'Ali al Husain Ibn Abdullah Ibn Sina, 980-1037) was an Islamic physician and philosopher, author of encyclopedias of medicine and philosophy which achieved wide circulation in the Moslem and medieval Christian world. Averroës (Abu'l-Walid Mohammed Ibn Ahmad Ibn Mohammed Ibn Rushd, 1129-98) was a Spanish Moslem, best known for his commentaries on Aristotle. Porphyry (233-*c.*304) was a Greek scholar, born in Syria and resident mostly in Italy, who devoted much of his efforts to popularizing the doctrines of Plotinus (205-70), the great Neoplatonist philosopher. Iamblicus (*c.* 250-*c.* 330) was Porphyry's student, who later established an influential Neoplatonic school in Syria, and who in his work contributed much to the systematizing and unfortunate complicating of Plotinus' thought.]

[6] [For *A—— of the C——*, read *arrêts du conseil* ("acts of the council"); *B—— and the C—— of the I——* is sometimes read *bulle et Constitution des Jésuites* ("bull and *Constitution* of the Jesuits"), but, more probably, means *banque* (or *bourse*) *et Compagnie des Indes* ("bank," or "exchange, and the Company of the Indies").]

AN EMETIC

Take six harangues, a dozen funeral orations (any will do, except be careful not to use those of M. of N.[7]), a collection of new operas, fifty romances, thirty recent memoirs. Put the whole in a large flask, let it dissolve for two days, then distill it in a sand bath. If this is not sufficient, here is:

A STRONGER EMETIC

Take a leaf of marbled paper which has been used to cover a collection of the literary pieces of the J. F.;[8] infuse it for three minutes; warm a spoonful of the infusion and swallow it.

A SIMPLE REMEDY FOR THE CURE OF ASTHMA

Read all the works of the Reverend Father Maimbourg,[9] ex-Jesuit, taking care only to stop at the end of each sentence. You will feel the ability to breathe gradually returning, and there is no need to repeat the treatment.

TO PREVENT ITCH, RASH, SCALDHEAD,[10] AND HORSE FARCY [11]

Take three of Aristotle's categories, two metaphysical degrees, one distinction, six of Chapelain's verses,[12] one phrase from the letters of the Abbé de St. Cyran.[13] Write all of this on a piece of paper, fold, attach to a ribbon, and wear about the neck.

---

[7] [Perhaps Esprit Fléchier (1632-1710), Bishop (M. = Monsieur?) of Nîmes and a well known if rather pedantic orator.]

[8] [Read as *Jésuites français* or, in this context more probably, as *Jeux Floreaux*, a Toulouse literary academy founded in 1324 to perpetuate the art of the *langue d'oc* troubadours.]

[9] [Louis Maimbourg (1610-86) was expelled from the Jesuit order in 1685 for defending the Gallican liberties in his *Traité historique de l'Église de Rome*.]

[10] [Popular term for any one of various scalp diseases characterized by pustules and falling hair.]

[11] [A dangerous and contagious disease of horses, communicable to man, characterized by ulcerating enlargement of the lymphatics, especially in the legs. It is similar to glanders.]

[12] [Jean Chapelain (1598-1674), minor poet and author of an epic poem on Joan of Arc. See also p. 126, footnote 2.]

[13] [Jean Duvergier de Hauranne (1581-1643), Jansenist theologian.]

A CHEMICAL WONDER, OF VIOLENT FERMENTATION, WITH SMOKE, HEAT, AND FLAME [14]

Mingle an infusion of Quesnel with one of Lallemand; [15] allow fermentation to proceed, with much violence, energy, and noise, as the acids fight and penetrate the alkaline salts: the fiery spirits will thus evaporate. Put the fermented liquid into an alembic: nothing will come out of it, and nothing will remain in it, but a dry, useless residue.[16]

A LAXATIVE

Take two papers of Molina for pain-killer, six pages of Escobar as a laxative, one sheet of Vasquez as emollient; infuse in four pounds of common water. When half has evaporated, strain and express, and into the expression dissolve three sheets of Bauny as a detergent, and three of Tamburini [17] to wash out impurities.

Apply as an enema.

FOR CHLOROSIS, COMMONLY CALLED GREENSICKNESS, OR HOT FIT OF LOVE

Take four figures from Aretino and two sheets from the Reverend Thomas Sanchez' work on marriage. Infuse in five pounds of common water.[18]

Apply as an aperient.

---

14 [This and the following two prescriptions are in Latin in the original texts.]

15 [The Jesuit Jacques-Phillippe Lallemand (*c.*1660-1748) defended the bull *Unigenitus* against the Jansenist Pasquier Quesnel (1634-1719) in his *Le Père Quesnel séditieux dans ses "Réflexions sur le Nouveau Testament"* (1704).]

16 [The text reads *caput mortuum,* which literally means "death's head." This was an expression used by alchemists to designate the nonliquid residue of their analyses.]

17 [Molina, Escobar, Vasquez, Bauny, and Tamburini were all casuists ridiculed by Pascal in *Les Lettres Provinciales.*]

18 [In this prescription Montesquieu combines the libertine works of Aretino (1492-1557) and the Jesuit Thomas Sanchez (1550-1610), author of *Disputationes de Sancto Matrimonio Sacramento,* a handbook on the intimacies of marriage.]

Such were the drugs which our physician put into practice, with predictable success. He said he prefers not to employ rare and almost unique remedies, which would be so expensive as to ruin his patients. For example: a dedicatory letter which made no one yawn, an excessively short preface, a pastoral charge written by a bishop, or a work written by a Jansenist and either scorned by another Jansenist or admired by a Jesuit. He held that such remedies were appropriate only to quackery, against which he had an invincible antipathy.]

LETTER CXLIV

Usbek to Rica[1]

Some days ago in a country house where I was visiting I met two scholars with a great reputation here. Their characters amazed me. The conversation of the first one, in essence, came to this: "What I have said is true, because I have said it." The second's conversation was different: "What I have not said is not true, because I have not said it."

I rather liked the first, for it makes little difference to me if a man is opinionated, but I cannot stand impertinence. The first defends his opinions, which are his property; the second attacks the opinions of others, which are the property of everyone.

Oh, my dear Rica![2] How poorly vanity serves those who have more of it than is needed for self-preservation! Such people seek to be noticed by being annoying. They would be superior but are not even ordinary.

Modest men, come forward, that I may embrace you! You make life gentle and charming. You believe you have nothing;

---

1 [Some texts have this letter *Rica to Usbek*.]

2 [The 1761 text has "Usbek," obviously a mistake not caught when the salutation to this letter was changed.]

I tell you, you have everything. You believe you humble no
one, and you humble everyone. And when, in my own mind,
I compare you with these imperious men I see everywhere, I
hurl them from their judgment seats to a position at your
feet.

Paris, the 22nd of the moon of Chahban, 1720

Usbek to ————

A man of wit and intellect is ordinarily a difficult person in
society. He selects few friends; he is bored with everyone in
that throng of people he chooses to term bad company; and,
as it is impossible that they do not sense some of his dislike, he
has many enemies.

Certain that he can make himself agreeable when he wishes,
he often neglects to do so.

He is inclined to be critical, because he sees more things
than other people and feels them more keenly.

He almost always ruins his fortune because his agile mind
shows him so many ways to do it.

He fails in his enterprises because he takes many chances.
His farsighted vision enables him to see things at too great a
distance. To this it must be added that at the beginning of a
project he is less struck with the difficulties of the scheme than
with the ways he can overcome them by his own resources.

He neglects particular details upon which, however, depends
the success of great undertakings.

The average man, on the other hand, seeks to turn everything to account, and he acutely feels that details are not to be
neglected.

Popular approval is usually for this average man. People
are pleased to give to him and to take from the other. The

man of wit is envied, and nothing is pardoned in him; everything is interpreted in the other's favor, because vanity takes his side.

But if a man of genius is under such a disadvantage, what can be said of the hard lot of the scholars?

I never think of this without recalling a letter from one of them to a friend of his. Here it is:

Sir:

I am a man whose nights are entirely occupied with looking through telescopes thirty feet long at the great bodies revolving over our heads; for relaxation I take my little microscope and study a maggot or a mite.

I am not at all rich, and I have only one room, in which I cannot even make a fire because I keep my thermometer there and unnatural heat would make it rise. Last winter I thought I would die of the cold, but even when my thermometer was at the lowest degree and warned me that my hands were about to freeze, I was not at all disturbed, and now I have the consolation of knowing exactly the slightest changes in temperature for all this past year.

I have almost nothing to do with people, and of all those I see, I do not really know one of them. But there is a man in Stockholm, another in Leipzig, and another in London, whom I have never seen and doubtless never will see, but with whom I correspond so regularly that the post never passes without my writing to them.

However, even though I know no one in this neighborhood, I have such a bad reputation here that sooner or later I will be obliged to move. Five years ago I was rudely insulted by one of my neighbors for having dissected a dog which she claimed belonged to her. A butcher's wife, who hapened to be present, took her side; and while the one loaded me with insults, the other pelted me with stones—and Doctor —— as well, who was with me and received a terrible blow on the frontal and occipital bone, which disordered his mind considerably.

Ever since then, whenever a dog strays away from the street, it is immediately decided that it has perished at my hands. A worthy housewife who had lost a little dog, which she loved, she said, more than her own children, came the other day to faint in my room; not finding her dog, she cited me before the magistrate. I believe

I will never be delivered from the persistent malice of these women, whose shrill voices ceaselessly deafen me with funeral orations on every creature that has died in the past ten years. I am, etc.

All scholars were formerly accused of magic. I am not surprised at this. For each would say to himself: "I have pushed my natural talents as far as they can go, yet a certain scholar has surpassed me. It must be that there is something diabolic in this."

Now that accusations of that sort have fallen into disrepute, a new twist is employed, and a scholar can hardly avoid the accusation of irreligion or heresy. It is unimportant that the people decide he is innocent; the wound is made, it never really heals, and for him it is always a sore spot. Perhaps thirty years later an adversary will unassumingly say to him, "God forbid that I should say that the accusation against you was true; still, you were obliged to defend yourself." And in this way even his justification is turned against him.

If he writes a history, however loftily he may conceive it, and however pure his intentions, a thousand persecutions must be suffered for it. The magistrate will use against him some point of fact that occurred a thousand years ago; and if his pen is not for sale, they will try to make it captive.

Yet even these are more fortunate than those miscreants who abandon their faith for some petty pension; who gain scarcely an obolus for all their impostures; who overturn the constitution of the empire by diminishing the rights of one group and augmenting those of another by giving to the princes what they take from the people, by reviving moribund rights, and by flattering the current passions and reigning vices; who impose themselves the more shamelessly upon posterity, because it has no means of nullifying their evidence.

But it is not enough for an author to have to endure these insults, not enough that he live in constant anxiety about the success of his work. Finally, that book appears which has cost him so much, and it is attacked from every direction. How could it be otherwise? He had an idea which he sustained in his writing; how could he know that a man two hundred leagues away had said exactly the contrary? And so war is declared.

Still, if he could hope to attain some fame! But no, at most he is esteemed by those whose work is in the same area as his own. A philosopher has a sovereign contempt for anyone whose head is stuffed with facts, and he in turn is regarded as a visionary by anyone with a good memory.

As for those whose profession is one of proud ignorance, they would have the entire human race buried in their own oblivion.

A man compensates for the lack of a talent by despising it. He removes the obstacle he finds between himself and merit, and so finds himself on a plane with those whose work he envies.

And finally, to achieve even such a dubious reputation, an author must sacrifice all pleasures and expect to lose his health.

Paris, the 26th of the moon of Chahban, 1720

LETTER CXLVI

Usbek to Rhedi, at Venice

Long ago it was said that sincerity was the soul of a good minister.

A private person may enjoy the obscurity of his position; he discredits himself only before a few people and turns a mask toward the others. But a minister who lacks probity has as many witnesses and as many judges as the people he governs.

Dare I say it? The worst evil done by a dishonorable minister is not in serving his prince badly and ruining his people; in my opinion there is another evil a thousand times more dangerous: the bad example he gives.

You know that I have traveled much in India.[1] There I have seen a naturally liberal people, from the meanest subject to the most elevated, instantly perverted by a minister's bad example. I have seen an entire nation, in whom generosity, honesty, candor, and good faith had always been accepted as natural qualities, become at once the basest of people. I have seen the infection spread, sparing not even the healthiest members; on the vain pretext that evil has been done to them, the most virtuous men did unworthy things and violated the first principles of justice.

They invoked odious laws to support the vilest acts; and injustice and perfidy they renamed necessity.

I have seen faith in contracts banished, the most sacred conventions annihilated, all the laws of the family overthrown. I have seen avaricious debtors, insolent in their poverty, unworthy instruments of the fury of the law and of the hardships of the time, feign payment instead of making it, and plunge a knife into the breast of their benefactors.

I have seen others, even more disgraceful, buy for almost nothing, or rather, pick oak leaves [2] from the ground and exchange them for the subsistence of widows and orphans.

I have seen suddenly born in every heart an insatiable thirst for wealth. In a moment, I have seen form a detestable conspiracy to acquire riches, not by honest toil and lawful industry, but by the ruin of the prince, the state, and its citizens.

In those unhappy times I have seen an honest citizen who never went to bed until he could say, "I have ruined one family today and will ruin another tomorrow."

"I am going," said another, "with a man in black, who carries an inkhorn in his hand and a sharp weapon on his ear, to assassinate everyone to whom I have an obligation." [3]

Another said, "I see my affairs are going well. It is true that

---

1 [The following lament over conditions in "India" is, of course, another attack on John Law's "system."]

2 [Shares of stock in Law's company.]

3 [Accompanied by a notary with a pen on his ear, the man is going to pay his debts in depreciated paper money.]

when I went to make a payment three days ago, I left an entire family in tears; that I wiped out the dowries of two virtuous girls and took away a little boy's education, so that the father and mother will perish brokenhearted. But I have done only what the law permits."

What crime can be greater than that committed by a minister, when he corrupts the morals of an entire nation, degrades the souls of the most upright, tarnishes the splendor of rank, obscures virtue itself, and confounds those of the highest birth with the most despised?

What will posterity say when it blushes over this shame of its fathers? What will the next generation say when it compares the iron of its ancestors with the gold of the generation which gave it birth? I do not doubt that the nobles will remove from their escutcheons a degree of unworthy nobility which dishonors them, and thus leave the present generation in the frightful oblivion into which it has sunk.

Paris, the 11th of the moon of Rhamazan, 1720

LETTER CXLVII

The chief eunuch to Usbek, at Paris

Things here have arrived at a state that can no longer be tolerated. Your wives have supposed that your departure gave them complete impunity and dreadful things have happened. I tremble myself at the terrible account I am about to give you.

Zelis, on her way to the mosque some days ago, dropped her veil and appeared before everyone with her face almost entirely exposed.

I have discovered Zachi in bed with one of her slaves, something absolutely forbidden by the laws of the seraglio.

I have intercepted, by the merest chance, a letter which I

am sending to you; I have never been able to discover to whom it was addressed.

Last evening a young man was found in the garden of the seraglio; he escaped over the walls.

Add to all this everything that has not come to my knowledge, and you will know that you have surely been betrayed. I await your orders, and until the happy moment when I receive them, I remain in a desperate situation. But if you do not put all these women at my discretion, I cannot answer for any of them and will have news as lamentable as the above to send you every day.

The seraglio at Ispahan, the 1st of the moon of Rhegeb, 1717

LETTER CXLVIII

Usbek to the chief eunuch, at the seraglio at Ispahan

Receive by this letter unlimited power over all the seraglio. Command with authority equal to mine. Let fear and terror run with you, as you move from apartment to apartment carrying penalty and punishment; let all be in consternation and in tears before you. Interrogate the whole seraglio. Begin with the slaves, but spare not my love; let all submit to your stern judgment. Bring to light the most deeply hidden secrets. Purify this infamous place and restore its banished virtue. For, from this moment on, I place upon your head the slightest fault committed. I suspect Zelis as the one to whom that letter was addressed; examine the matter with the eyes of a lynx.

————, the 11th of the moon of Zilhage, 1718

LETTER CXLIX

Narsit to Usbek, at Paris

The chief eunuch has died, magnificent lord; as the oldest of your slaves, I have taken his place until you make it known upon whom you choose to cast your eyes.

Two days after his death there was brought to me one of your letters addressed to him. I have taken care not to open it, but have respectfully put it in an envelope and locked it away until you make your sacred will known to me.

Yesterday a slave came in the middle of the night to tell me that he had seen a young man in the seraglio. I got up, investigated the matter, and found that it was a vision.

I kiss your feet, sublime lord, and I pray you to trust my zeal, my experience, and my age.

The seraglio at Ispahan, the 5th of the moon of Gemmadi II, 1718

LETTER CL

Usbek to Narsit, at the seraglio at Ispahan

Wretch that you are! You have in your hands letters which contain immediate and severe orders; the slightest delay makes me despair, and you rest peaceful under a vain pretext!

Horrible things are happening; perhaps half of my slaves deserve to die. I send to you the letter which the chief eunuch wrote on this subject before his death. If you had opened the packet addressed to him, you would have found bloody orders. Read them; you perish if they are not executed.

———, the 25th of the moon of Chalval, 1718

LETTER CLI

Solim to Usbek, at Paris

If I guarded my silence any longer, I would be as guilty as every criminal in your seraglio.

I was the confidant of the chief eunuch, the most faithful of your slaves. When he saw that his end was near, he called me to him and said this: "I am dying, but the only regret I have in leaving life is that my dying eyes have discovered the guilt of my master's wives. May heaven protect him from all the miseries I foresee! After my death may my menacing shade return to tell these traitresses of their duty and to intimidate them still! Here are the keys to those fearful places; take them to the oldest of the black eunuchs. But if, after my death, he lacks vigilance, be sure to advise my master of it." With these words he expired in my arms.

I know that he wrote to you some time before his death about the conduct of your wives, and in the seraglio there is a letter which would have brought terror with it, had it been opened. What you have written since has been intercepted three leagues away. I do not know why, but everything turns out badly.

Meanwhile, your wives show no restraint whatever; since the chief eunuch's death, it seems that everything is permitted to them, and only Roxana respects her duty and retains her modesty. Morals are daily becoming more visibly corrupt. No longer do the faces of your wives show the stern and austere virtue which formerly reigned; a new gaiety prevails—an in-fallible sign, in my opinion, of some new satisfactions. In the slightest things I note liberties hitherto unknown. Even among your slaves there is a certain neglect of duty and rule, which surprises me; they no longer have that ardent zeal for your service, which once animated the entire seraglio.

Your wives have been in the country for a week at one of the most secluded houses. It is said that the slave in charge was bribed, and that a day before they arrived he hid two men in a secret recess in the wall of the main room, from which they emerged at night after we had retired. The old eunuch, who is presently our head, is an imbecile who can be made to believe anything.

I am moved by a vengeful wrath against all these perfidies; and if heaven willed for the good of your service that you might judge me capable of rule, I promise that if your wives were not virtuous, at least they would be faithful.

> *The seraglio at Ispahan, the 6th of the moon of Rebiab I, 1719*

LETTER CLII

Narsit to Usbek, at Paris

Roxana and Zelis wished to go to the country; I did not think it my duty to refuse them. Happy Usbek! You have faithful wives and vigilant slaves; I command in a place which virtue herself seems to have chosen as her abode. Be assured that nothing will happen here which would offend your eyes.

A misfortune has occurred which annoyed me greatly. Some Armenian merchants newly arrived in Ispahan brought one of your letters to me; I sent a slave to get it; he was robbed on the way back, and the letter is lost. Write to me then immediately, for I suppose that with all these changes you must have important things to communicate to me.

> *The seraglio at Fatima, the 6th of the moon of Rebiab I, 1719*

LETTER CLIII

Usbek to Solim, at the seraglio at Ispahan

I put the sword in your hand. I entrust to you the dearest
thing I presently have in the world: my vengeance. Enter into
your new position, bring with you neither pity nor remorse. I
have written to tell my wives that you are to be blindly
obeyed; in the confusion of so many crimes, they will fall before your glances. To you must I entrust my happiness and
my peace of mind. Return the seraglio to me as I left it. Begin my expiation: exterminate the guilty and make those
tremble who consider being so. What rewards can you not
expect from your master for such signal services? It is up to
you whether you will rise even above your present state and
gain a recompense even beyond your desires.

Paris, the 4th of the moon of Chahban, 1719

LETTER CLIV

Usbek to his wives, at the seraglio at Ispahan

May this letter fall upon you like the thunder amidst lightning and tempests! Solim is your chief eunuch, not to guard
you, but to punish. Let all the seraglio abase itself before him.
He is to judge your past actions, and in the future he will
make you live under a yoke so rigorous that you will regret
your liberty, even if you do not regret your virtue.

Paris, the 4th of the moon of Chahban, 1719

LETTER CLV

Usbek to Nessir, at Ispahan

Happy is he who, knowing the value of a gentle and peaceful life, makes his family the center of his existence and knows no country other than that which gave him birth!

I live in a barbarous country, surrounded by everything offensive to me, absent from all my interests. A somber sadness grips me; I am sinking into a frightening depression; it seems I am annihilating myself, and I recover only when dark jealousies come to kindle and nurture fear, suspicion, hate, and regrets in my soul.

You understand me, Nessir; you have always seen as well into my heart as into your own. You would pity me, if you knew my deplorable state. I sometimes wait six whole months for news of the seraglio; I count every passing moment, and my impatience lengthens them; and when that long-awaited time finally arrives, a revolution suddenly occurs in my heart, my hand trembles in opening the fatal letter, and I find that a state of despairing anxiety is the happiest one possible for me, for I fear being forced out of it by a blow more cruel to me than a thousand deaths.

Whatever the reason I had to leave my country, and even though I owe my life to my flight from it, yet, Nessir, I can no longer endure this dreadful exile. Will I not die just the same, a victim to my grief? I have urged Rica a thousand times to leave this alien land, but he is opposed to all my resolution and keeps me here with a thousand excuses. It seems he has forgotten his country, or rather, he seems to have forgotten me, so indifferent is he to my well-being.

Wretch that I am! I want to see my country again, perhaps to become more wretched still! Ah! What can I do there? I shall only submit my head to my enemies. And that is not all: I shall return to the seraglio, where I must demand an account of the calamitous time of my absence; and if I find some guilty, what am I to do? And if the simple thought of it overwhelms me at this distance, what will it be when intensified by my presence? What will it be if I must see and hear things which I cannot even imagine without a shudder? What will it be, finally, if the punishments which I myself proclaim must stand forever as the marks of my confusion and despair?

I shall return to shut myself behind walls more terrible to me than to the women they guard. I shall carry with me all my suspicions, which all their eagerness will not remove; in my bed, in their arms, I will enjoy only my anxieties; at a time when reflections are entirely inappropriate, my jealousy will manufacture them. Unworthy refuse of human nature, base slaves whose hearts are forever closed to all sentiments of love—you would not complain so of your condition, if you knew the misery of mine.

Paris, the 4th of the moon of Chahban, 1719

LETTER CLVI

Roxana to Usbek, at Paris

Horror, darkness, and terror reign in the seraglio; a terrible gloom enfolds it; a tiger constantly exercises his rage upon us. He has put two white eunuchs to torture, but they only swear their innocence. He has sold a number of our slaves and has required that we change around those who remain. Zachi and Zelis have received, in their rooms and in the dark of night, a most unworthy treatment; the sacriligious one has not feared even to lay his vile hands upon them. He has shut us all into our own apartments, and though we are alone, he insists that we be veiled. We are no longer permitted to talk together; it would be criminal to write; we retain only the freedom to weep.

A swarm of new eunuchs has entered the seraglio to afflict us day and night; our sleep is continually interrupted by their feigned or real distrust. My only consolation is that all of this cannot last long and that these miseries will end with my life. It will not be long, cruel Usbek; I will not even give you time to end these cruel outrages.

The seraglio at Ispahan, the 2nd of the moon of Maharram, 1720

LETTER CLVII

Zachi to Usbek, at Paris

O heavens! A barbarian has outraged me even in his manner of punishing me! He has inflicted on me that chastisement which begins by alarming the sense of decency—that most humiliating of all punishments, which takes one, so to speak, back to childhood.

My soul was at first paralyzed with shame, but it recovered its proper indignation, and my cries resounded to the vaults of my apartment. I was heard begging mercy from the vilest of the human race, trying to arouse his pity, while he became even more inexorable.

Since then, his insolent and servile soul dominates mine. His presence, his looks, his words, his total malignancy overwhelm me. When I am alone, at least I have the consolation of my tears; but when he appears, I am seized by a fury I know is impotent, and I fall into despair.

The tiger dares to tell me that you are the author of all these barbarisms. He seeks to alienate my love for you and to profane even the sentiments of my heart. When he utters the name of him whom I love, I can no longer complain but only die.

I have endured your absence and retained my love by the strength of that love. Nights and days, every moment, have been for you. I was proud of that love, and it made me respected here. But now. . . . No, I can no longer tolerate the humiliation into which I have sunk. If I am innocent, return to love me; if I am guilty, return that I may die at your feet.

> *The seraglio at Ispahan, the 2nd of the moon of Maharram, 1720*

LETTER CLVIII

Zelis to Usbek, at Paris

A thousand leagues distant and you judge me guilty; a thousand leagues away from me and you punish.

That a barbarous eunuch laid his foul hands on me was by your order; I am outraged by the tyrant, not by him who exercises that tyranny.

You may, at your fancy, redouble your evil treatment. My heart is peaceful, since it can no longer love you. You have degraded your soul and become cruel. Be certain that you will not be happy. Farewell.

> *The seraglio at Ispahan, the 2nd of the moon of Maharram, 1720*

LETTER CLIX

Solim to Usbek, at Paris

I pity myself, magnificent lord, and I pity you: never has a faithful servant sunk to my present level of despair. Behold your misfortunes and mine; I tremble as I write them.

I swear by every prophet in heaven that since you entrusted

your wives to me, I have watched them night and day; my anxiety never relaxed even for a moment. I began my ministry with punishments and suspended them without altering my accustomed severity.

But what am I saying? Why do I boast of a fidelity which has been useless? Forget all my past services; regard me as a traitor and punish me for all the crimes I have been unable to prevent.

Roxana, the proud Roxana—O heaven! Whom can we henceforth trust? You suspected Zelis and felt entirely secure about Roxana; but her fierce virtue was a cruel imposture, the veil of her treachery. I have surprised her in the arms of a young man, who, perceiving that he was discovered, attacked and struck me twice with his dagger. The eunuchs, brought running by the noise, surrounded him; he defended himself for a long time, wounded several of them, and even tried to regain Roxana's bedroom—to die, he said, before her eyes. But he finally succumbed to numbers and fell at our feet.

I do not know, sublime lord, if I can wait for your stern orders. You have put your vengeance in my hands, and I must not let it languish.

> *The seraglio at Ispahan, the 8th of the moon of Rebiab I, 1720*

LETTER CLX

Solim to Usbek, at Paris

I have made my decision; your misfortunes are about to end. I am going to punish.

Already I feel a secret joy. My soul and yours are to be appeased; we are going to exterminate crime and make even innocence turn pale.

O all you women who seem to be created only to treat your

senses with contempt, you who are ashamed of your own desires, you everlasting victims of shame and modesty—could I
but bring you in crowds into this unhappy seraglio, that you
might be astonished to see all the blood I am about to spill!

> *The seraglio at Ispahan, the 8th of the moon of
> Rebiab I, 1720*

LETTER CLXI

Roxana to Usbek, at Paris

Yes, I deceived you; I corrupted your eunuchs, made sport of
your jealousy, and learned how to make your frightful seraglio
into a place of delight and pleasure.

I am about to die of the poison now running through my
veins; for what should I do here, now that the only man who
held me to life is no more? I die, but my spirit will be well
accompanied in its ascent, for I have dispatched before me
all those sacrilegious jailors who shed the sweetest blood in
the world.

How could you have imagined me credulous enough to believe that I existed only to adore your caprices, that in permitting yourself everything, you had the right to thwart my
every desire? No: I have lived in slavery, but I have always
been free. I reformed your laws by those of nature, and my
spirit has always held to its independence.

You ought to thank me for the sacrifice I have made to you,
by abasing myself even to the point of appearing faithful; by
cravenly hiding in my heart what I should have proclaimed to
the world; finally, by profaning virtue, in permitting my submission to your fantasies to be called by that name.

You were surprised not to find in me the transports of love.
Had you known me well, you would have found all the violence of hate.

But for a long time you had the satisfaction of believing that a heart like mine was submissive to you. So we were both happy: you believed I was deceived, and I deceived you.

No doubt this language seems strange to you. Is it possible that after crushing you with sorrow, I may yet force you to admire my courage? But all this is done now. The poison consumes me; my strength departs and the pen falls from my hand. I feel even my hate grow weaker; I die.

> *The seraglio at Ispahan, the 8th of the moon of Rebiab I, 1720*